D1062490

FATIMA
MYSTERIES

ignatius PRESS

GRZEGORZ GÓRNY
JANUSZ ROSIKOŃ

MACIEJ MARCHEWICZ

FATIMA MYSTERIES

Mary's Message to the Modern Age

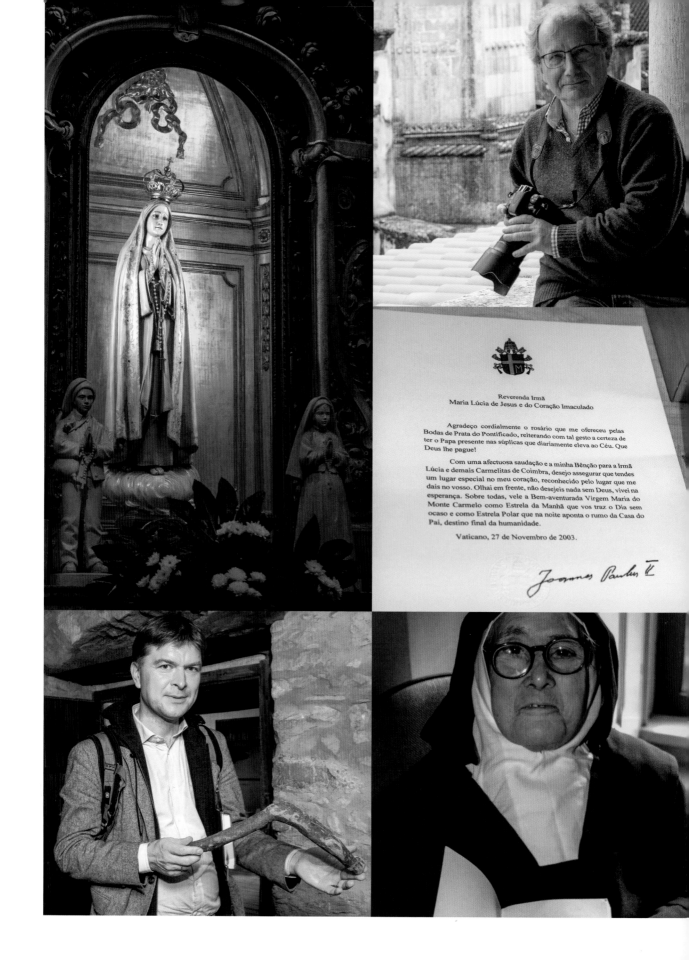

Reverenda Irmã
Maria Lúcia de Jesus e do Coração Imaculado

Agradeço cordialmente o rosário que me ofereceu pelas Bodas de Prata do Pontificado, reiterando com tal gesto a certeza de ter o Papa presente nas súplicas que diariamente eleva ao Céu. Que Deus lhe pague!

Com uma afectuosa saudação e a minha Bênção para a Irmã Lúcia e demais Carmelitas de Coimbra, desejo assegurar que tendes um lugar especial no meu coração, reconhecido pelo lugar que me dais no vosso. Olhai em frente, não desejeis nada sem Deus, vivei na esperança. Sobre todas, vele a Bem-aventurada Virgem Maria do Monte Carmelo como Estrela da Manhã que vos traz o Dia sem ocaso e como Estrela Polar que na noite aponta o rumo da Casa do Pai, destino final da humanidade.

Vaticano, 27 de Novembro de 2003.

PROLOGUE

The apparitions that occurred in Fatima, Portugal, in 1917 were the most important private revelations not only of the twentieth century, but also of the whole history of the Catholic Church. They gave rise to one of the most frequently visited shrines in the Christian world, led to two of the youngest people ever to be beatified in Church history, inspired millions throughout the world to embark on a prayer crusade, and captured the attention of as many as six popes, who personally responded to their requests. No other private revelations have seen such elaborate interpretations by the Holy See, and no others have been associated with such an important "secret", nor stirred up so many emotions.

The Fatima message, as attested to by two popes – John Paul II and Benedict XVI – changed the course of history. It contained information as to the only hope of deliverance from the madness of the bloodiest century in human history. It occupied the very center of the struggle over the world's soul, reconciling man's free will with Providence, and it showed that moral strength was able to crush the walls of empires. As Cardinal Joseph Ratzinger stated in 2000, the Fatima revelations proved that God is the Lord of history, that the whole world is in His hands.

Many people do not acknowledge the possibility of supernatural interventions in their everyday lives. They do not entertain the possibility of some deity intervening in human history. Hence, to them, revelations are but illusions. St. Paul the Apostle wrote of such an attitude: "The unspiritual man does not receive the gifts of the Spirit of God, for they are folly to him, and he is not able to understand them because they are spiritually discerned" (1 Cor 2:14).

Christianity, however, is based on the Incarnation, a historical event, which is not at all a closed chapter. Although God's revelation to mankind is complete in Christ, the paths of the Almighty and those of men are intertwined to this day. Before the Ascension, Jesus said: "Behold, I am with you always, to the close of the age" (Mt 28: 20). Who can impose on Christ the manner of this presence? Who can limit the Creator as to how He might wish to reveal Himself to His creatures? Who can forbid Him to send His Mother to His people? All the more so when she is to charge us with a mission concerning the fate of all humanity.

The year 2017 marks the one hundredth anniversary of the Fatima apparitions. These private revelations never cease to amaze people, including the authors of this book when travelling around the world, seeking new dimensions to this most singular message. During the successive stages of our journeys, we became convinced that Benedict XVI was quite right when he said that Fatima had not as yet exhausted its prophetic potential and that it is still relevant today.

5

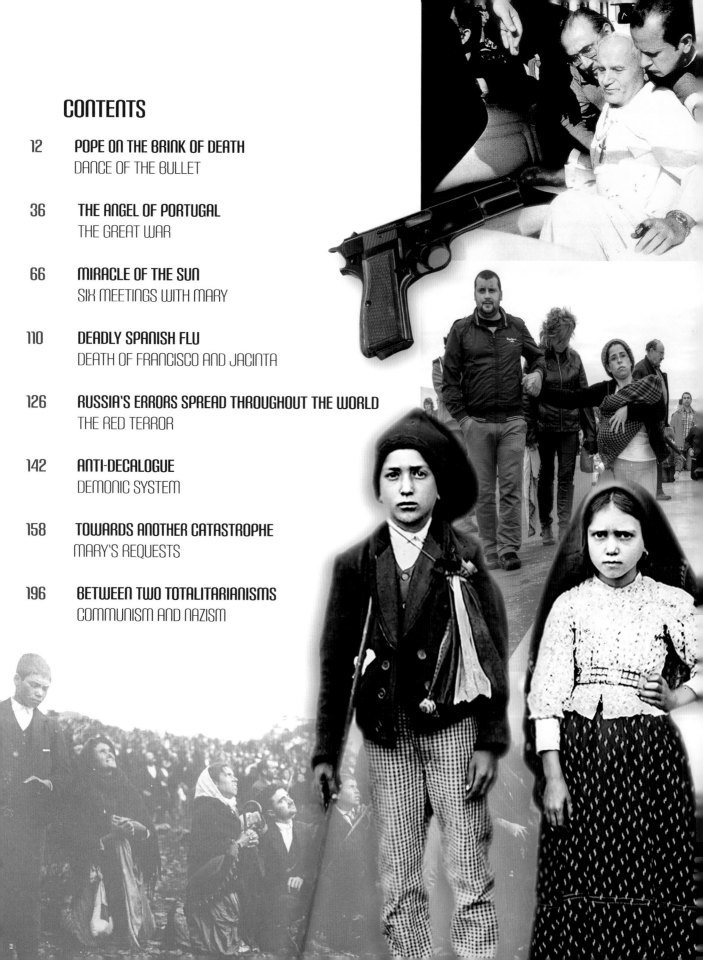

CONTENTS

7

SPAIN

PORTUGAL

Pontevedra
Tui
Valinhos
Valenca
Vilar

Leiria
Ourem Coimbra
Fatima
Lisbon

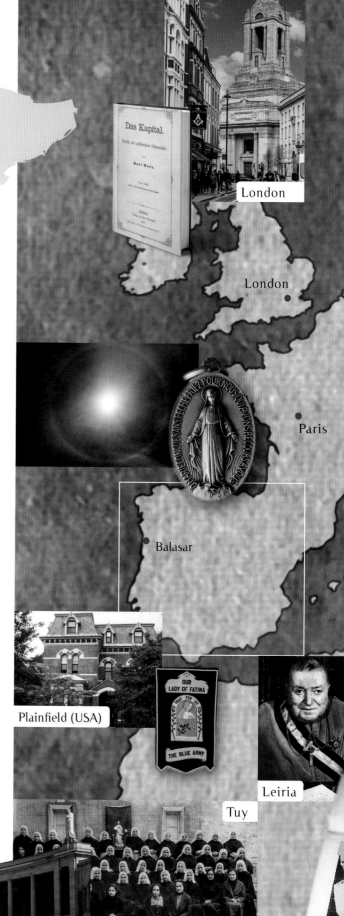

London

London

Paris

Balasar

Plainfield (USA)

OUR LADY OF FATIMA
PRAY FOR US
THE BLUE ARMY

Leiria

Tuy

Petersburg

Warsaw

Kiev

Moscow

Moscow

Moscow

БЕЗБОЖНИК У СТАНКА

Warsaw
Niepokalanow
Berlin
Czestochowa
Krakow
Zakopane
Rozniawa
Berlin
Bratislava
Vienna
Budapest
Kiev

Vatican
Vienna

Petersburg

Rome

Rome

Yekaterinburg

Fatima

Aurora

9

Kamchatka

BEMUS · PAPAM
NNEM PAULUM II
Karol Wojtyła
Świętego Piotra
SŁOWO
powszechne

Severomorsk

FATIMA TIMELINE

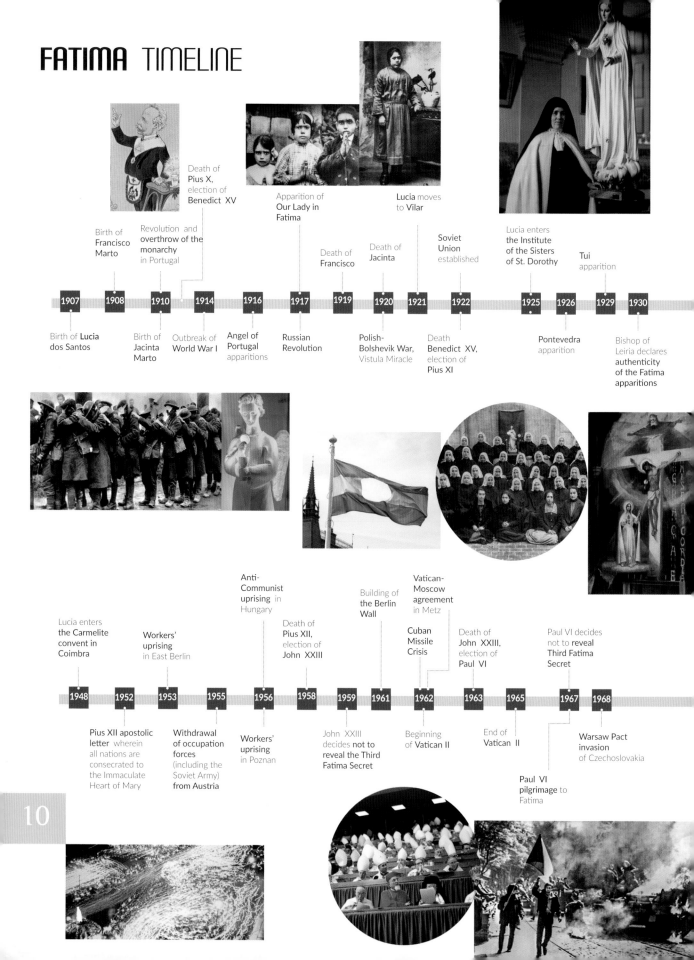

Death of Pius X, election of Benedict XV

Apparition of Our Lady in Fatima

Lucia moves to Vilar

Birth of Francisco Marto

Revolution and overthrow of the monarchy in Portugal

Death of Francisco

Death of Jacinta

Soviet Union established

Lucia enters the Institute of the Sisters of St. Dorothy

Tui apparition

| 1907 | 1908 | 1910 | 1914 | 1916 | 1917 | 1919 | 1920 | 1921 | 1922 | 1925 | 1926 | 1929 | 1930 |

Birth of Lucia dos Santos

Birth of Jacinta Marto

Outbreak of World War I

Angel of Portugal apparitions

Russian Revolution

Polish-Bolshevik War, Vistula Miracle

Death Benedict XV, election of Pius XI

Pontevedra apparition

Bishop of Leiria declares authenticity of the Fatima apparitions

Lucia enters the Carmelite convent in Coimbra

Workers' uprising in East Berlin

Anti-Communist uprising in Hungary

Death of Pius XII, election of John XXIII

Building of the Berlin Wall

Vatican-Moscow agreement in Metz

Cuban Missile Crisis

Death of John XXIII, election of Paul VI

Paul VI decides not to reveal Third Fatima Secret

| 1948 | 1952 | 1953 | 1955 | 1956 | 1958 | 1959 | 1961 | 1962 | 1963 | 1965 | 1967 | 1968 |

Pius XII apostolic letter wherein all nations are consecrated to the Immaculate Heart of Mary

Withdrawal of occupation forces (including the Soviet Army) from Austria

Workers' uprising in Poznan

John XXIII decides not to reveal the Third Fatima Secret

Beginning of Vatican II

End of Vatican II

Warsaw Pact invasion of Czechoslovakia

Paul VI pilgrimage to Fatima

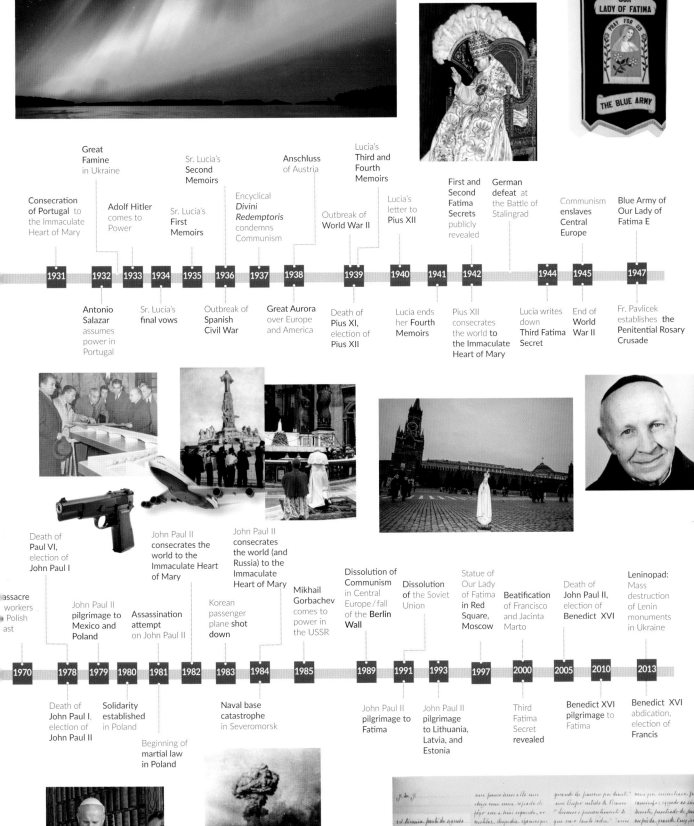

Consecration of Portugal to the Immaculate Heart of Mary

Great Famine in Ukraine

Adolf Hitler comes to Power

Sr. Lucia's **First Memoirs**

Sr. Lucia's **Second Memoirs**

Encyclical *Divini Redemptoris* condemns Communism

Anschluss of Austria

Outbreak of World War II

Lucia's **Third and Fourth Memoirs**

Lucia's **letter to Pius XII**

First and Second Fatima Secrets publicly revealed

German defeat at the Battle of Stalingrad

Communism enslaves Central Europe

Blue Army of Our Lady of Fatima E

| 1931 | 1932 | 1933 | 1934 | 1935 | 1936 | 1937 | 1938 | 1939 | 1940 | 1941 | 1942 | 1944 | 1945 | 1947 |

Antonio Salazar assumes power in Portugal

Sr. Lucia's **final vows**

Outbreak of Spanish Civil War

Great Aurora over Europe and America

Death of Pius XI, election of Pius XII

Lucia ends her **Fourth Memoirs**

Pius XII consecrates the world **to the Immaculate Heart of Mary**

Lucia writes down **Third Fatima Secret**

End of **World War II**

Fr. Pavlicek establishes the **Penitential Rosary Crusade**

Death of Paul VI, election of John Paul I

John Paul II **consecrates the world to the Immaculate Heart of Mary**

John Paul II **consecrates the world (and Russia) to the Immaculate Heart of Mary**

Mikhail Gorbachev comes to power in the USSR

Dissolution of Communism in Central Europe / fall of the **Berlin Wall**

Dissolution of the Soviet Union

Statue of Our Lady of Fatima in Red Square, Moscow

Beatification of Francisco and Jacinta Marto

Death of John Paul II, election of Benedict XVI

Leninopad: Mass destruction of Lenin monuments in Ukraine

...assacre ...workers ...Polish ...ast

John Paul II **pilgrimage to Mexico and Poland**

Assassination attempt on John Paul II

Korean passenger plane shot down

| 1970 | 1978 | 1979 | 1980 | 1981 | 1982 | 1983 | 1984 | 1985 | 1989 | 1991 | 1993 | 1997 | 2000 | 2005 | 2010 | 2013 |

Death of John Paul I, election of John Paul II

Solidarity established in Poland

Beginning of martial law in Poland

Naval base catastrophe in Severomorsk

John Paul II **pilgrimage to Fatima**

John Paul II **pilgrimage to Lithuania, Latvia, and Estonia**

Third Fatima Secret revealed

Benedict XVI pilgrimage to Fatima

Benedict XVI abdication, election of Francis

Pope on the Brink of Death

CHAPTER 1

Pope on the Brink of Death

The shots changed the world's fate. The man who fired at the pope was aware of that. However, he did not imagine that the changes initiated by his assassination attempt would redirect world history on a course that was totally different from the one that he and his superiors had imagined. Let us go back in time.

It is 5:17 p.m., May 13, 1981, St. Peter's Square, Rome. The popemobile, registration number SCV3, driven by Sebastiano Baglioni, is moving slowly through the crowd of pilgrims, gawkers, and tourists from all over the world. The pope, in white, is standing in the vehicle. John Paul II is the first Pole to ascend St. Peter's throne. It is said that he has changed the image of the papacy. Thanks to his charisma and resoluteness, his numerous pilgrimages around the world, and the all-pervasive media, he has become the most recognizable person in the world. Twenty thousand have gathered here to see him.

As on every Wednesday, the pope is being driven around St. Peter's Square, blessing people. From time to time he takes a child held out to him, cuddles it, and kisses its forehead. The pope is smiling and relaxed. The pope's butler, Angelo Gugel, and his personal secretary, Fr. Stanislaw Dziwisz, are sitting next to him. Fr. Dziwisz

Rome

ITALY

JOHN PAUL II during general audiences frequently took children into his hands. A catechist from a parish in Lariano decided to take her 18-month-old daughter to Rome on May 13, 1981. The girl was Sara Bartoli, who saved the pope's life in unwittingly delaying the terrorist's pistol shot.

15

ASSASSIN'S
PISTOL
– aimed at the
pope.

is holding the text that John Paul II is to read. It includes a request that the Virgin Mary teach us to so transform our fate, one that is leading us to the cross – together with her – that it might be of credit to us.

In a moment the tranquil spring afternoon will suddenly end. There is a young, serious-looking black-haired man in a blue jacket in the crowd. He has a passport in his pocket under the name of Farum Ogzum. In reality he is Mehmet Ali Agca, a contract killer. A year earlier a court in Ankara had sentenced him to death in absentia. His documents tally only with regard to his age, twenty-three, and his citizenship, Turkish. He, like the pilgrims all around, is taking photos. Agca positions himself so as to be as close as possible to John Paul II when he passes by. He had chosen the place the day before: sector E, second row. The sun is behind him, so his target will be well lit.

As the vehicle comes within ten feet of him, Agca is about to fire. But at that moment a parish priest from Lariano, Italy, holds out eighteen-month-old Sara Bartoli to the pope. He takes her in his hands. Tourists all around, arms extended, are taking photos. Agca waits until John Paul II returns the

LETHAL WEAPON

THE BROWNING HI POWER GUN was designed in 1928 by a Belgian small arms designer, Dieudonne Saive, at a munitions factory in Herstal. The gun was named after the main designer, John Moses Browning, an American who died in 1926. Initially not many were keen on the gun. But the situation changed in 1937, when the Chinese Army began to purchase it. Mass production, however, did not begin until 1940, when the Third Reich attacked Belgium and took over the factory. Then 319,000 were produced for the German Army, mainly for the Waffen-SS. The postwar years saw updated versions that were often ordered by armies and police forces from all over the world. The gun is also used by terrorists and assassins because of its ease of use and effectiveness.

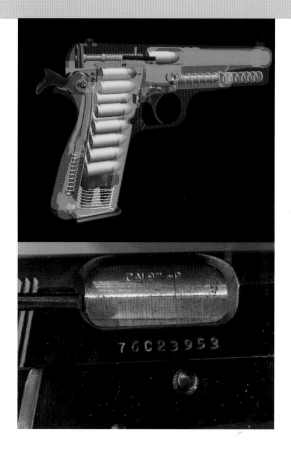

BROWNING HI POWER 9 mm magazine – holds 13 cartridges.

MEHMET ALI AGCA'S gun – John Paul II Family Home Museum, Wadowice.

AGCA'S BROWNING serial number: 76C23953.

ALOIS ESTERMANN, a Swiss Guard, shielding the pope with his body.

THREE TURKISH TERRORISTS who were in St. Peter's Square on May 13, 1981: ❶ Mehmet Ali Agca, the only one apprehended by the Italian police, ❷ Oral Celik, ❸ Omer Ay.

girl. Then he lowers his camera and pulls out a gun from under his belt. It is a Belgian Browning Hi Power pistol, a reliable weapon favored by assassins. Agca had prepared for this moment for a long time. He is certain that he will kill the pope.

The assassin is convinced that the pope is wearing a bulletproof vest. He does not know that John Paul II had refused to wear one in November 1979, a year before his pilgrimage to Ireland, saying that danger was an "occupational hazard". So, holding his gun with both hands, Agca aims at the pope's stomach.

He squeezes the trigger twice. At the sound of the shots dozens of pigeons around St. Peter's Square take flight. During the second shot, Agca said later, he felt someone pulling his arm violently. This is still a mysterious, or unexplained, matter.

Swiss Guard Alois Estermann throws himself at the pope to shield him with his own body. Years later, on May 4, 1998, he will be elected commander of the Swiss Guards, but he and his wife, Gladys Romero, will be murdered by

JOHN PAUL II slumps into the arms of his secretary, Fr. Stanislaw Dziwisz.

19

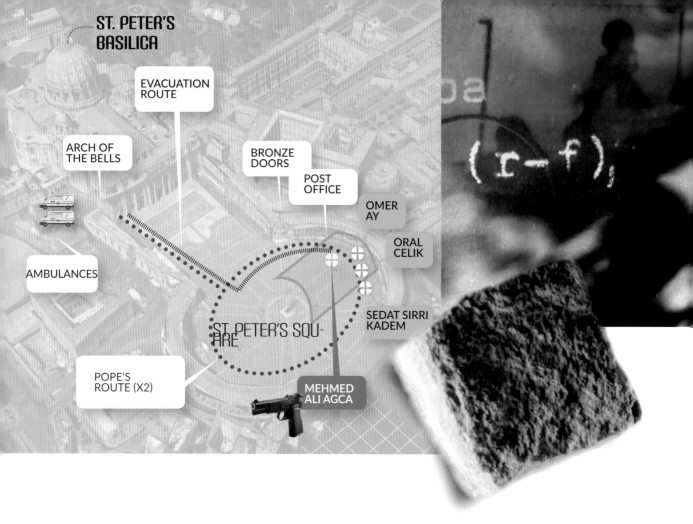

ST. PETER'S
BASILICA

EVACUATION
ROUTE

ARCH OF
THE BELLS

BRONZE
DOORS

POST
OFFICE

OMER
AY

ORAL
CELIK

AMBULANCES

ST. PETER'S SQU-
ARE

SEDAT SIRRI
KADEM

POPE'S
ROUTE (X2)

MEHMED
ALI AGCA

ST. PETER'S SQUARE
– scene of events
on May 13, 1981.

A SETT STONE from
St. Peter's Square.
Agca tripped over
such a stone when
attempting to flee
from the scene of
the crime.

a Swiss Guard corporal Cedric Tornay, who will then commit suicide.

The first bullet passes through the pope's abdominal cavity, injuring his index finger on the way, and falls on the vehicle's floor between the pope and his personal secretary. The second hits the pope's left elbow. Other shots were fired, but to this day it is not known how many. Witnesses speak of three, four, and even five. An expert ballistic evaluation was prepared. The trajectory of the bullets showed that the shots came from two different points. Three bullets were found at the scene of the crime. There is another assassin in section E, not far from a fountain: twenty-six-year-old Oral Celik, Agca's friend. He is armed with an Italian 7.65 mm Beretta. They are in eye contact and have arranged that the one who had a more favorable position would nod his head and start to shoot. Celik also has a bomb, which he intends to detonate if the assassination attempt were to fail. He does not detonate the bomb and withdraws. There are yet two

more Turkish terrorists: Omer Ay and Sedat Sirri Kadem, who are to cover the withdrawal of their companions.

The public prosecutor Rosario Priore, who will lead the assassination attempt investigation, does not rule out that Celik might have fired the third shot, and that his bullet and not Agca's might have hit the pope's elbow. However, this could not be confirmed as the third bullet was never officially examined by specialists. Hidden away by Camillo Cibin, papal bodyguard and inspector general of the Vatican Gendarmerie, it eventually became part of the crown of Our Lady of Fatima.

The bullets wound two American tourists. Rose Hall, hit in her left arm, and Ann Odre, whose throat was grazed. Both are treated at a nearby hospital. The papal photographer Arturo Mari, who is half a yard from the pope, hears four shots. He is convinced that the bullets did not come from one gun, as the American women were on opposite sides of the vehicle. Agca rushes towards the Bernini colonnades. He is convinced that he has killed the pope. He suddenly trips over a sett stone and falls down. Franciscan Sister Letizia Giudici jumps on him, pressing him to the ground with her body. Police appear and arrest the assassin.

The pope slumps into the arms of his secretary, who asks, "Where?" John Paul, with a wince of pain on his face, replies, "The stomach." "Does it hurt a lot?" asks Fr. Dziwisz. "Yes," whispers the pope and then repeats with difficulty,

TERRORIST'S HAND – finger squeezing the trigger.

21

SERIOUSLY WOUNDED
John Paul II supported by his coworkers. The assassination attempt became headline news throughout the world.

BLOOD-STAINED STOLE
which the pope was wearing at the time of the assassination attempt - kept at the Jasna Góra Monastery.

"It hurts… it hurts…" The popemobile abruptly sets off towards the Arco delle Campane (Arch of the Bells). Brother Kamil, that is, Franciszek Kipiel, a Knight Hospitaller from Poland and a Vatican medic, jumps onto the vehicle's bumper. The papal bodyguards push people aside, clearing the way for the vehicle to make its way through the terrified crowd. Some onlookers are frozen with terror; others are shouting and lamenting.

The popemobile draws up to an ambulance parked near a first aid station. The pope is stretchered into the ambulance. It turns out, however, that there are problems with the ambulance. After a while another ambulance appears with more modern equipment, which had in fact been bought by the Vatican. A day earlier the pope had visited a medical center and had blessed this new ambulance. He then said, "I also give my blessings to this ambulance's first patient."

The pope's personal doctor, Renato Buzzonetti, appears in the ambulance. Brother Kamil is also there. John Paul II is bleeding profusely. Everyone realizes that every minute counts. Fr. Dziwisz must decide on the way to Gemelli Clinic: the shorter or longer route? He quickly decides on the longer route.

It turns out to be a providential choice; the shorter route via the city center is jammed with traffic. After only a few hundred yards the ambulance's siren and lights fail. Despite that, the ambulance races through the city at high speed. Now and again

SARA BARTOLI has been called "bambina del Papa" ever since her childhood. She said that the assassination attempt of 1981 had become an inseparable part of her life.

TELEGRAM REGARDING the attempted assassination – Polish Press Agency correspondent in Rome Zdzislaw Morawski.

BULLET HOLE in the pope's cassock – traces of blood to the left.

the driver uses his horn. Several times he avoids crashes at the last second. In the rush the pope's bed had not been secured. So every now and then his head hits the knee of the medic sitting next to him. The ambulance takes eight minutes to cover the route, which normally takes thirty minutes.

At this time Dr. Francesco Crucitti, an experienced surgeon at Gemelli Clinic, is visiting a patient at a hospital on the Via Aurelia. A nun, who had been listening to the radio, rushes into the ward shouting that the pope has been shot and is on his way to Gemelli Clinic. Crucitti quickly takes off his apron, puts on his jacket, and runs to his car. He is about two miles from the clinic, and the city is jammed with traffic. Initially he races along the left lane,

GEMELLI CLINIC

AN ITALIAN DOCTOR, Agostini Gemelli, who became a Franciscan, initiated the founding of the clinic. It is not an exclusive clinic, but an ordinary Roman hospital, except for its considerable size, as it employs 4,000 people (including 500 doctors) and has 1,800 beds. One of the beds had been allotted to the pope long ago.

When John Paul II began his pontificate, he made it clear that – were it to be necessary – he did not want to be hospitalized in the Vatican. That was the case with Paul VI, who had a prostate operation at the papal apartments in 1967. The Pius XII Hall was then changed into a sort of hospital for one patient. Dr. Pietro Valdoni carried out the operation, assisted by Dr. Corrado Manni, who later participated in saving John Paul II.

GEMELLI CLINIC, Rome – John Paul II monument commemorating his stay at the hospital.

He, unlike Paul VI, demanded a normal hospital. He chose the Gemelli Clinic. Hence a special room had been organized for the pope on the 10th floor, which had not been used until the assassination attempt.

every now and again sounding his horn and overtaking vehicles. He squeezes himself between cars in a police convoy. One of the policemen threatens him with his machine gun. But the doctor does not bother about that and races on. After a while he sees a policeman in his mirror chasing him on a motorbike. He is convinced that the policeman wants to stop him. When the motorbike is alongside his car, Crucciti opens the window and shouts, "I have to get to the Gemelli Clinic as quickly as possible!" The policeman replies, "Foot down! I shall help you", and escorts the doctor at high speed.

The pope is losing a lot of blood in the speeding ambulance (he will lose over three-quarters of his blood), but through sheer will power he remains conscious. Eyes closed, he prays with an ever weaker voice. He keeps repeating: "Mary! My Mother! Mary! My Mother!" He loses consciousness before he reaches the clinic.

Hospital staff are awaiting the pope. At 5:25 p.m. Dr. Trisalti takes a phone call from the Vatican: "Il papa e stato colpito." The news is not precise. The word *colpito* may mean a number of things. Trisalti, who knows nothing about the assassination attempt, is wondering whether it is a heart attack, a

WOUNDED POPE
in film excerpt – part of Barbara and Jaroslaw Klaput's exhibition at the John Paul II Family Home Museum in Wadowice, Poland.

25

THANKSGIVING MASS celebrated in a corridor at the Gemelli Clinic by John Paul II.

FR. AGOSTINO GEMELLI, Franciscan doctor, founder of the clinic.

cerebral hemorrhage, or an injury from a fall. He instructs the staff to prepare the pope's room. No one at the hospital knows that the pope is in a critical condition.

When the ambulance arrives at the clinic, the pope is stretchered in, laid on a mobile bed, and taken to the tenth floor. It is only there that the doctors realize that the pope's condition is more serious than they had thought. It is decided to immediately take the pope to a lower floor, to the surgical ward. The theater is already prepared as another operation was about to take place. The pope is taken in. His blood pressure is falling rapidly, his pulse is weakening, his heartbeat is barely perceptible. Fr. Dziwisz administers extreme unction to his superior.

A question arises: Who is to carry out the operation? Ordinarily Dr. Castiglione, the senior surgeon at Gemelli, would, but he is in Milan. Next in line is Dr. Crucitti, but he is off duty. Hence the responsibility falls on Dr. Angelo di Marzio. Francesco Crucitti suddenly rushes into the ward. The assistants know there is no time to lose. They literally pull off the doctor's jacket and trousers. Coins, keys, and documents fall out of his pockets, but no one takes any notice of this. The assistants quickly dress the surgeon for the operation.

As Crucitti enters the theater, the pope's blood pressure falls further. The anaesthetist Dr. Corrado Manni administers an anaesthetic. The pope is put on a drip, and the blood transfusion begins. He is lying with arms outstretched. Dr. Manni has the impression that he, as it were, has the crucified Christ before him. The operation begins at 5:55 p.m. Dr. Manzoni, a cardiologist, and Dr. Breda, an internist, are also present. The surgeon slits the pope's stomach with a scalpel.

News about the attempted assassination travels around the world like lightning. People gather in cathedrals, churches, and chapels all around the world to pray for the pope. At that time Primate Stefan Wyszynski, seen as the "uncrowned king of Poland", is dying. He is in bed with cancer. He had said his last Mass on April 30, and on May 9 he developed a heart condition. On hearing of this, John Paul II sent Fr. Dziwisz to Warsaw to visit the dying cardinal on May 11, two days before the assassination attempt. When the primate learned of the attempt, he said: "I was always afraid of that."

THE POPE'S white cassock with traces of blood – relic at the John Paul II Shrine in Krakow, Poland.

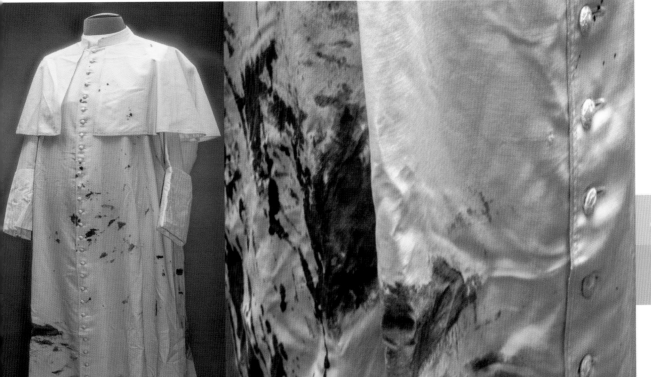

27

✢

ABORTION IN ITALY

ABORTION WAS ILLEGAL in Italy until 1976, when poisonous substances leaked from a factory in Sevese. It was suspected that unborn children in that region had suffered damage. At that time the Christian Democratic Party governed Italy. The Christian Democratic health and justice ministers, with the approval of the prime minister Giulio Andreotti, allowed for exceptions and permitted women from Sevese to have, as it was defined, "a therapeutic abortion".

Abortion was fully legalized in Italy two years later. Only one party was seriously involved in the campaign against the legal sanctioning of abortion: the right-wing Italian Social Movement. At that time the Christian Democrats had a minority government. Mainly through the votes of Socialists and Communists, Italy allowed abortion on request to the third month, and to the sixth month in cases of risk to the health or the life of a mother.

It is the only pro-abortion law in the world that was signed solely by Catholic politicians: Christian Democrats President Giovanni Leone, Prime Minister Giulio Andreotti, Minister of Health Tina Anselmi, Minister of Justice Francesco Bonifacio, Minister of Administration Tommaso Morlino, and Minister of the Treasury Filippo Pandolfi. The Christian Democrats admittedly voted against the new law, but later they did not do anything to stop it from coming into effect. President Leone could have had the law returned for another vote in parliament, but he did not do so, and Prime Minister Andreotti instructed the prosecutor general to defend its conformity with the constitution before the high court.

On May 17, 1981, when John Paul II was in the hospital, there was a referendum on abortion, and two-thirds of Italians were for its legalization.

ITALIAN CHRISTIAN DEMOCRATIC PARTY politicians contributed to the enactment of the abortion law. The then prime minister, Giulio Andreotti, is on the left.

POLISH PILGRIMS praying before the vacant papal throne in the Vatican, awaiting news from the hospital.

A PAINTING of Our Lady of Czestochowa on the papal throne.

RELIQUARY with the pope's blood – John Paul II Shrine in Krakow, Poland.

Only an hour earlier Italy was engrossed with a completely different event, a forthcoming referendum – on May 17 – legalizing abortion. The pope was absolutely opposed to it, stating that one could not murder the most defenseless, that is, the unborn, with the full sanction of the law. It was no accident that several hours before the assassination attempt the pope had the eminent French geneticist Jerome Lejeune at dinner. Lejeune not only discovered the causes of such chromosomal abnormalities as Down syndrome but defended human life from the moment of conception. That evening the Italian Communist Party announced the organization of a large demonstration in the center of Rome in favor of legalizing abortion. After the assassination attempt, the Communist Party secretary general Enrico Berlinguer called off the demonstration.

In St. Peter's Square there is a ceaseless prayer vigil. Once the popemobile disappeared, pilgrims from Poland placed a copy of the image of Our Lady of Czestochowa on the papal chair. Thousands of people from all over the world are deep in prayer in various languages, awaiting official information from the hospital.

WHITE MARCH after the assassination attempt – Market Square, Krakow.

POLISH PRIMATE Cardinal Wyszynski predicted the assassination attempt.

Dr. Crucitti is opening the pope's abdominal cavity. He first removes three quarts of blood, sucking and wiping it away in order to be able to get to the source of the bleeding and stem the flow. The pope's blood pressure rises slowly. After the bleeding is under control, the surgeon continues the operation. He sees a number of wounds. He cuts out twenty-two inches of the intestine and stitches the colon in several places. There is a larger wound in its posterior part, which is bleeding the most. Dr. Crucitti coats it with sterilized wax. Near the end of the operation Dr. Castiglione, the senior surgeon, returns from Milan. The operation finishes at 11:25 p.m.

The doctors are astonished that the bullet had not damaged any vital organs. The bullet had as if slalomed through the body, missing the spine and the major blood vessels. Dr. Crucitti said later that the bullet zigzagged and did not cause irreparable damage.

Cardinals, Roman Curia employees, and the most important Italian politicians, headed by President Sandro Pertinim and Prime Minister Arnaldo Forlanim, arrive at the clinic during the operation. All wait for the outcome. After a while surgery

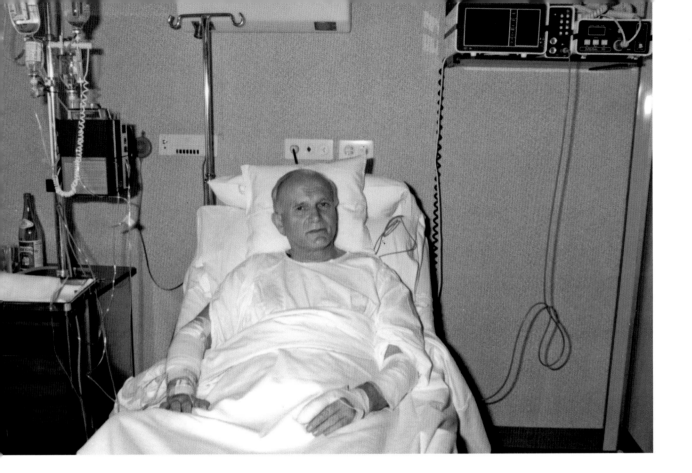

JOHN PAUL II
at the Gemelli
Clinic during his
convalescence
after a successful
operation.

assistants inform them that the pope's condition is improving. Before midnight the clinic officially announces that the operation was a success and that the pope's life is out of danger.

Telegrams from leaders from all over the world flood into the Vatican. Leonid Brezhnev, leader of the Soviet Union, writes: "I am very indignant at the criminal assassination attempt on you. I wish you a quick and complete return to health." Ronald Reagan, president of the United States, assures the pope that he will pray for him. Reagan was also recovering after an assassination attempt. He was shot in Washington eighteen months earlier, March 30, 1981. The bullet fired by John Hinckley missed the president's heart by barely an inch.

The pope remains in the hospital for three weeks. He records speeches that are broadcast by radio all over the world. On May 17 he says: "Pray for the brother that wounded me, whom I sincerely forgive. United with Christ, Priest and Victim, I offer up my suffering for the Church and for the world." On the May 25, at 12:15 p.m., John Paul II had his last telephone discussion with

Cardinal Wyszynski. Three days later – the Feast of the Ascension – the Polish primate died.

John Paul II returns to the Vatican on June 3. Four days later, on the Feast of Pentecost, he appears publicly for the first time in several weeks. From the inner balcony of the basilica he blesses those gathered in St. Peter's Square.

On June 9, however, his health suddenly worsens. His temperature rises to nearly 104 degrees. The pope sweats and shivers with cold by turns. He also complains of pains. He is ever weaker. Antibiotics do not help, and the doctors do not know what is happening. There is a case conference. One of the doctors is Gabriel Turowski, an immunology professor from Krakow, a friend of the pope. It is decided that the pope must return to hospital.

DR. GABRIEL TUROWSKI, a friend of the pope. Thanks to him the pope survived an infection.

On June 20, at 4:30 p.m., the pope returns to Gemelli Clinic. Further examinations, however, do not reveal the cause of the problem. It is not until June 22 that the virus causing the infection is isolated. The matter is clarified: On May 13, when blood was quickly

32

JOHN PAUL II and Slovakian Bishop Pavol Hnilica with a statue of Our Lady of Fatima.

required for a transfusion for the pope, essential tests were not carried out because of the rush. One of the doses was infected with a virus. Thanks to the discovery, effective treatment was possible but took several weeks. It is not until after July 16, the Feast of Our Lady of Mount Carmel, that the pope's health gradually improved.

During the pope's second stay at the hospital, the July, 17, Prof. Gabriel Turowski points out a puzzling coincidence to him: On May 13, 1917, Our Lady appeared to three Portuguese shepherd children from Fatima for the first time; on May 13, 1981 – precisely sixty-four years later – John Paul II became the victim of an assassination attempt. The pope sees this as a sign.

He requests a Slovak archbishop, Pavol Hnilica, who has lived in Rome for years, to visit him. They know each other from Vatican II. The

INCONSPICUOUS ENVELOPE containing the third Fatima secret.

SITE of the assassination attempt in St. Peter's Square.

Slovak is a great advocate of the Fatima message. It was he who, several days after Karol Wojtyla's election as pope, told him something memorable. He declared that God had chosen John Paul II for an extraordinary mission, the consecration and conversion of Russia. The Holy Father asks the archbishop to bring all the documentation concerning the Fatima apparitions to him in the hospital. The archbishop takes a briefcase containing the documentation to the clinic. The pope becomes engrossed in the documentation. His thoughts turn to Portugal, to the memorable year of 1917, when Our Lady appeared to three little shepherds in the little village of Fatima. John Paul II knows that history, marked by great figures and well-known events, has, in parallel, the history of redemption woven into it, wherein barely noticeable people, hidden in the shadows, not seeking fame, power, or wealth, at times play the leading roles. He is perfectly aware that world history is full of such quiet heroes like Paul, the First Hermit, Margaret Mary

STANISLAW GRYGIEL, philosophy professor – and friend of the pope.

ATTACK ON THE FAMILY

ON MAY 13, 1981, John Paul II intended to announce, during the general audience, the proposed establishment of a new research center in Rome, that is, the Institute for Studies on Marriage and Family. The assassination attempt prevented it, a project that he had cherished for some time. The Holy Father wanted the institute to realize the idea of a medieval university, a community of professors and students who worked and prayed together, and, first and foremost, sought the truth together.

Thus arose the John Paul II Institute for Studies on Marriage and Family at the Pontifical Lateran University in Rome (December 13, 1981), with Our Lady of Fatima as its patroness. Among its directors were the future cardinals Carlo Caffara and Angelo Scola.

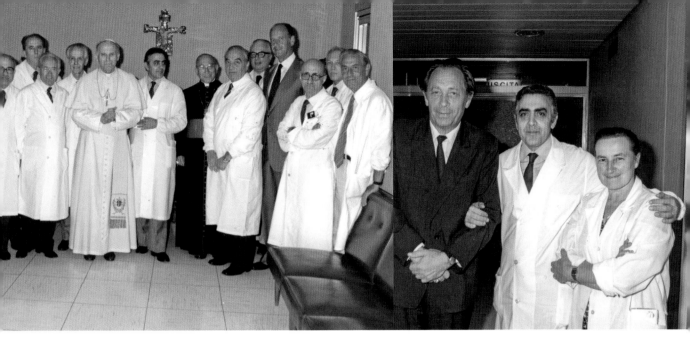

Alacoque, Catherine Labouré, Bernadette Soubirous, Faustina Kowalska, Marthe Robin... Such inconspicuous figures, frail children with brave hearts, emerge from the accounts of the extraordinary apparitions in Portugal. The documentation mentions the greatest secret of the twentieth century – the third Fatima secret.

On closing the dossier the pope requests one of the world's most guarded documents to be delivered to the hospital. The prefect of the Congregation for the Doctrine of the Faith, a Croatian cardinal, Franjo Seper, makes his way to a secret dicastery archive and takes out two sealed envelopes from the safe of the former Holy Office: one white and the other orange. The white envelope contains the original text of the third Fatima secret in Portuguese, written by Sr. Lucia; the other holds an Italian translation of the text. The prefect gives the envelopes to his deputy, a Spanish bishop, Eduardo Martinez Somalo, who takes it to the Gemelli Clinic. John Paul II carefully reads the writing on a sheet of paper, folded several times, sentence after sentence. Fr. Stanislaw Dziwisz will say later that the pope will discern his own destiny within it.

The Holy Father appears in the Fatima message as many as ten times. The bishop of Rome, St. Peter's successor, the Vicar of Christ on earth, is at the very center of Lucia's vision. John Paul II's thoughts turn to events in Europe at the beginning of the twentieth century.

MEDICAL TEAM that attended to John Paul II during his stay in the hospital in 1981.

HE SAVED THE POPE: Dr. Francesco Crucitti (center), an Italian surgeon, with Gabriel Turowski and Wanda Poltawska.

The Angel of Portugal

ARCHDUKE FRANZ FERDINAND of Austria with his wife shortly before their deaths in Sarajevo on June 28, 1914.

CHAPTER 2

The Angel of Portugal

The Serbian nationalist from the Black Hand terrorist organization, in firing
at the heir of the Austro-Hungarian throne, did not know that his action
would begin a chain reaction that would lead to World War I, to the death of millions of soldiers on many fronts, and would change the fate of the world.

It was 10:15 a.m., June 28, 1914. An olive-grey Graf & Stift limousine with a convertible roof was gliding along the streets of Sarajevo, conveying Archduke Franz Ferdinand of Austria and his wife, Sophie Chotek, a Bohemian aristocrat. They were celebrating their first wedding anniversary. One and a half hours earlier they had participated in a solemn Mass for the occasion. When the limousine slowed down, a twenty-year-old terrorist, Gavrilo Princip, suddenly ran up to the vehicle and fired two shots from a pistol at the couple. Both shots turned out to be lethal.

The assassination occasioned a series of events that ran out of control. The conflict between Austria-Hungary and Serbia – a consequence of a complicated system of international alliances – turned into a conflict on a continental scale. The Great War broke out on July 28. The Central Powers on one side: Germany,

39

GAVRILO PRINCIP unleashed World War I.

BIG BERTHA – pride of the German artillery

GERMAN SOLDIERS on their way to the western front, full of enthusiasm, counting on a speedy victory over France as in 1871.

POPE BENEDICT XV ceaselessly attempted to end World War I.

40

Austria-Hungary, Turkey and Bulgaria; and on the other, the Triple Entente countries: Great Britain, France, Russia, Serbia, Romania, Italy, Belgium, Portugal, and Montenegro, as well as the United States and Japan. Conflict will also arise in the colonies – Africa and Oceania.

In the meanwhile, Pope Pius X died in Rome on August 20. Two weeks later the cardinals gathered at the conclave to elect his successor, Giacomo della Chiesa, a sixty-year-old from the Bologna Diocese. As he had become a cardinal barely three months earlier, on May 20, he was the least senior at the conclave. However, the hierarchs elected him as they nurtured a conviction that at a time of a global war the Vatican needed an experienced international mediator. Giacomo della Chiesa had worked as a Vatican diplomat for twenty-five years and had even achieved the rank of deputy secretary of state. So it seemed that he was the best candidate. The new pope took the name Benedict XV.

BRITISH MARK I
TANKS were the
first tanks to
be used in war
– Battle of the
Somme, 1916.

CHATEAU
WOOD near
Passchendaele,
Belgium, the site
of one of the
bloodiest battles
of World War I. It
lasted from July 31
to November 6,
1917. The battle
was undecided.
The Triple Entente
had 448,000
killed, wounded, or
lost, the Germans
260,000.

On September 8, just five days after his election, the Holy Father appealed to the leaders of the warring states to make peace. On November 1, 1914, he issued the encyclical *Ad Beatissim Apostolorum*, wherein he called on the belligerents to cease the conflict. He was to make many more such appeals throughout the war – all futile. The majority of countries were ruled by elites who were ill-disposed towards the Catholic Church. Only Charles Hapsburg, who assumed the dual monarchy of Austria-Hungary after the death of Emperor Franz Joseph, supported papal peace initiatives. Although other European heads of state were unimpressed by him, the Church showed her official appreciation for his efforts in 2004, when he was beatified by Pope John Paul II.

In 1915 Benedict XV ordered all Catholic churches in Europe to pray the devotion to the Most Sacred Heart of Jesus for peace. France, Spain, and Germany ignored the pope's wishes. The desire for war turned out to be stronger than the desire for peace. In Europe

41

the conviction that force was the best way to resolve the conflicts prevailed.

Hitherto the world had not experienced such a terrible war. It broke out in 1914, and is known as the Great Slaughter. Barely several months after the start of the war, two hundred thousand soldiers perished in one battle alone, the Battle of Lodz (November 11 to December 6, 1914). Though Russian and German soldiers had faced each other, many of those that perished were Poles who fought on both sides. Not having their own state, they were forced into the occupying armies as cannon fodder.

Germany was the first country in history to use poisonous gases during a war – the Battle of Ypres in Belgium (April 22, 1916). Two days later, Turkey, taking advantage of the wartime confusion, began the extermination of the Armenian civil population. About one and a half millon Armenians were victims of the genocide.

TRIPLE ENTENTE SOLDIERS – first victims of the first use of gas in war.

42

They were tortured, massacred, mutilated, murdered and executed, or forced to march to the Deir ez-Zor camps in the Syrian desert, where they died of thirst, hunger, and exhaustion.

In 1916, three hundred thousand soldiers perished, and four hundred thousand were wounded at the nine-month Battle of Verdun. In all, nine million soldiers perished during World War I, and twenty-nine million were wounded.

When the attention of Europeans was concentrated on ministerial offices in the capitals of the great powers, as well as on the fronts of the Great War, an event in a distant Portuguese province went unnoticed by all the politicians and the journalists on the Old Continent. There was nothing odd in that, however, as only three little shepherd children knew of it.

It was the spring of 1916, near a rocky outcrop, Loca do Cabeco, close to the village of Fatima in central Portugal. Three children were grazing sheep in a meadow: nine-year-old Lucia, eight-year-old Francisco, and six-year-old Jacinta. They hardly seemed to be the sort that would shortly become the central figures of the most important apparition of the twentieth century. We do not know the exact date of the apparition, as children of this age do not attach much significance to times and dates. They were carefree, but unlike their peers, they not only played together but also prayed together. So it was on that spring day.

DEATH MARCH – Armenians forced into Syrian desert, 1915.

MOTHER MOURNING over a child – Armenian victims of the genocidal policy of the Ottoman government.

ROAD LEADING to Loca do Cabeco hill – 100 years ago and today.

PORTUGAL

Fatima
●Lisbon

Before we move on to the events that will preoccupy thousands of theologians and several popes, let us take a closer look at the main dramatis personae. Firstly, Lucia dos Santos – the cousin of the other two children, who were brother and sister. She came from a large, pious peasant family with a small farm. Though the youngest of seven siblings, she helped her parents by grazing the sheep. Of the three, she alone had been catechized and had had First Communion. Lucia mentioned that Holy Communion strongly affected her, drew her closer to God.

Secondly, her cousin Francisco Marto, an exceptionally quiet and level-headed boy for his age. He seemed to be indifferent to everything and did not feel the need to compete with his friends. He livened

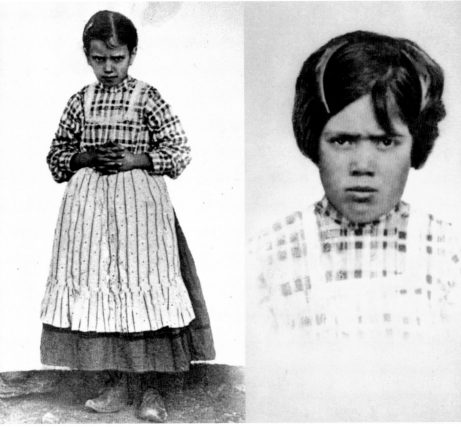

up whenever he left the village for the mountains. When communing with nature, he regained an interest in the world.

And finally his sister, Jacinta Marto, the youngest of the group. She was the complete opposite of her brother: a strong character, imposing her will on her peers, full of energy and new ideas. The three children lived in the hamlet of Aljustrel on the outskirts of Fatima.

The children were grazing sheep near Loca do Cabeco. After reciting the Rosary they started to play. They suddenly stopped when they heard a strong wind and saw a youth of about fifteeen years of age in front of them. He was no ordinary youth: whiter than snow, transparent as crystal, and of great beauty. The children were simultaneously fascinated and troubled by the sight. The stranger said: "Do not be afraid, I am the Angel of Peace. Pray with me."[1] He knelt, bowed down, and touched the ground with his forehead. The children did the same. Then the angel said a prayer three times: "My God, I believe, I adore, I hope, and I love You. I

LITTLE ENRICO – Francisco and Jacinta's nephew – next to his home with the family sheep.

JACINTA MARTO, the youngest of the visionaries (1917).

LUCIA DOS SANTOS, the principal visionary.

45

BOWING IN CHRISTIAN TRADITION

THE TRADITION OF BOWING one's head to the ground has been preserved in the Eastern churches, both the Orthodox and the Greek Catholic. It is particularly evident on the Monday, Tuesday, Wednesday, and Thursday of the first and the fifth weeks of Lent, when the Great Canon of St. Andrew of Crete is read in churches. St. Andrew was an outstanding Greek poet and preacher who lived in the 18th century.

This penitential canon is a lament over one's sinfulness and hard-heartedness, a demeaning of oneself, and an expression of bitter remorse for one's own faults, but at the same time one of faith in God's boundless mercy. This expiatory prayer, in a church plunged in darkness, is accompanied by 240 bows by the faithful.

ST. ANDREW of Crete – Orthodox icon.

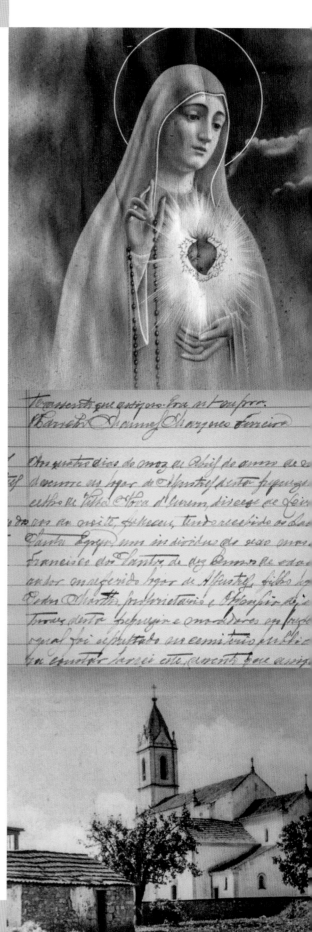

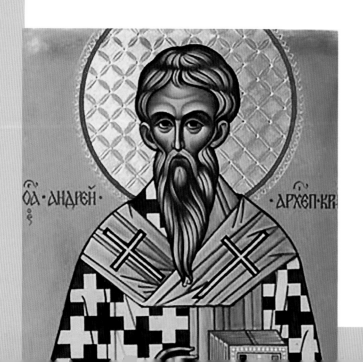

ask pardon of You for those who do not believe, do not adore, do not hope, and do not love You." Then the angel rose and said, "Pray thus. The Hearts of Jesus and Mary are attentive to the voice of your supplications."

Years later Lucia wrote: "The supernatural atmosphere which enveloped us was so intense, that we were for a long time scarcely aware of our own existence, remaining in the same posture in which he had left us, and continually repeating the same prayer. The presence of God made itself felt so intimately and so intensely that we did not even venture to speak to one another. Next day, we were still immersed in this spiritual atmosphere, which only gradually began to disappear."[2]

The children decided not to tell anyone of the extraordinary event. Thenceforth they constantly said the prayer that the stranger from another world had taught them.

PICTURE OF MARY – from Lucia's family home.

LUCIA'S MANUSCRIPT – account of the first apparition.

PARISH CHURCH – St. Anthony's, Fatima.

JACINTA, LUCIA, AND FRANCISCO – photo taken in the Martos' garden in Aljustrel.

TREE next to the path to the Santos' well.

GARDEN WELL – where the angel appeared.

Several months later, the summer of 1916, the children were sheltering from a heat wave in the shade of some trees. The angel appeared before them for the second time, near the well of the Santos' farm. The children gazed at him enraptured and astonished. He encouraged them to pray and to make sacrifices, as Jesus and Mary wanted to show the world a great deal of mercy through them. When they asked how they were to mortify themselves, he said: "Make of everything you can a sacrifice, and offer it to God as an act of reparation for the sins by which He is offended, and in supplication for the conversion of sinners. You will thus draw down peace upon your country. I am its Angel Guardian, the Angel of Portugal. Above all,

accept and bear with submission, the suffering which the Lord will send you."[3]

Let us pause for a moment and take a closer look at this celestial stranger. The mysterious visitor introduced himself to the children as the guardian angel of Portugal. The Church teaches that everyone is called to eternal life, that God sends everyone a guardian angel to help in fulfilling the will of God. If nations have such celestial guardians, it follows that they also have missions to fulfill. This is in accord with the Bible, as in the Book of Daniel Michael the Archangel kept watch over the Chosen People.

As Portugal saw the most momentous apparitions of the twentieth century, let us give some thought for a while to that country's mission. Geographically it is on the western edge of Europe, the edge of the Atlantic. In ancient times that territory was part of the

VIEW of Lucia's family house from the garden.

STATUES OF THE VISIONARIES where the angel appeared for the second time.

49

VANQUISHER OF THE MOORS – Alfonso the Conqueror.

CISTERCIAN Gothic church in Alcobaca – its central nave is 348 feet long.

STONE FOUNTAIN – monastery courtyard in Alcobaca.

Roman Empire. Christianity appeared there in the first centuries after Christ. In the eighth century Portugal, like the whole of the Iberian Peninsula, was conquered by invaders from North Africa, the Muslim Moors.

Throughout the following centuries, Christian knights attempted to liberate Portugal, succeeding in 1139 when Alfonso the Conqueror defeated the Muslims at the Battle of Ourique and became the first crowned ruler of the country. The king, as a votive offering of gratitude, built a huge church and monastery in honor of Our Lady in Alcobaca, where over one thousand Cistercians soon settled.

It is in those days that Fatima appeared on maps of Portugal. This was connected with the fervent love of the Christian knight Don Goncalo for Fatima, a Muslim princess. In Islam, her name is highly esteemed, as it was the name of Muhammad's youngest, beloved daughter. Princess Fatima returned Don Goncalo's love. She was baptized, taking the name Oureana, and married him, but she died a year later. Devastated, Don Goncalo became a Cistercian monk in

Alcobaca. Later he moved to another monastery. There he buried his wife's remains and named the place Fatima.

The valor of the Portuguese in battle is second only to their religious zeal. At a time when the Orthodox East and the Catholic West were having bitter arguments about the Holy Spirit, Queen Elizabeth of Portugal, under the influence of the Franciscans, established among her countrymen festivals in honor of the Holy Spirit. As a result, devotion to the third Person of the Trinity took root in Portugal in a way unparalleled anywhere else.

In the fourteenth century, Portugal was invaded by Spain, which laid claim to the throne of Lisbon. The Portuguese implored Our Lady for help, and despite being outnumbered they won the Battle of Aljubarrota in 1385. A monument was built to commemorate the deliverance of the country – a monastery complex in Batalha, funded by King John I of Portugal, which he bequeathed to the Dominicans.

JOHN I OF PORTUGAL.

BATTLE OF ALJUBARROTA – Portugal defeats Spain.

BATALHA MONASTERY – votive offering for the deliverance of the country.

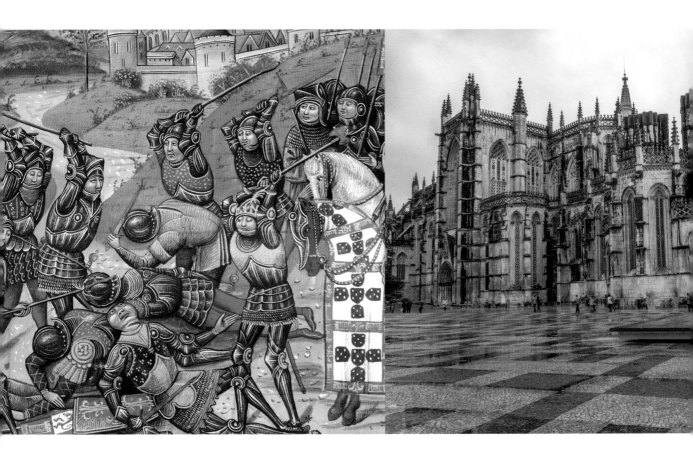

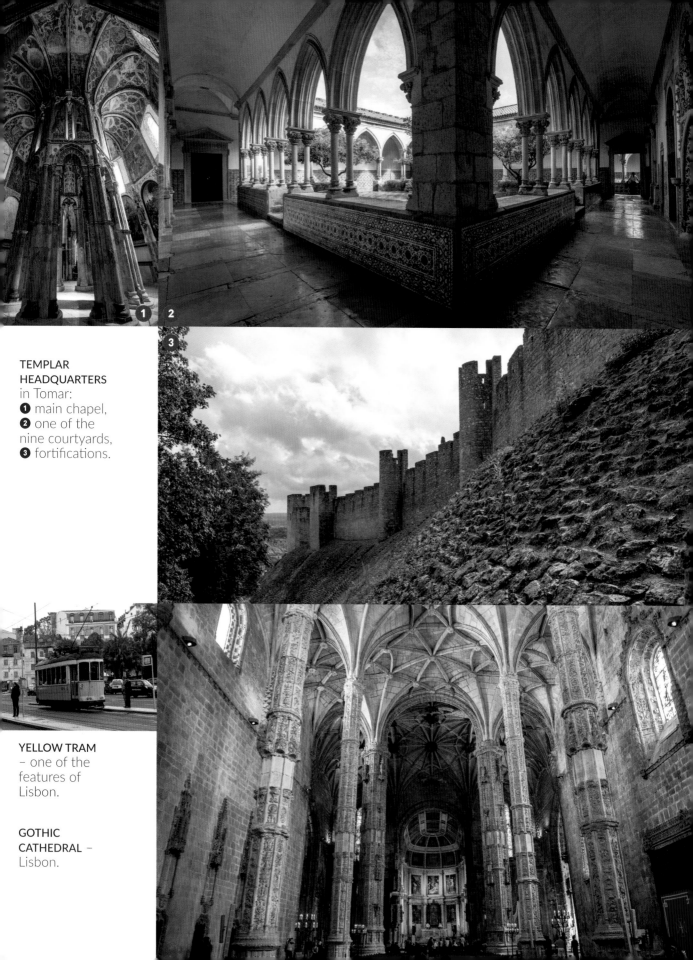

TEMPLAR HEADQUARTERS in Tomar:
❶ main chapel,
❷ one of the nine courtyards,
❸ fortifications.

YELLOW TRAM – one of the features of Lisbon.

GOTHIC CATHEDRAL – Lisbon.

LUIS DE CAMOES – Portugal's greatest poet.

DISCOVERIES MONUMENT – River Tagus, Lisbon.

PORTUGUESE GALLEON – sails with a red cross.

Portugal's geographical location meant that its history was inextricably linked with long ocean expeditions and great geographical discoveries. The conquest of overseas lands under the standards of the Holy Spirit is connected with the desire to evangelize and win over exotic peoples to the Church. Thus arose a specific Portuguese messianism that marked out a particular place for this nation in God's plan of salvation. Luis de Camoes, the greatest Portuguese poet, wrote in his *The Lusiads* that Lisbon, by the will of heaven, would become a new Rome.

In the fourteenth century, King Denis of Portugal granted asylum to the Knights Templar, an order that had been suppressed throughout Europe. With the pope's consent, he changed its name to the Military Order of Christ. The Templar monastery in Tomar became the order's headquarters. Its first task was to defend Portugal against the Moors. Henry the Navigator later enlisted their help with colonizing Africa and spreading the Faith there. The Templars'

VASCO DA GAMA – discovered the sea route to India.

53

HENRY THE NAVIGATOR established the world's first maritime academy.

MARQUIS OF POMBAL – best-known figure of the Portuguese Enlightenment.

characteristic cross, known from the Holy Land Crusades, marked the sails of Portuguese ships.

In 1646, King John IV, "the Restorer", declared Our Lady Immaculate, Queen and Patroness of Portugal. Henceforth the Lisbon monarchs did not wear a crown as this insignia of royalty was reserved for the Virgin Mary alone.

In the eighteenth century Portugal was regarded as one of the most religiously fervent countries in Europe. According to the 1750 General Census, of the three million inhabitants, two hundred thousand were monks and nuns in more than five hundred monasteries. The same century, however, saw the beginnings of secularization, personified by the Enlightenment prime minister, the Marquis of Pombal. In the nineteenth century the state's Catholic character was undermined, mainly through the efforts of Freemasons. Masonry sought to overthrow the old social order, the main pillar of which was Catholicism.

On October 3, 1910, the *Sao Paulo*, a Brazilian battleship, sailed into Lisbon. The president of Brazil Hermes Rodrigues da Fonseca was on board, on an official visit to Portugal. The opposition to the Portuguese monarchy organized a manifestation in the capital in

KING JOHN IV "THE RESTORER" renounced his throne for Luisa Maria.

PORTUGUESE COAT OF ARMS

PORTUGAL is the only country that has a symbol of Christ's five wounds as part of its national emblem. It appeared in the 12th century and is connected with the first king of Portugal, Alfonso the Conqueror, who defeated five Muslim rulers. He placed five small shields on his coat of arms to commemorate these victories.

On July 25, 1139, during the Battle of Ourique, Alfonso had a vision of the crucified Christ. The vision inspired him to believe in victory though he was greatly outnumbered by the Islamic soldiers, led by Ali ibn Yusuf. The king commemorated his victory by adding five silver bezants, symbolizing Christ's wounds, on the five blue shields. In the 15th century Henry the Navigator became the grand master of the sea-going Military Order of Christ (formerly the Templars) and organized expeditions along the western coast of Africa. He established the world's first maritime academy, and great Portuguese mariners entered history: Vasco da Gama, discoverer of the sea route to India, and Pedro Cabral, who discovered Brazil.

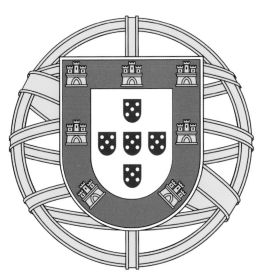

BRAZILIAN BATTLESHIP, the *Sao Paulo*, one of the symbols of the Portuguese revolution of 1910. Its presence in Lisbon instigated a revolt.

KING MANUEL II was forced to abdicate. He fled to Gibraltar on a yacht.

honor of the guest, a Republican. Demonstrations turned into riots, and the riots into a revolution. Members of the Republican Party and Freemasonry organized a coup. The colonial fleet turned the scales in favor of the rebellion. King Manuel II, just a twenty-one-year-old youth, escaped to Gibraltar on a yacht. On October 5, the victors proclaimed the First Republic.

Freemasonry had a great influence on shaping the state. Over half the ministers were Freemasons, as were the three successive presidents: Bernardino Machado, Sidonio Pais, and Antonio Jose de Almeida. It was the members of clandestine lodges that imparted an anti-clerical nature to the revolution. During clashes, a dozen or so priests were murdered and over one hundred assaulted. Shortly the Church began to suffer repressions. Alfonso Costa, a Mason, the minister of justice, enacted anti-clerical laws: He banned Catholic schools, removed religious

ENTHUSIASTIC WELCOME for the Brazilian president in Lisbon in October 1910.

PRESIDENT OF BRAZIL Hermes Rodriguez da Fonseca – in office from 1910 to 1914.

symbols from public places, abolished Church feast days (e.g., Christmas was changed into Family Feast Day), dismissed priests from the army, severed diplomatic relations with the Vatican, and confiscated Church possessions. Bishops were driven out of the country when they protested.

In January 1913, Alfonso Costa became prime minister. The war against Christianity escalated. Costa decided to send lay missions to the colonies to replace Catholic missionaries and to convince the natives of the benefits of atheism. On June 10, 1913, a procession in honor of St. Anthony in the center of Lisbon had bombs hurled at it – about twenty people perished, including several children. The murderers were terrorists called White Ants, who had the support of the prime minister.

In 1914 there was a rift in the Republican camp. In large measure it coincided with a conflict in Masonry between the Supreme Council of the Thirty-Third Degree, led by Gen. Augusto Ferreira de Castro, and the Great United Portuguese East, led by the grand master

57

BATTLE OF THE LYS
in Belgium, April
1918. Portuguese
Expeditionary
Corps soldiers in
trenches.

Magalhaes Lima. Part of the ruling faction thought that the radical anti-Catholic policy threatened to occasion too much social tension and civil war. So in January 1914, Costa was forced to resign. He was replaced by Bernardino Machado, who somewhat toned down the policy with regard to the Church.

But not for long. On May 14, 1915, the radicals staged a putsch, during which three hundred people perished. Not long afterwards, Alfonso Costa returned to power. The battle with religion began anew. The new government closed seminaries and Catholic editorial offices. The White Ants murdered believers unhindered, both religious and lay. Hundreds were assassinated or executed. Over a hundred churches were burnt, and several hundred plundered and profaned. Costa was nicknamed "Mata-Frades" (Monk Killer).

The majority of Portuguese disapproved of the government's anti-clerical policy, but they were mainly rural people, predominantly passive and incapable of self-organization. The most active urban circles supported the revolution, particularly in Lisbon.

**BERARDINO
MACHADO**
– Mason,
prime minister,
and president
of Portugal.

**MACHADO
CARICATURE**
– the
beginning
of the 20th
century.

PORTUGUESE SOLDIERS training before their departure to the front.

COIMBRA MONUMENT commemorating soldiers killed in action during World War I.

In March 1916, Portugal, hitherto neutral, at the instigation of the British, commandeered German ships moored in Portuguese ports. In response, Germany declared war. It is then that the Angel of Portugal appeared to three children in Fatima. They knew nothing of Masonry, but they heard of wars somewhere far off, and that young men from neighboring villages were being called up for military service.

Lucia, Francisco, and Jacinta not only prayed for the conversion of sinners, as the angel had instructed, but they also made sacrifices for their sake. They daily united their little offerings, like denying themselves pleasures or conveniences, with Christ's suffering. Though they had not as yet experienced much in life, they sensed that to love someone meant to be with that person in the most difficult situations. It was to do everything to lighten, though a little, a dear person's load. The Passion was such a time for Christ. Hence the children wanted to accompany Christ at such times. They, though but for a moment, wanted to share their own suffering with Him, and thus draw closer to Him. Since Christ died to save everyone, the children, uniting with Him spiritually, desired to make amends for people's sins, which so offended God.

MARTO FAMILY FARMSTEAD in Aljustrel. View from the garden.

MONUMENT OF THE SHEPHERDS in Fatima.

The children often went to Loca do Cabeco, where the angel first appeared to them. One autumn day they were there on their knees praying, when they suddenly found themselves in an incredibly intense light. The messenger from heaven appeared before them for the third time. As Lucia recalled, he held a chalice in his hands "with a host above it from which some drops of blood were falling into the sacred vessel". Leaving the chalice and the host suspended in the air, the angel knelt down and said the following prayer three times: "Most Holy Trinity, Father, Son, and Holy Spirit, I adore You profoundly, and I offer You the most precious Body, Blood, Soul, and Divinity of Jesus Christ, present in all the tabernacles of the world, in reparation for the outrages, sacrileges, and indifference with which He Himself is offended. And, through the infinite merits of His most Sacred Heart, and of the Immaculate Heart of Mary, I beg of You for the conversion of poor sinners."[4]

The angel asked the children to say the prayer three times. He then stood up, took the chalice and the host, and proffered them to the children. Lucia was the first to receive the Most Blessed Sacrament.

OLIVE GARDEN between Aljustrel and Valinhos.

STATUE OF AN ANGEL with a chalice – House of Light, Fatima.

61

CHAPLET OF DIVINE MERCY

ON SEPTEMBER 13, 1935, Sr. Faustina Kowalska had two visions in her convent cell in Vilnius: first of an angel, the executor of God's wrath, and then the Holy Trinity. The angel was preparing to punish humanity for its sins, but God was prepared to show people His mercy. The nun began to beg for mercy for the world when she heard a prayer in her heart, very like the one the angel had taught the children in Fatima. The prayer is known as the Chaplet of Divine Mercy. It is as follows:

> Eternal Father, I offer You the Body and Blood, Soul and Divinity of Your Dearly Beloved Son, Our Lord, Jesus Christ, in atonement for our sins and those of the whole world.

Thirty years later, a dispute about Sr. Faustina arose among Polish theologians, particularly about the dogmatic correctness of the Chaplet of Divine Mercy. The prayer, according to the then vice chancellor of the Catholic University of Lublin, Rev. Wincenty Granat, contained serious theological errors. The opinion of his adversary, Rev. Ignacy Rozycki, ultimately prevailed. He, referring to St. Paul's letters and Council of Trent statements, established that the chaplet was completely in accord with Catholic teaching. He also referred to the prayer the angel had taught the children in Fatima.

Vilnius

● Warsaw

POLAND
before 1939

ST. FAUSTINA KOWALSKA.

MERCIFUL JESUS – painting by Eugeniusz Kazimirowski

FRAGMENT OF A DIARY – Sr. Faustina's: "Jesus I Trust in You."

ANGEL
MONUMENT
commemorating
the Loca
do Cabeco
apparition.

Jacinta and Francisco were bashful as they had not yet received Holy Communion. The angel proffered the chalice to them. They drank while he said: "Take and drink the Body and Blood of Jesus Christ, horribly outraged by ungrateful men. Repair their crimes and console your God."[5] He then knelt down again, said the prayer he had taught the children three times, and then disappeared.

There is another element in these visions that, besides the bows, turns our attention to Eastern Christianity. It is the reception of Holy Communion under both kinds, practiced by the Orthodox and the Greek Catholic Churches, whereas the Roman Catholic Church has usually restricted it to the Lord's Body.

The children were alone, in a state of bliss. They sensed the presence of God so strongly, filling them with happiness, that they lost all sense of time and place. The children were unfamiliar with theology, but they had a sense of faith, that which the Church Fathers defined as *sensus fidei*. The revelation of the angel showed them how spiritually life-giving the Most Blessed Sacrament is. During the eucharistic ecstacy they experienced the real presence of Christ in the form of bread and wine. They began to comprehend that God's love very often met with man's ingratitude. They, with all their childlike simplicity and sincerity, wanted to comfort God. But how could one comfort God?

In the meantime, the warring sides in Europe continued to lose a lot of men in the long, drawn-out war. At the beginning of 1917 the Portuguese Expeditionary Corps reached France and set out for the front. Lists of the dead and wounded were regularly displayed in town and city squares. The Portuguese were seized with fear. By the end of the war over seven thousand of their countrymen had perished and twice as many had been wounded.

Let us take a look at what was happening in Rome. On February 17, 1917, the Italian Masons organized an event to celebrate three anniversaries. The first was February 17, 1600, when a former Dominican, Giordano Bruno, an esoteric philospher and occultist, was burned at the stake. The Freemasons regard him as a hero. The second was the four hundredth anniversary of the appearance of Martin Luther's Ninety-Five Theses in Wittenberg, which historians see as the beginning of the Reformation. The third was the two hundredth anniversary of the establishment of the Premier Grand Lodge of England in London.

GIORDANO BRUNO monument, Campo di Fiori, Rome.

64

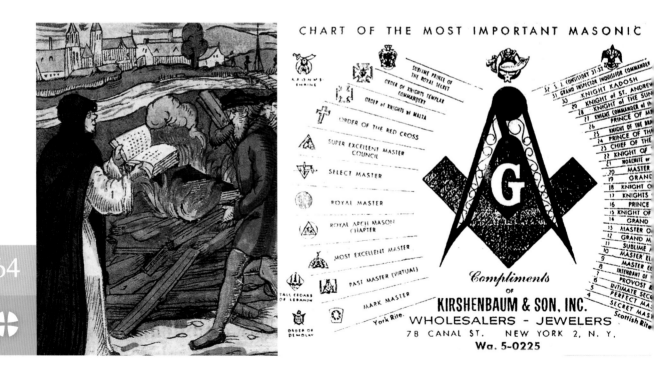

MARTIN LUTHER burning a papal bull.   **IMPRESSIVE CHART** of the most important Masonic symbols.

The demonstrators were making their way along the streets of Rome, carrying standards with an image of Lucifer and Michael the Archangel at his feet. They were shouting anti-papal slogans, claiming that the devil would shortly begin to rule in the Vatican and that the pope would serve him as a doorman. An infuriated twenty-five-year-old Polish cleric from the Seraphic College, Maximilian Maria Kolbe, observed the demonstrators. He went to his vice chancellor, Fr. Stefan Ignudi, and asked him if he could go and see the grand master of Masonry so as to convert him. The experienced priest did not give his consent, and he gave the young student some advice: to pray for the leader of the Masons and particularly to request the intercession of Our Lady Immaculate. Kolbe took this to heart, and a certain idea began to dawn on him.

Meanwhile, Benedict XV, more and more horrified by the bloody conflict, which he called the "suicide of Europe", decided to seek Our Lady's aid. On May 5, 1917, he added a new petition to the Litany of the Blessed Virgin Mary: "Queen of peace, pray for us." He also summoned people to pray the Novena to Our Lady, Queen of Peace in her honor. In a document issued for the occasion, he asked the Blessed Virgin Mary to hear the cries of children, of mothers and wives, that she might help to end the terrible war. An answer came eight days later in Fatima.

MASONIC LODGE near Covent Garden, London.

MASONIC INITIATION

Miracle of the Sun

CHAPTER 3

Miracle of the Sun

On October 13, 1917, thousands of people witnessed an event that convinced them three shepherd children had received messages from heaven.

WOODEN STATUE of the Blessed Virgin Mary – House of Light, Fatima.

On Sunday, May 13, 1917, Lucia, Francisco, and Jacinta were at morning Mass. Then they went to graze the sheep at the Cova da Iria. They suddenly saw lightning in the sky. Certain that a storm was approaching, they started to drive the sheep off the meadow and headed home. After a while they saw another flash of light, hence they began to hurry. But they stopped when they saw a figure of an unknown woman in white hovering above a holm oak. She was so radiant that it was as if her mantle and gown were made of light. She had a small, luminous sphere hanging from her neck, a bright rosary in her hands, and a star at her feet.

The overawed children stood trembling. As yet they did not know that they were in the presence of the Blessed Virgin Mary. She, in order to reassure them, said: "Do not be afraid. I will do you no harm."[6] She looked about seventeen years of age. A dialogue ensued between her and Lucia:

"Where are you from?"

"I am from heaven"

"What do you want of me?"

"I have come to ask you to come here for six months in succession, on the 13th day, at this same hour. Later on I will tell you who I am and what I want. Afterwards, I will return here yet a seventh time."

"Shall I go to heaven too?"

"Yes, you will."

68

LUCIA, FRANCISCO, AND JACINTA – Martos' garden October 13, 1917.

Fatima

• Lisbon

PORTUGAL

CHURCH OF ST. ANTHONY of Padua, Fatima. St. Anthony, born in Lisbon in 1195, was an outstanding Portuguese theologian and preacher.

LUCIA'S FAMILY HOME in Aljustrel: ❶ contemporary view from the street, ❷ Manuel dos Santo's room, ❸ kitchen, ❹ 1917 photo, ❺ utility room, ❻ crucifix.

"And Jacinta?"

"She will go also."

"And Francisco?"

"He will go there too, but he must say many Rosaries."[7]

Lucia asked about two deceased friends, Maria and Amelia. The Lady told her that Maria was already in heaven, and that Amelia would stay in purgatory until the end of the world.

Only Lucia conversed with the Lady. She alone of the three saw, heard, and spoke to her. Jacinta only saw and heard the Lady. Francisco only saw her.

When Lucia was silent, the Lady asked questions. The most important of which was: "Are you willing to offer yourselves to God and bear all the sufferings He wills to send you, as an act of reparation for the sins by which He is offended, and of supplication for the conversion of sinners?"[8]

3 5

6

When the children replied in the affirmative, the Lady told them that they would have to suffer a great deal, but that God's grace would not desert them. After a while the Lady, as Lucia recalled, opened her hands. "Rays penetrated our hearts and the innermost depths of our souls, making us see ourselves in God, Who was that light, more clearly than we see ourselves in the best of mirrors. Then, moved by an interior impulse that was also communicated to us, we fell on our knees, repeating in our hearts: 'O most Holy Trinity, I adore You! My God, my God, I love You in the most Blessed Sacrament!'"[9]

This experience helped them at times of tribulation, for suffering soon came, as the Lady had said. Before she departed from the Cova da Iria, she asked the children to pray the Rosary daily for world peace and the end of the war. Then she rose up in the air and disappeared.

The children promised that they would not tell anyone about the extraordinary event. But that was difficult. On the one hand they wanted to be silent, but on the other they were bursting with

71

CHURCH OF ST. ANTHONY – where Lucia received her first Holy Communion

FR. MANUEL FERREIRA – Fatima parish priest from 1914 to 1919 – questioned the visionaries.

the urge to tell everyone. Jacinta was the first to reveal the secret and confided to her mother, Maria Rosa, who did not believe her, as was the case with her brothers and sisters. Francisco's testimony did not help, although it confirmed Jacinta's account. They were subjected to mockery and snide remarks in their own home. News of their adventure quickly spread, and they soon became the laughing stock of the whole village. Their father, Manuel Marto, was the only one in the family who believed them.

Lucia's parents learnt of her visions from a third party. Her mother was furious. She thought that her daughter had made everything up and was causing amongst their neighbors a growing aversion towards the family. Constantly hearing people scorning her behind her back, she took Lucia by the hand to see the parish priest, Fr. Manuel Ferreira. She counted on the priest to force her daughter to admit the story was a hoax. But after listening to Lucia's account, he did not reject it. He recommended prudence:

SPIRITUAL VISIONS

CATHOLIC THEOLOGY distinguishes three kinds of private revelation: sensory (*visio sensibilis*), interior (*visio imaginativa*) and spiritual (*visio intellectualis*). In the first case we are dealing with sensory perception, bodily perception. In the third category we have imageless visions, characteristic of profound mystical experiences.

The apparitions in Fatima were of the interior kind. They were seen solely by the visionaries, while witnesses around them did not see anything. The visions were not, however, products of the imagination, but a real way of perceiving reality, which can be called supersensory. Some theologians say that images in such visions are accessible thanks to "interior senses".

Such apparitions are not photographic recordings of the material world, but images from another dimension of reality, the sense of which can be expressed by symbolic language.

to await further developments. He also suggested that the children be allowed to continue going to the Cova da Iria.

After those experiences Lucia herself decided not to go there. She had the parish priest's words in mind, that the vision might well be a demonic delusion. This possibility sowed doubts in her heart. One night, a nightmare tormented her. She saw the devil laughing at her, as she had allowed him to deceive her. She awoke terrified. On the morning of June 13 she did not want to go to the place where the apparitions occurred, but she changed her mind as an inner force urged her to go.

On the day that the Lady spoke of for her next visit, the three visionaries made their way to the Cova da Iria once again. To their amazement awaiting them were about fifty people who had heard of the anticipated revelation. At that time the majority of the inhabitants of Fatima were making their way to the Church of St. Anthony to celebrate the parish patron's feast day.

The people gathered at the Cova da Iria were praying the Rosary. On ending, the children saw a light approaching them from a distance. Like the first time, the Virgin Mary appeared above the holm oak. No one saw her apart from the three visionaries. Nobody heard her voice. But all saw the little shepherds, having lost all sense of time and space, standing enraptured, eyes fixed on some invisible reality.

Our Lady and Lucia conversed for the second time. She asked the children to come there again in a month, recite the Rosary daily, and learn to read, as all three were illiterate. Lucia asked Our Lady about curing a certain acquaintance. She said: "If he is converted, he will be cured during the year."[10]

And so it was. The acquaintance, Joao Carreira, was lame. His mother prayed that he might be healed and that he might find a job. The boy was healed and later became a sacristan at the sanctuary in Fatima, a position he held for almost fifty years.

Lucia also begged Mary to take all three of them to heaven. Our Lady replied: "Yes. I will take Jacinta and Francisco soon. But you are to stay here some time longer. Jesus wishes to make use of you to make me known and loved. He wants to establish in the world devotion to my Immaculate Heart."[11]

TYPICAL FATIMA landscape

MARTO FAMILY HOME in Aljustrel – photo from the early 20th century.

Lucy became sad, as she would not be able to go to heaven just yet, and because she was to remain alone, without her cousins. Mary reassured her. She told her that she would never abandon her, and that she would always be of aid to her. The children then saw a light akin to the one during the May apparition. But this time they saw a heart surrounded by thorns in front of her right hand. It was obvious to them that it was an image of the Immaculate Heart of Mary, affronted by the sins of humanity, and desiring reparation.

From that day on, news of the events in Fatima spread throughout Portugal. Eyewitnesses related that they saw the children, in a state of ecstacy, conversing with an invisible person. The news began to live a life of its own, moving some, irritating others. The children's village was divided into two camps: Some believed them; the majority remained distrustful. The event aroused curiosity and emotions to the point that on July 13, 1917, four thousand people appeared at the Cova da Iria.

A situation akin to the one a month earlier arose. The visionaries again saw Mary in bright white. As before she instructed them to come back in a month and recite the Rosary. Mary added, however, that it should be in honor of Our Lady of the Rosary to pray

SALE OF FATIMA DEVOTIONAL objects in Aljustrel, including *azulejos*, ornate ceramic tilework characteristic of Portugal.

75

FRANCISCO AND JACINTA'S family home: contemporary view from the street; garden gate; wall separating the garden from the footpath.

for the end of the war and world peace as that was the only way to achieve it.

The incident was disagreeable to politicians, generals, and diplomats. Their views about war and peace were determined by economic advantages, military power, a network of mutual alliances and commitments, and most frequently a combination of all these factors – not prayer, especially not the Rosary, a prayer despised and ridiculed by enlightened intellectuals, a prayer of the illiterate who repeated it over and over again.

There was yet one more reason to mock. The message, of the highest importance, determining the fate of the continent, and perhaps even the fate of the world, turned out to be addressed not to emperors, kings, presidents, prime ministers or millionaires, but to three illiterate shepherd children from a hitherto unknown village, which alone was enough to make one shrug one's shoulders contemptuously on hearing of it.

Such thoughts did not preoccupy Lucia, who asked the Lady who she was. She also asked for a miracle, thanks to which all might be convinced that she was telling the truth. Mary assured her that she would reveal her identity in October, when she would occasion a miracle so that people might believe.

Lucia conveyed requests to Our Lady from people who had come to her during the last month. She mentioned those she remembered. Most frequently they were matters concerned with physical and spiritual healing. Mary promised favors, but on one condition – the recitation of the Rosary. She also told the children: "Sacrifice yourself for sinners, and say many times, especially whenever you make some sacrifice: O Jesus, it is for love of You, for the conversion of sinners, and in reparation for the sins committed against the Immaculate Heart of Mary."[12]

Then Our Lady spread out her hands, as in May and June. The children were convinced that the same thing would happen for the third time, the more so because Mary's hands were again emanating rays of light. However, something suddenly occurred that was simultaneously surprising and terrifying. Lucia recalled:

"The rays of light seemed to penetrate the earth, and we saw as it were a sea of fire. Plunged in this fire were demons and souls in human form, like transparent burning embers, all blackened or burnished bronze, floating about in the conflagration, now raised into the air by the flames that issued from within themselves together with great clouds of smoke, now falling back on every side like sparks in huge fires, without weight or equilibrium, amid shrieks and groans of pain and despair, which horrified us and made us tremble with fear. (It must have been the sight that caused me to cry out, as people say they heard me.) The demons could be distinguished by their terrifying and repellent likeness to frightful and unknown animals, black and transparent like burning coals. Terrified and as if to plead for succor, we looked up at Our Lady, who said to us kindly but so sadly: 'You have seen hell where the souls of poor sinners go. To save them, God wishes to establish in the world devotion to my Immaculate Heart. If what I say to you is done, many souls will be saved and there will be peace.' "[13]

JOAO MARTO, Francisco and Jacinta's brother, witness of the apparition in Valinhos.

FRANCISCO'S BED, where he spent his last days.

KEROSENE
LAMP from
Lucia's home.

Our Lady continued, but let us pause for a while to make a small digression. Lucia said later that it was at that moment that the first Fatima secret ended. It included a vision of hell and an explanation as to how to save sinners from eternal damnation.

The existence of hell is a truth of the Faith, present in Holy Scripture and the Tradition of the Church, and repeatedly confirmed by papal documents, the statements of councils, and the revelations of mystics. It is not connected with God's vengeance, but the free will of man, who can choose between good and evil. Ultimately, he can side with sin, Satan, and death. Hence one condemns oneself to eternal damnation.

Many, however, even Christians, do not accept the existence of hell, and they do not believe in the possibility of losing their souls.

Sr. Faustina Kowalska, who had a vision similar to the Fatima vision of hell, said that most souls in hell had not believed in its existence. In her *Diary*, she wrote that this terrible afterlife reality was shown to her solely so that she might testify to its existence. It was so with the Portuguese children. Our Lady assured them that they would go to heaven, but she showed them the infernal abyss to warn all against it. Then she passed on to the next part, later called the second Fatima secret:

"The war is going to end; but if people do not cease offending God, a worse one will break out during the pontificate of Pius XI. When you see a night illumined by an unknown light, know that this is the great sign given you by God that He is about to punish the

JACINTA AND Lucia – cousins from Fatima (September 1917).

FRANCISCO MARTO – an introvert.

WOODEN STOOL from the Martos' home.

79

MARTO FAMILY in 1920. Front – Manuel and Olimpia, Francisco and Jacinta's parents. Back – Antonio and Manuel, Olimpia's sons from her first marriage, as well as Joao and Teresa, the Martos' children.

PANTRY in the Martos' house.

DOS SANTOS FAMILY in 1920. Front- Maria Rosa (widow) and her fourteen-year-old daughter, Lucia. Back – Lucia's brother, Manuel, and her sisters, Maria dos Santos holding her daughter, Carolina de Jesus, and Gloria de Jesus.

MANUEL AND OLIMPIA Marto, Francisco and Jacinta's parents.

world for its crimes, by means of war, famine, and persecutions of the Church and of the Holy Father. To prevent this, I shall come to ask for the consecration of Russia to my Immaculate Heart, and the Communion of Reparation on the First Saturdays. If my requests are heeded, Russia will be converted, and there will be peace; if not she will spread her errors throughout the world, causing wars and persecutions of the Church. The good will be martyred, the Holy

FRANCISCO AND his brothers' room: Antoni, Manuel, Jose, and Joao.

Father will have much to suffer, various nations will be annihilated. In the end my Immaculate Heart will triumph. The Holy Father will consecrate Russia to me and she will be converted, and a period of peace will be granted to the world. In Portugal, the dogma of the Faith will always be preserved."[14]

Our Lady said other things that became known as the third secret of Fatima. Until the third secret was revealed by the Vatican in 2000, there was much speculation about it.

Let us first take a look at the second secret, which concerns war, Russia's errors, persecutions of the Church, and the pope's suffering. Mary spoke of the end of the war, but at the same time foresaw another, a much more terrible war. She explained that the cause of the war would be people's sins. What Our Lady said was incomprehensible to the illiterate Lucia. It would have even been incomprehensible to the educated, had they been in her place, for in July 1917, no one had heard of Pius XI or of Russia's godless propaganda.

Russia was at the center of Mary's message. When Lucia first heard the word "Russia", she thought it was the name of a sinful woman who needed to be converted. Francisco was convinced that it concerned his uncle's stubborn mule, which was called Russa.

There was more to the July revelation. Our Lady instructed the children to add the following to every mystery of the Rosary: "O my Jesus, forgive us our sins, save us from the fires of hell. Lead all souls to heaven, especially those most in need of Thy mercy. Amen." This is known as the "Fatima addition", which became an inseparable part of the Rosary throughout the world.

The children did not reveal what they had seen or heard to anyone. They were obedient to Mary, who told them to keep everything

OBJECTS OF DAILY USE from the Martos' home.

ROOM where Francisco died on April 4, 1919.

a secret. She allowed Lucia and Jacinta to tell Francisco, as he did not hear anything. As a result, the first two secrets were not revealed for almost twenty-five years, while the third intrigued the curious until 2000.

Lucia did not want to disclose everything she had heard from Mary to those gathered at the Cova da Iria. She did tell them that a great miracle would occur on October 13 and confirm the authenticity of the revelations. This announcement heightened the crowd's curiosity. News of the promised miracle spread rapidly throughout the country. The inquisitive began to arrive in Fatima. Articles about the little visionaries appeared in the press. The majority of journalists were skeptical and anti-clerical. They ridiculed the villagers'

HOUSE IN ALJUSTREL – birthplace of Francisco and Jacinta.

83

TO THIS DAY members of the Marto family preserve objects associated with the visionaries.

ignorance, accused the clergy of spreading superstitions, and criticized the local authorities for their lack of a robust response.

Fatima and the neighboring villages were then part of the administrative district of Vila Nova de Ourem, where Arturo de Oliveira Santos was the chairman of the council, hence the most important representative of the state authorities. Baptized a Catholic, he abandoned the faith of his ancestors, became a Mason, and enthusiastically supported the 1910 revolution. Disturbed by religious incidents in his district, he decided to put things in order. He summoned the three little shepherds.

Lucia and her father, Antonio, turned up. Manuel Marto came instead of his children Jacinta and Francisco. He stated that the ten miles from Fatima to Ourem was too far for them to come personally. So the administrator questioned Lucia, without witnesses. He urged her to admit to a fabrication, and to reveal the secret. He categorically forbade her to go to the Cova da Iria, threatened to impose a fine on her parents, and even threatend her with death. The ten-year-old was frightened but unyielding. Then Arturo Santos asked the fathers for their opinions. Antonio dos Santos replied evasively, saying that it was all just a lot of female prattle. Manuel

HEARTH AND HOME.

LUCIA'S SIBLINGS in 1968: Maria Gloria, Manuel, Maria dos Anjos, Maria Carolina, and Maria Teresa.

85

WEAVING WORKSHOP at the dos Santos home.

FRANCISCO'S canvas bag

Marto, however, admitted that he believed his children. The administrator remained dissatisfied.

On August 13, Arturo Santos arrived in Aljustrel in his carriage. He told the children that he wanted to witness the apparition, as he was like doubting Thomas, who did not believe until he saw for himself. He proposed to take them to the local parish priest and then to the Cova da Iria. The little visionaries willingly agreed and got into the carriage. They headed towards the church, but the carriage suddenly changed direction and sped to Ourem.

Meanwhile an enormous crowd had gathered in the valley of the Cova da Iria. People awaited the three little shepherds and the promised revelation. But the children did not appear. No one knew

PUBLIC AND PRIVATE REVELATIONS

CATHOLIC THEOLOGY distinguishes public revelations from private revelations. The former concern the numerous works of God recorded in the Old and the New Testaments. An acquaintance with them – as Cardinal Joseph Ratzinger noted – is not a purely intellectual activity, but a process that involves the whole person in order to draw one into the mystery of God and a personal relationship with Him. The Church states that public revelation has definitively ended (nothing more can be added), and that belief in it is necessary for every Christian.

It is otherwise with visions experienced by believers like the Fatima children. According to the *Catechism of the Catholic Church*: "Throughout the ages, there have been so-called 'private' revelations, some of which have been recognized by the authority of the Church.... It is not their role to improve or complete Christ's definitive Revelation, but to help live more fully by it in a certain period of history."[15] Belief in such revelations, even when they have been officially recognized by the Church, is not obligatory to Catholics. One can accept them to better understand the Faith and to experience one's relationship with God more profoundly.

THE FOLLOWIG had private revelations: ❶ Marthe Robin, ❷ St. Padre Pio, ❸ Sr. Stanislawa Barbara Samulowska from Gietrzwald, ❹ St. John Bosco, ❺ Miguel Juan Pellicer from Calanda.

ARTURO DE OLIVEIRA SANTOS – official who arrested the visionaries.

ADMINISTRATOR'S HOUSE – where the childern were detained.

ADMINISTRATOR'S HOME – now the Ourem City Museum.

FRAGMENT OF Arturo de Oliveira Santos' account.

what had happened. People were concerned. Suddenly someone shouted that the little visionaries had been kidnapped by the administrator. There was an uproar. People were furious, shouting. Suddenly there was a thunderclap. All fell silent. Lightning flashed, and then a thin white cloud floated down from the sky and settled on a holm oak. Some fell to their knees. All were amazed to see that everything around them was shimmering with all the colors of the rainbow. Shortly afterwards, the little cloud rose into the sky and disappeared. Many came to believe in the authenticity of the apparitions.

People were angry. They wanted to go to the administrator's house and free the children. Manuel Marto feared that the disturbances would only make matters worse for his children. So he tried to calm the outraged crowd. Some, however, went off to protest at the rectory as they were convinced that the parish priest was in league with the administrator.

In the meantime, the frightened children arrived at Arturo de Oliveira Santos' home in Ourem. The host invited them in

for dinner. His wife was a pious woman, who had to conceal her faith from her husband. She prepared a refined meal for her little guests. Everyone was unusually pleasant and friendly to them. The politician hoped that he could convince the children through goodness. He questioned them again, trying to win them over by requests rather than by threats. The children stopped being afraid but stuck to their guns. They spent the night of August 13 at the administrator's home.

The following day, Santos changed his approach. He stopped appearing to be gentle, and he imprisoned the children in a cell together with some criminals. The children were scared, but they kept up their spirits through prayer. They said that they were offering their suffering for the conversion of sinners. Their attitude moved the criminals, who also recited the Rosary.

Santos was convinced that their stay in a dark prison with dangerous thugs would break the children's resistance. He summoned them for questioning, and he urged them to admit the visions were a hoax. The children categorically refused. Then he tried a different

PRISON BARS in Ourem – where the visionaries were detained.

CITY HALL in Ourem – where the visionaries were questioned.

Ourem

Fatima
Lisbon

PORTUGAL

89

ADMISTRATOR'S ROOM, where Arturo de Oliveira Santos questioned the children.

FR. MANUEL FERREIRA, Fatima parish priest, many years after the apparitions.

90

✜

tack and demanded to know the secret. The administrator threatened them with a very painful death – in boiling oil. They, however, preferred martyrdom to revealing the secret.

The administrator came to the conclusion that the visionaries were steadfast because they were together. Hence he decided to separate them, question them individually, and break them one by one. He started with Jacinta, for as the youngest she was – so he thought – the weakest link. He tried to frighten her in various ways. He even called a guard and asked if the boiling oil was ready. The guard reported that it was. Finally he pretended that the seven-year-old girl was being led out to be boiled. Yet she, shaking with fear, said that she preferred to die. Francisco and Lucia were subjected to the same ordeal.

The administrator was impressed by the children's courage. He detained them for another day, and on August 15 – the Feast of the Assumption – he sent them back to Fatima. The coachman dropped

off the children at the rectory just as people were coming out of the church. Not only Catholics, but also those who were anti-clerical were outraged by the administrator's disgraceful behavior. He had abused his power by kidnapping the little children and by threatening them with death.

Arturo Santos attempted to justify himself by claiming that Fr. Manuel Ferreira, the Fatima parish priest, was his accomplice. The priest wrote an open letter to the local newspaper, *O Ouriense*, saying that the accusation concerning his alleged participation in kidnapping the children was an unjust and base slander. In the same letter he explained that he did not attend the apparitions because he did not want to give nonbelievers any pretext to see him as inspiring

STATUE OF MARY in Valinhos – fourth apparition occurred there on August 19, 1917.

JACINTA, LUCIA, AND FRANCISCO (July 13, 1917) after the vision of hell – their anguish is evident.

[Handwritten parish register document in Portuguese — Jacinta Marto's baptism and death record]

PARISH REGISTER – Jacinta Marto's baptism and death dates.

the activities of the visionaries. Hence he preferred to stay on the sidelines.

Four days after being released, Sunday, August 19, the children were grazing sheep near the hamlet of Valinhos when Our Lady appeared. It was the only apparition that did not occur in the Cova da Iria. As before, she instructed them to pray the Rosary and told them of her coming on September 13 and October 13, when she would occasion a miracle. She stressed that the miracle would have been greater had the children not been arrested in Ourem. Joao, Francisco and Lucia's brother, was present, but he did not see or hear anything.

Lucia asked Our Lady what she was to do with the money people had left at the Cova da Iria. The site of the apparitions was then being looked after by Maria de Carreira, known as "de Capelinha", who was one of the first to believe the children. She collected the

92

donations that were spontaneously offered by pilgrims. Our Lady said that two moveable Marian altars ought to be made and the rest of the money spent on building a chapel.

Lucia also asked Our Lady for the cure of several people, the relatives of whom had turned to Lucia for help. Mary promised to help some, but she said that they had to change their lives and, first and foremost, recite the Rosary. Finally, Our Lady instructed the children to pray a great deal and to make sacrifices for sinners, as many souls were heading for eternal damnation because they did not have anyone to intercede for them.

The little shepherds took Our Lady's words to heart. They not only prayed, but also outdid one another in little mortifications; for example, they gave poorer children their own food. One day,

FRANCISCO AND JACINTA'S parents: Olimpia and Manuel Marto.

OUR LADY'S second apparition at the Cova da Iria on June 13, 1917. Painting by Sr. Maria Conceicao.

93

BOYS FROM FATIMA grazing sheep.

JESUIT CHURCH of the Immaculate Conception of the Blessed Virgin Mary in Santarem, the town where the Fatima apparitions were ridiculed.

PORTUGAL

Santarem

•Fatima

• Lisbon

Lucia found some rope on a road and wound it around her arm so that the coarse twine might dig into her flesh and cause her pain. She did this as a penance, out of love for Jesus. Jacinta and Francisco did the same.

News of the apparitions reached ever-widening circles. Newcomers continued to appear in Fatima asking about the visionaries and wanting to meet them. Towards the end of August someone distributed leaflets in the village, accusing the little visionaries and priests, who were allegedly behind it all, of fraud. An invitation to an anti-clerical rally was attached to the leaflets. It was to take place on Sunday, September 9, at 11:00 a.m., in front of the church.

In fear of the disturbances, the parish priest decided not to celebrate Mass at 10:00 a.m. Contrary to the organizer's expectations, only a handful of people appeared for the rally. Its initiator, editor-in-chief of the *O Mundo* newspaper Jose do Valo, an anti-clerical atheist, did not conceal his disappointment. He and his companions made their way to the Cova da Iria, where they expected to find the inhabitants of Fatima. Instead, however, they found a herd of several dozen mules tied to trees. Boys, concealed amongst the mules, thrust a foul-smelling substance under their noses. The mules began to bray dreadfully. The anti-clerical demonstration

ended in a fiasco. Instead of ridiculing the religious frauds, the demonstrators were ridiculed by the mules.

The nearer to September 13, the more the tension grew in Fatima. Twenty-five thousand people appeared at the Cova da Iria on the day of the foretold apparitions. Lucia was shocked by the sight of such a large crowd. Years later, she recalled: "As the hour approached, I set out with Jacinta and Francisco, but owing to the crowds around us we could only advance with difficulty. The roads were packed with people, and everyone wanted to see us and speak to us…. Some climbed up to the tops of trees and walls to see us go by, and shouted down to us. Saying yes to some, giving a hand to others and helping them up from the dusty ground, we managed to move forward, thanks to some gentlemen who went ahead and opened a passage for us through the multitude.

HOUSE IN SANTAREM – the arched wooden gate and the holm oak that were brought here from the Cova da Iria were derided from this balcony (October 23, 1917).

95

PORTUGAL

Fatima

● Lisbon

A HUGE NUMBER of people turned up at the Cova da Iria on October 13, 1917, to see the foretold miracle.

"Now when I read in the New Testament about those enchanting scenes of Our Lord's passing through Palestine, I think of those which Our Lord allowed me to witness, while yet a child, on the poor roads and lanes from Aljustrel to Fatima and on to the Cova da Iria! I give thanks to God, offering Him the faith of our good Portuguese people, and I think, 'If these people so humbled themselves before three poor children, just because they were mercifully granted the grace to speak to the Mother of God, what would they not do if they saw Our Lord Himself in person before them?' "[16]

When the visionaries reached the site of the apparitions, they began to recite the Rosary. As previously, there was a flash of light in the sky prior to Our Lady's appearing above the holm oak. Only the children saw Mary. The people all around saw only the children enraptured, with eyes fixed, on some invisible thing above the oak. Our Lady said to them: "Continue to pray the Rosary in order to obtain the end of the war. In October Our Lord will come, as well

as Our Lady of Dolours and Our Lady of Carmel. Saint Joseph will appear with the Child Jesus to bless the world."[17] Mary praised them for their sacrifices and mortifications, but asked them not to overdo it and to wear the penitential rope only during daytime. Finally, she again promised to perform a miracle in October to prove the authenticity of the revelations.

As Our Lady was departing, Lucia shouted out that if anyone wanted to see her they should look eastwards. People looked in that direction and saw something like a bright cloud disappearing into the distance.

Fatima was on the lips of people throughout the country. People spoke of it on the streets. Newspapers constantly printed new articles about it. The liberal press did the most to promote the revelations, writing at length of the foretold miracle in October. Editors were convinced that nothing of the sort would occur, and that Catholicism would be ridiculed. They hoped that the more they publicized the event, the more it would turn out to be an embarrassment for the Church.

JACINTA HELD
by a policeman,
who was
to protect
her from an
outraged crowd
in the event of
no miracle.

97

CROWDS DRAWN by the foretold miracle (October 13, 1917).

THE THREE VISIONARIES – Francisco, Lucia, and Jacinta – at the site of the apparitions.

During the night of September 22, unknown perpetrators vandalized the site of the apparitions at the Cova da Iria. They destroyed the fence around the site, stole all the devotional objects left by pilgrims, and uprooted a holm oak. But, by mistake, it was not the oak that Mary had appeared above. In nearby Santarem, about one hundred local Masons organized a blasphemous procession to parody the apparitions.

People from all over Portugal continued to arrive in Fatima. They enquired about the visionaries and wanted to talk to them. Most of the neighbors mocked the children. Even relatives did not believe them. Lucia was particularly hurt by her mother's disbelief. Maria Rosa dos Santos was depressed. She did not believe her daughter's account about Our Lady from the outset. She too was the object of rumors and ridicule. In addition, the thousands that arrived in Fatima trampled over the family fields and completely destroyed the harvest. Some of the neighbors blamed Lucia for everything. Whenever they came across her, they threatened her, even beat her. They were afraid that when the hoax was exposed they would become the laughing stock of all Portugal.

MASSES OF PEOPLE at the Cova da Iria – despite torrential rain – awaiting a miracle.

Tired of the atmosphere around them, the children accepted an invitation from Maria do Carmo da Cruz Menezes, a friend of their parents, with relief. She took them to her home in Reixida, where they were able to rest.

The day before the promised apparition, Lucia's mother asked Lucia to go to confession with her. Her mother was convinced that a miracle would not occur and that her daughter would be lynched by the outraged crowd. She decided to share her daughter's fate. Hence she wanted to be well prepared for death. The certainty of Lucia, who had no doubts that Our Lady would keep her promise, did not convince her.

The eagerly awaited day, October 13, began with a downpour. It rained continously for several hours. But that did not deter the large number of people who had come from the furthest corners of Portugal. There were about fifty-five thousand people around the Cova da Iria, and about twenty thousand more in the vicinity. All were freezing, and those without umbrellas were soaked. The ground underfoot had turned into mud. But they stayed put.

The little shepherds pushed their way through the crowd to get to the Cova da Iria. They were protected by policemen, who feared that that they might well be harmed were a miracle not to occur. On arrival, Lucia asked everyone to close their umbrellas and recite the Rosary. Shortly after, preceded by a flash of light, Mary appeared above the holm oak. As before, only the visionaries saw her. Our Lady addressed Lucia: "I want to tell you that a chapel is to be built here in my honour. I am the Lady of the

WITNESSES OF THE FATIMA MIRACLE gazing at the sky. All were shocked by the spinning sun. It could not have been a collective illusion as it was seen even as far as 20 miles away.

...ILAGRE DE FÁTIMA

Rosary. Continue always to pray the Rosary every day. The war is going to end, and the soldiers will soon return to their homes."[18]

As usual Lucia asked for the healing and conversion of several people whose families had turned to her for help. Mary said that she would help some, but not others, as an intention to improve oneself and remorse for one's sins were the most important things. She added, with a sad look: "Do not offend the Lord our God any more because he is already so much offended."

Then Our Lady opened her hands wide and rose into the sky. A bright light emanated from her. Lucia shouted to people to look in that direction. Then an event occurred that thousands of people would remember for the rest of their lives.

Suddenly the rain stopped. The clouds parted, and the sun appeared behind them and shone more brightly than usual. It

101

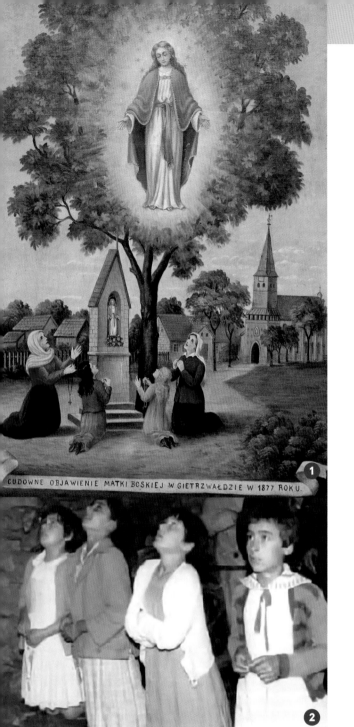

CUDOWNE OBJAWIENIE MATKI BOSKIEJ W GIETRZWAŁDZIE W 1877 ROKU.

①

②

③

FALSE AND AUTHENTIC REVELATIONS

THE CHURCH believes that authentic private revelations are inspired by the Holy Spirit. The basic criterion as to their authenticity is whether or not they are Christ-oriented. Authentic revelations do not contain anything that is contrary to Catholic belief and morality. They also ought to help people to better understand and experience Christian truths and to discern "the signs of the times", so as to be able to respond to challenges in the light of faith.

A false revelation does not draw one to Christ, but distances one from Him, and sometimes even aims to supersede the biblical message or obscure it. It often refers to prophecies, but the sole aim is to fuel and satisfy curiosity.

An authentic prophecy is – as Cardinal Joseph Ratzinger noted – not to foretell the future, but to clarify God's will for today, and also to indicate the road for the future. St. Paul recommends discernment: "Do not quench the Spirit, do not despise prophesying, but test everything; hold fast what is good" (I Thess 5:19–21).

THE CHURCH has authenticated, for example, the apparitions of Our Lady in Gietrzwald, Poland **①** and Our Lady of Kibeho in Rwanda **③**, but not the Garabandal apparitions in Spain **②**.

became increasingly larger and brighter, but did not dazzle those that gazed at it. Then it glowed and dimmed, and then spun round, emitting multicolored rays in all directions. The whole landscape changed in turn into various colors: blue, yellow, red, green. All were enchanted, speechless with delight.

But after a while their mood changed. The sun suddenly stopped spinning and started falling. The enormous, bright sphere sped towards the terrified crowd. People shouted in fear, cried, fainted, fell to their knees, calling for mercy, regretting their sins. When the sun was just above the ground, it suddenly stopped and returned to its place. All were amazed that their clothes were dry, that the ground was sun-cracked, as if it had not rained for ages.

The author of one of the most precise accounts of this event is a professor from Coimbra, Jose Maria de Almeida Garrett. He wrote:

THE FATIMA VISIONARIES beneath the wooden arch at the Cova da Iria, which was made by pilgrims.

WITNESSES OF THE MIRACLE gazing at the sky.

103

AT THE SIGHT OF THE MIRACLE OF THE SUN people fell to their knees and prayed fervently. Many were converted.

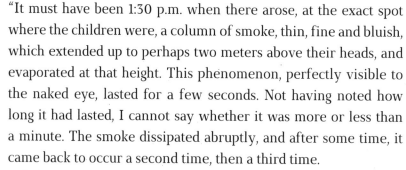

"It must have been 1:30 p.m. when there arose, at the exact spot where the children were, a column of smoke, thin, fine and bluish, which extended up to perhaps two meters above their heads, and evaporated at that height. This phenomenon, perfectly visible to the naked eye, lasted for a few seconds. Not having noted how long it had lasted, I cannot say whether it was more or less than a minute. The smoke dissipated abruptly, and after some time, it came back to occur a second time, then a third time.

"The sky, which had been overcast all day, suddenly cleared; the rain stopped and it looked as if the sun were about to fill with light the countryside that the wintery morning had made so gloomy. I was looking at the spot of the apparitions in a serene, if cold, expectation of something happening and with diminishing curiosity because a long time had passed without anything to excite my attention. The sun, a few moments before, had broken through the thick layer of clouds which hid it and now shone clearly and intensely.

"Suddenly I heard the uproar of thousands of voices, and I saw the whole multitude spread out in that vast space at my feet … turn their backs to that spot where, until then, all their expectations had been focused, and look at the sun on the other side. I turned around, too, toward the point commanding their gaze and I could see the sun, like a very clear disc, with its sharp edge, which gleamed without hurting the sight. It could not be confused with the sun seen through a fog (there was no fog at that moment), for it was neither veiled nor dim. At Fatima, it kept its light and heat, and stood out clearly in the sky, with a sharp edge, like a large gaming table. The most astonishing thing was to be able to stare at the solar disc for a long time, brilliant with light and heat, without hurting the eyes or damaging the retina. [During this time], the sun's disc did not remain immobile, it had a giddy motion, [but] not like the twinkling of a star in all its brilliance for it spun round upon itself in a mad whirl.

"During the solar phenomenon, which I have just described, there were also changes of color in the atmosphere. Looking at the sun, I noticed that everything was becoming darkened. I looked first at the nearest objects and then extended my glance further afield as far as the horizon. I saw everything had assumed an amethyst color. Objects around me, the sky and the atmosphere, were of the same color. Everything both near and far had changed, taking on the color of old yellow damask. People looked as if they were suffering from jaundice and I recall a sensation of amusement at seeing them look so ugly and unattractive. My own hand was the same color.

"Then, suddenly, one heard a clamor, a cry of anguish breaking from all the people. The sun, whirling wildly, seemed all at once to loosen itself from the firmament and, blood red, advance threateningly upon the earth as if to crush us with its huge and fiery weight. The sensation during those moments was truly terrible.

"All the phenomena which I have described were observed by me in a calm and serene state of mind without any emotional disturbance. It is for others to interpret and explain them. Finally, I must declare that never, before or after October 13 [1917], have

HIGINO FARIA witnessed the miracle on October 13, 1917. That same day he was inexplicably healed.

MIRACLE WITNESS – Carlos de Azevedo Mendes, author of an extensive account of this event.

105

I observed similar atmospheric or solar phenomena."[19]

One could see the miracle as a product of an unbridled religious imagination were it not for the fact that thousands of eyewitnesses bore testimony to it. A poet, Antonio Lopez Vieira, saw it from his home, twenty miles from Fatima. Many were converted in a flash. The very people who had ridiculed the superstitious simpletons that morning, knelt and prayed loudly.

One of them was an engineer, Antonio da Silva, one of the most influential Masons in Portugal, a member of the Carbonaria, a clandestine anti-clerical organization. After being converted he was repeatedly defamed and ridiculed in the liberal press. Pio Sciatizzi, a scientist, was also an eyewitness. He acknowledged that there was not the least doubt as to the authenticity of the miracle.

Avelino de Almeida, a journalist from the pro-government and anti-clerical newspaper *O Seculo*, was in the crowd. He had come from Lisbon to expose the Catholic hoax, certain that he would obtain unique newspaper material. He was not mistaken. His account is truly exceptional, but in a way that he had not imagined. He confirmed the miracle, publishing a long article about it.

People from all professions and classes saw the miracle: men and women, young and old, highly educated and uneducated, aristocrats and peasants, rich and poor,

AVELINO DE ALMEIDA, a Portuguese journalist who went to Fatima to negate the apparitions, became an eyewitness.

Avelino de Almeida

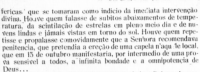

REPORTER'S ACCOUNT

AN ACCOUNT from Fatima in the *O Seculo* newspaper of October 15, 1917.

The following is from Avelino de Almeida's story published on October 15, 1917, on the first page of the newspaper *O Seculo*:

"**FROM THE ROAD,** where the vehicles were parked and where hundreds of people who had not dared to brave the mud were congregated, one could see the immense multitude turn toward the sun, which appeared free from clouds and in its zenith. It looked like a plaque of dull silver, and it was possible to look at it without the least discomfort. It might have been an eclipse which was taking place. But at that moment a great shout went up, and one could hear the spectators nearest at hand shouting: 'A miracle! A miracle!'

"Before the astonished eyes of the crowd, whose aspect was biblical as they stood bareheaded, eagerly searching the sky, the sun trembled, made sudden incredible movements outside all cosmic laws – the sun 'danced' according to the typical expression of the people.

"Standing at the step of an omnibus was an old man. With his face turned to the sun, he recited the Credo in a loud voice. I asked who he was and was told Senhor Joao da Cunha Vasconcelos. I saw him afterwards going up to those around him who still had their hats on, and vehemently imploring them to uncover before such an extraordinary demonstration of the existence of God.

"Identical scenes were repeated elsewhere, and in one place a woman cried out: 'How terrible! There are even men who do not uncover before such a stupendous miracle!'

"People then began to ask each other what they had seen. The great majority admitted to having seen the trembling and the dancing of the sun; others affirmed that they saw the face of the Blessed Virgin; others, again, swore that the sun whirled on itself like a giant Catherine wheel and that it lowered itself to the earth as if to burn it in its rays. Some said they saw it change colors successively."[20]

107

PORTUGUESE POET
Antonio Lopez Vieira witnessed the miracle of the sun from his home 20 miles from Fatima.

POSTCARD WITH A VIEW
of the Cova da Iria (October 13, 1917).

believers and atheists, those close to the visionaries and those twenty miles away.

At a time when masses of people were passing from a state of rapture to terror, the children had another vision. Lucia related it thus: "We beheld St. Joseph with the Child Jesus and Our Lady robed in white with a blue mantle, beside the sun. St. Joseph and the Child Jesus appeared to bless the world, for they traced the Sign of the Cross with their hands. When, a little later, this apparition disappeared, I saw Our Lord and Our Lady; it seemed to me that it was Our Lady of Dolours. Our Lord appeared to bless the world in the same manner as St. Joseph had done. This apparition also vanished, and I saw Our Lady once more, this time resembling Our Lady of Carmel."[21]

News of the miracle spread rapidly throughout the country. Witnesses spoke of it excitedly to everyone they met. The little village of Fatima, hitherto unheard of, was soon on the lips of people throughout the world.

FATIMA IN THE LIGHT OF SCIENCE

SCIENCE CANNOT EXPLAIN the miracle of the sun satisfactorily. No astronomical observatory in the world observed any such solar phenomenon that day. Besides, if the sun had even minimally changed its natural position, the whole solar system would have collapsed.

British zoologist Richard Dawkins, known for his promotion of atheism, thinks that the miracle was a collective hallucination, a mass hysteria. While Auguste Meessen, a Belgian physicist, thinks that the miracle was an optical illusion caused by gazing at the sun for too long. But how does one explain the fact that about 20,000 people within a 20-mile radius of Fatima saw the phenomenon, but had not gazed at the sun?

American astronomer Carl Sagan did not rule out the appearance of a UFO at that time. But no one has as yet proved the existence of extraterrestrial life, much less aliens visting this planet.

A theory appeared about a stratospheric dust cloud, which was to have distorted a view of the sun. This theory also did not withstand scientific verification. However, the question of how an illiterate girl could have foreseen many months earlier such an extraordinary event remains unexplained. Even if we accept that it was a meteorological phenomenon, how could she have known about it?

SCIENTISTS ARE STILL TRYING to find a rational explanation for the Fatima phenomenon: from a gigantic halo to glimmering particles of charged ice concentrated in a gigantic cloud. Such theories are stubbornly based on just one – optical – aspect of the phenomenon, but ignore, for example, the instant drying of people's clothes after many hours of heavy rain.

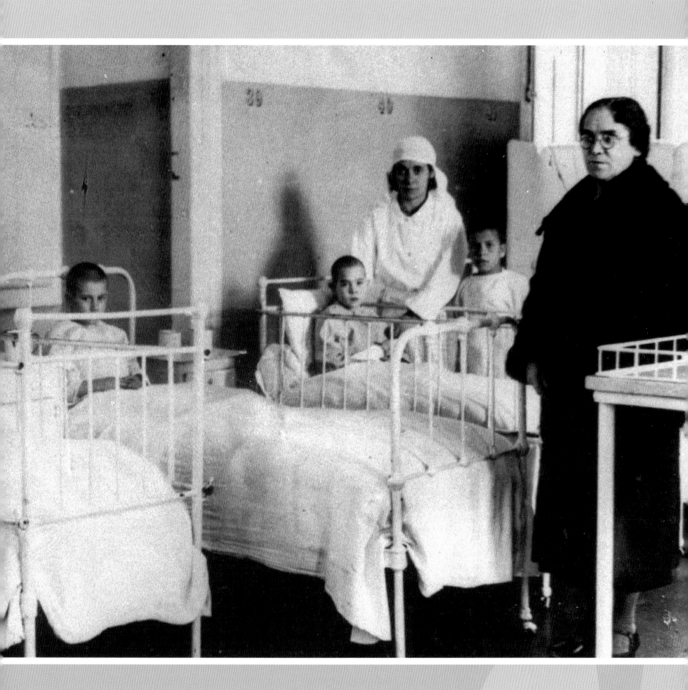

Deadly Spanish Flu

112

FRANCISCO AND JACINTA often recited the Rosary.

CHAPTER 4

Deadly Spanish Flu

It was the evening of October 16, 1917, three days after the last apparition in Fatima. One of the cells in the Seraphic College in Rome was in semidarkness. Seven hooded men in black habits were gathered around a table, a statue of Our Lady in the middle, candles burning at its sides.

They were Franciscans: three priests and four brothers, four of whom were Italians and three were Poles. Brother Maximilian Maria Kolbe, who had called the meeting, related how shocked he was to read banners at a Masonic demonstration in Rome saying that Lucifer would rule in the Vatican in 2017.

In view of the ever-increasing attacks on the Catholic Faith, he proposed to form a Militia Immaculata. As yet, none of them knew of the Fatima apparitions, nor that they were centered on the Immaculate Heart of the Blessed Virgin Mary. Yet they were convinced that they ought to seek aid for the world and the Church through her intercession.

Brother Maximilian reached into his pocket for a small folio volume and read the Militia's program. Its aim, to convert sinners, heretics, and schismatics, but primarily Masons. The means would be prayers for the intercession of Our Immaculate Lady and the

OFFICIAL EMBLEM – Militia Immaculata.

YOUNG SEMINARIAN MAXIMILIAN KOLBE and three fellow brothers – the first members of the Militia Immaculata, established exactly three days after the Fatima apparitions.

Saint Catherine Laboure

ST. CATHERINE LABOURE. Chapel at the Rue du Bac, Paris.

MIRACULOUS MEDAL and its propagator Alphonse Ratisbonne.

MIRACULOUS MEDAL

THE NIGHT of July 18, 1830, at the convent of the Sisters of Charity of Saint Vincent de Paul, 140 Rue du Bac, Paris, a 24-year-old novice, Catherine Laboure, heard a voice in her cell that told her to go down to the chapel. On entering, she saw Our Lady, who told her that she was to be charged with a mission.

This occurred during the next apparition (November 27, 1830), when Our Lady appeared to Catherine while she was at evening prayer in the chapel. Our Lady stood on a globe, a serpent underfoot. She had 30 rings on her fingers that emitted rays of light, which, she said, symbolized God's mercy for humanity. There was an oval frame around her, on which was written, in French: "O Mary, conceived without sin, pray for us who have recourse to thee." The vision changed and the novice saw two hearts, the Most Sacred Heart of Jesus, surrounded by a crown of thorns, and the Immaculate Heart of Mary, pierced by a sword. Above them there was a large letter *M* surmounted by a cross.

Our Lady told the nun to produce a medal with the images she had seen during the apparition. She promised that all who wore the medal would be granted many graces.

There were three more apparitions. Catherine convinced her superiors of the authenticity of the visions, and the first medal was cast in 1832. In view of the numerous cures and conversions, as well as other graces connected with the medal, the Holy See officially permitted it to be called the Miraculous Medal. The Rue du Bac apparitions were also seen as a sign for the Catholic Church to declare the Immaculate Conception of the Blessed Virgin Mary a dogma of the Faith.

FRANCE Paris

SERAPHIC COLLEGE, Rome. Room where Maximilian Kolbe and his companions established the Militia Immaculata.

promotion of Marian devotion, particularly through the Miraculous Medal.

Brother Kolbe knew that his proposition seemed to be a laughable one – to overcome the high and mighty of this world through prayer. Hence he referred to one of his cobrothers of six hundred years ago, Blessed Ramon Llull, a Spanish courtier who after a conversion became a Franciscan tertiary. After the failures of the Crusades, he realized that the Holy Land could not be taken by force, not to mention the conversion of Muslims. The only effective weapons the Christian world could use against Islam were prayer, fasting, and alms. Hence Llull advocated a new kind of knighthood – the conquest of the world via love and sacrifice. That was what Maximilian Kolbe proposed to his brothers – a six-hundred-year-old vision.

He envisioned his ideal knight as one who did not attack, rob, or destroy, but always defended the honor of his Lady. God's one and only Lady, the Blessed Virgin Mary, whom our Savior gave us as the treasure of His heart. Hence her honor was to be defended, her love sought. The most direct road to her Son's Heart, according to Kolbe, was through Our Lady's Heart.

A similar vision raised the spirits of the little shepherds from Fatima. Before the apparitions, they recited the Rosary in their own shortened way, not saying the whole Our Father or the whole Hail Mary, but only the first two words of each prayer, that is,

Rome

ITALY

115

"Our Father" and "Hail Mary" without continuing. But everything changed after the apparition. They became aware of the importance of the words to which they had hitherto not given due attention. Henceforth, they fervently recited the Rosary, certain that they would thus hasten the end of the war. When Lucia asked for the conversion of Russia, she did not know that it was the largest country in the world. Yet she said the prayer so zealously that years later people posed a basic question: Did an illiterate peasant girl from central Portugal do more to prevent conflicts than any diplomat?

The children, according to Our Lady's instructions, were taught to read and to write. But Francisco and Jacinta lacked motivation, as they knew that they were shortly to be taken to heaven. Francisco in particular did not want to learn, preferring to recite the Rosary for hours. Unlike them, Lucia quickly made progress as she wanted to fulfill Mary's wishes.

The war ended on November 18, 1918. At that time there was an exceptionally virulent flu pandemic throughout the world, known as Spanish Flu. Contrary to the name, it first appeared in Kansas, the result of a dangerous mutation of an influenza A (H1N1)-type

SPANISH FLU – millions died from this virus.

THE MOST SERIOUS CASES OF THE SPANISH FLU were children, not adults.

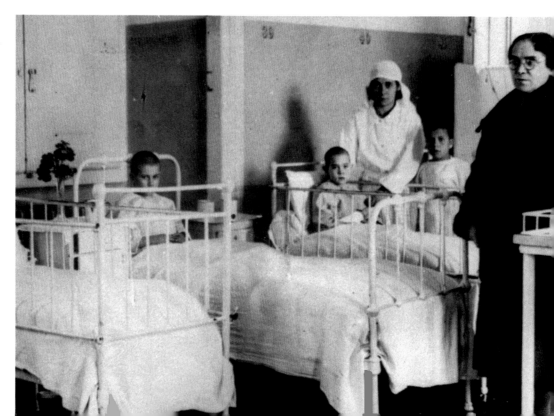

virus. Within two years it had infected five hundred million people, one-third of the world's population. Epidemiologists are still arguing about the number of victims: twenty, fifty, or perhaps one hundred million deaths. An unusual feature of this pandemic was that it was more dangerous to the young than to the old.

The Spanish Flu also reached Fatima. Mr. and Mrs. dos Santos and their children Lucia, Gloria, and Manuel helped those in need, heedless of the danger. They prepared meals for seriously ill villagers, which they personally distributed, and even fed their neighbors' children at their own home if their parents were too ill to feed them themselves. Manuel Marto strongly advised them against it, while he himself did not allow his family to leave the farm. But protective measures failed, and all his children were infected. Four of them – Francisco, Jacinta, Florinda, and Teresa – died within several years, whereas no one perished in the dos Santos family.

Jacinta and Francisco fell ill in the autumn of 1918. The siblings had another apparition of Our Lady at that time. She told them that she would shortly take Francisco to heaven, while Jacinta had a choice – to be taken to heaven immediately or to stay on earth for a time to suffer for the conversion of sinners. Since the vision of hell in July 1918, the youngest of the three seemed to have been distressed the most by the fate of the damned. She physically suffered at the thought of the everlasting torments of so many people. She did not hesitate, deciding on the latter option. Our Lady told her that she would end up in a hospital, where she would suffer a great deal for the salvation of souls, and that she would die alone.

After the end of the Fatima apparitions, Francisco had at least several more visions. It is known that he also conversed with Jesus. Lucia recalled one such occasion. Lucia's sister Teresa, who was recently married and living in another town, visited Lucia to ask for prayers on behalf of a man falsely accused of a crime. If he could not prove his innocence, he would be exiled or imprisoned for a long time. After receiving the message, Lucia set out for school, and on the way she told her cousins all about the case. When the children reached Fatima, Francisco said to Lucia, "Listen! While you go to school, I'll stay with the Hidden Jesus, and I'll ask Him for that grace."[22] When Lucia returned from school, she asked Francisco whether he had

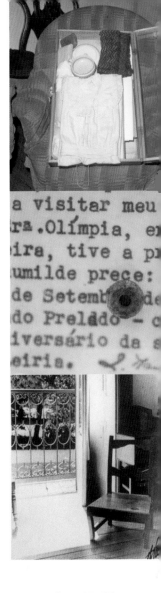

JACINTA'S CLOTHES AND ARTICLES – Lisbon orphanage.

FRANCISCO'S ROSARY BEAD – found in his grave during his exhumation.

ORPHANAGE OF OUR LADY of Miracles in Lisbon, where Our Lady appeared to Jacinta.

prayed for the man. "Yes, I did," he said. "Tell your Teresa that he'll be home in a few days' time." A few days later the man returned home, and he and his entire family thanked Our Lady for answering their prayers.

Jacinta also had more apparitions, which mainly concerned the future. Lucia recalled that she saw her cousin after one of those visions: "One day, I went to Jacinta's house to spend a little while with her. I found her sitting on her bed, deep in thought. 'Jacinta, what are you thinking about?' 'About the war that is coming. So many people are going to die, and almost all of them are going to hell! Many homes will be destroyed, and many priests will be killed. Look, I am going to heaven, and as for you, when you see the light which the Lady told us would come one night before the war, you run up there too.' 'Don't you see that nobody can just run off to heaven?' 'That's true, you cannot! But don't be afraid! In heaven I'll be praying hard for you, for the Holy Father, for Portugal, so that the war will not come here, and for all priests.'"[23]

Francisco had serious postflu complications, but he did not seem to be at all concerned. He was cheerful and repeatedly told everyone how pleased he was that he would shortly go to heaven, where he would finally meet Jesus and Mary. He offered all his suffering for the conversion of sinners without complaining. He received his very first Holy Communion on his deathbed in his family home in Aljustrel (not counting the Lord's Blood proffered him in a chalice by an angel). The morning of April 4, 1919, he asked his nearest and dearest to forgive him. At 10:00 a.m., he smiled and told his mother

PORTUGAL

Fatima

● Lisbon

HOSPITAL REGISTER – date of Jacinta's death in Lisbon.

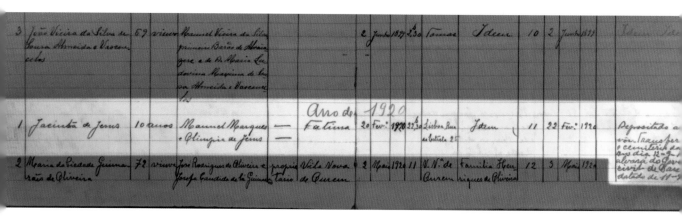

DONA ESTEFANIA HOSPITAL in Lisbon, where Jacinta died 10 days after an operation.

ST. AUGUSTINE HOSPITAL STAFF in Vila Nova de Ourem, where Jacinta spent two months.

that he could see a very beautiful light in the doorway. And then he died. He was ten years and ten months old and was buried on April 5 at the parish cemetery in Fatima.

After Jacinta contracted influenza, she ended up in the hospital in Ourem, where she stayed for two months. She returned home, but her condition became worse as she developed tuberculosis. In January 1920, she was sent to the sick ward at the Catholic Orphanage of Our Lady of Miracles in Lisbon. Before being admitted, Jacinta told Lucia that her task was to bring about a worldwide devotion to the Immaculate Heart of Mary. The thirteen-year-old cousin nodded in agreement, though she really did not know what she was agreeing to.

As there was a chapel at the orphanage, Jacinta was able participate in Mass and receive Communion. But she shortly found herself in a Lisbon hospital (February 2), greatly weakened by her deadly illness. Doctors discovered, apart from a purulent infection of the left pluera, acute inflammations of the seventh and eighth ribs on

DEATH CERTIFICATE – of Jacinta Marto, who died on February 20, 1920.

119

CATHOLIC ORPHANAGE of Our Lady of Miracles, Lisbon, where Jacinta spent thirteen days.

ORPHANAGE ❶, chapel ❷. A grilled window ❸ enabled Jacinta to participate in Mass.

the left side of her rib cage. She was in great pain day and night as the infection had spread more and more; her wounds exuding an odor.

On February 10, she had two ribs removed without having had a full dose of anaesthetic because of her weak condition. The operation, however, did not bring the desired effects, but solely caused her more pain. Though she suffered agony every time she had her dressing changed, she did not complain. Like her brother, she offered up all her suffering for the conversion of sinners.

Jacinta had further apparitions when she was ill and alone. She had two visions of the Holy Father, during the first of which she saw him in a large house kneeling by a small table, crying, his hands covering his face. Outside, a crowd was shouting, insulting him, throwing stones. After the vision, Jacinta had a strong urge to pray more for the pope. In the second vision, the Holy Father was in a world full of famine and suffering, praying with many others in a church before the Immacuate Heart of Mary.

In other visions, Our Lady told Jacinta that times were approaching when many couples would live together without the Sacrament of Matrimony, and most people would end up in hell because of the sin of impurity. She said that there were certain fashions that offended

GRILLED WINDOW, through which Jacinta could see into the chapel.

ORPHANAGE ROOM, where Jacinta stayed during her illness.

COMO HOMENAGEM À MINHA E NUNCA ESQUECIDA AFILHADA A QUEM NOSSA SENHORA APAREC JACINTA MÁRTO VIDENTE DE FÁTIMA ONDE EM MEADOS DE JANEIRO ATÉ 2 DE FEVEREIRO DE 1? QUANDO NO DECURSO DO SEU REPOUSO FEITO NESTE ORFÃ LHE APARECEU NOVAMENTE NOSSA SENHORA. ANTES DE SER INTERNADA NO HOSPITAL DE D. ESTEFA

JACINTA'S MEMENTOES – her dress at the orphanage.

PLAQUE COMMEMORATING Jacinta's stay in the orphanage.

PORTUGAL

Fatima
Lisbon

CHURCH OF THE ANGELS, Lisbon.

JACINTA - she looked as if she were asleep.

God, that a great misfortune would befall Spain, and that priests ought to be chaste and obedient to the pope and their superiors. Mary appeared to Jacinta for the last time on February 16, 1920, when she consoled her, assuring her that she would shortly take her to heaven.

Four days later Jacinta kept on asking for the sacraments. A priest arrived, heard her confession, and promised to return with Holy Communion the following day. But she knew that she would not live till then. She died that evening, all alone, as Our Lady had told her, just a few days before her eleventh birthday.

Problems arose as to where she was to be buried. The doctors, priests, and her family could not agree, hence her coffin was taken to the sacristy in the Church of the Angels, and left in the darkest corner until the problem was sorted out. But news of this spread around the town, and crowds from all over Lisbon arrived to pay their last respects.

Eventually the problem of the burial place was resolved. A baron from Alvaiazere, one of the first to believe in the authenticity of the apparitions, made room for the little mystic in his family tomb at a cemetery in Vila Nova de Ourem. On February 24, Jacinta's remains were transferred from the wooden coffin to a zinc one. Witnesses were astounded that her lips were pink and that her remains gave off a pleasant fragrance, alike to flowers, as Jacinta's purulent body had given off an unbearable stench even before her death and she had lain dead for four days in the sacristy, where her body ought

PORTUGAL

Ourem

Fatima

Lisbon

CENTRAL NAVE – Church of the Angels.

to have decayed further and should have continued to give off an unbearable odor. Her funeral took place on the same day, attended by many despite the torrential rain.

Meanwhile believers from all over Portugal continued to arrive at the Cova da Iria. They prayed at the site of the apparitions, asking for favors. Portuguese peasants quickly built the first chapel there, but no priest wanted to consecrate it as the apparitions had not as yet been approved by the Church. Furthermore, disgruntled state officials issued a directive hindering the influx of pilgrims, but nothing could stop them streaming into Fatima.

A certain inhabitant of Torres Novas commissioned a local sculptor, Jose Ferreira Thedim, to sculpt a statue of Our Lady as depicted by the little shepherds. The parishioners wanted to take the statue to the chapel at the Cova da Iria on May 13, 1920, in order to commemorate

TOMB IN FATIMA – built in 1935 for Francisco and Jacinta.

PORTUGUESE SCULPTOR – Jose Ferreira Thedim sculptured a statue of Our Lady of Fatima.

CATHOLIC COLLEGE, Vilar, on the outskirts of Porto. Lucia stayed there from 1921 to 1925.

COVA DA IRIA – chapel was blown up by unknown perpetrators on March 6, 1922.

PILGRIMS IN FATIMA gathered around the damaged chapel.

JACINTA'S FAVORITE PICTURE Our Lady of Sameiro, Braga. It reminded her of Our Lady of Fatima.

Virgem Immaculada do Sameiro
BRAGA

the third anniversary of the first apparition. The authorities heard about this and cordoned off the benefactor's house. But the sculpture was smuggled out in an ox-drawn wagon, hidden amongst farming equipment. As it approached the chapel, the road was blocked by units of the Republican Guard. A clash between the soldiers and the crowd of pilgrims ensued. The soldiers offered little resistance as the majority were Catholics and could not bear to obey their orders. The statue was placed in the chapel, and Fatima became famous for numerous miracles and conversions.

Bishop of Leiria Jose Alves Correia da Silva took a lively interest in the apparitions. His diocese was a new one, established on January 17, 1918, and included Fatima. The new ordinary purchased the whole Cova da Iria valley, intending to establish a Marian center there. But a lack of drinking water for pilgrims posed a problem. In November 1921 the bishop instructed workers to dig a well. Having but begun, they discovered three springs, a find some people saw as a miracle.

Lucia was not in Fatima at that time. Exhausted by people constantly visiting her – seeking advice on family matters, asking her to foretell the future, and so forth – she wanted to move to Lisbon or Santarem, where she had acquaintances prepared to take her in. Her parents agreed to this, but she changed her plans. She had a meeting with the vicar general of the Leiria Diocese in Olival, a nearby town, who told her that Bishop Correia da Silva wanted her to commence studies at the Catholic college in Vilar, on the outskirts of Porto. She had other plans. But in another apparition Mary told her that the bishop's request was the will of God. Hence Lucia departed for the College of the Sisters of St. Dorothy in Vilar, where she remained for four years.

On the night of March 6, 1922, unknown perpertrators planted five explosive charges under the chapel at the Cova da Iria. The chapel was blown up, yet the statue of Our Lady stood unscathed. From then on believers prayed before it daily, but at night it was taken to people's homes. One night, someone planted a bomb under the oak where the apparitions had occurred, but it did not explode. Later, the tree itself was cut into pieces by pilgrims and taken away. Attacks on the Faith, instead of deterring people, attracted more and more to Fatima, as evidenced by a 1922 pilgrimage of sixty thousand.

On May 3, 1922, Bishop Correia da Silva opened a canonical process to evaluate the apparitions. He appointed a commission of seven to determine what had occurred in Fatima between May 13 and October 13, 1917. Seven years later they submitted a report to the bishop, and on October 13, 1930, he officially approved the apparitions.

PORTUGAL — Vilar, Fatima, Lisbon

LUCIA DOS SANTOS during her stay in Vilar.

CHAPEL – Dorothean College, Vilar.

125

Russia's Errors Spread throughout the World

AT THE BEGINNING of the 20th century Russia was the largest country in the world. Its economy was developing dynamically. The rouble was convertible into gold from 1897 to 1914. All the economic forecasts predicted that Russia would become one of the richest countries in the world.

RUSSIAN EMPIRE

CHAPTER 5

Russia's Errors Spread throughout the World

In October 1917 Lucia had no idea of the existence of the professional revolutionary Vladimir Ilyich Ulyanov, who used one hundred sixty Communist Party aliases, of which one is permanently associated with him: Lenin.

Several weeks after the last Fatima apparition there was an event that is now closely connected with Lucia's later life: The Bolsheviks, led by Lenin, assumed power in St. Petersburg, the capital of the Russian Empire.

On the evening of November 7 (October 25, according to the old Julian calendar), Vladimir Ulyanov sneaked into the Smolny Institute, the revolutionaries' headquarters. He had earlier called for a coup, but he himself hid in a flat in the Kirovsky District. When he appeared at the Bolshevik headquarters, disguised as a worker, face bandaged, and a wig on his balding head, the fate of the revolution had already been practically decided. Earlier, on the orders of Leon Trotsky, Red Guard units had cut the telephone and telegraph lines that connected the government with the military headquarters. They then took over all the strategic points in St. Petersburg without resistance: post office, power station, gasworks, railway stations, telephone and telegraph exchanges, and bridges over the Neva River. Some soldiers from the St. Petersburg garrison joined the Bolsheviks,

CRUISER *AURORA*, moored on the Neva in St. Petersburg, was to have – according to Communist legend – fired a salvo as a signal to start the Russian Revolution.

VLADIMIR LENIN, leader of the Russian Communists, wearing a wig, disguised as a worker.

129

and the military headquarters at St. Michael's Castle was taken without a shot being fired. Captured last was the Winter Palace, the seat of the provisional government led by Prime Minister Alexander Kerensky, who had fled to Pskov to bring Cossack reinforcements. The building was defended by pathetic forces for such an enormous empire: a batallion of one hundred forty women, forty war invalids led by a cripple, and a handful of teenage students from military schools. There was no storming of the palace, as Sergei Eisenstein depicted in a propaganda film, because the Bolsheviks quite simply entered through open doors and windows. Only five people perished during the whole of the take-over.

Meanwhile no one in St. Petersburg even knew that there had been a coup. Like every evening, the pubs were full and vodka flowed. Politicians in European capitals did not even imagine that Bolshevik governments would last for over seventy years and leave a bloody mark in world history. Communism turned out to be the most criminal system ever, and it left an unimaginable one hundred million or more dead in in its wake. In 1917, however, foreign commentators predicted that the Communist government in Russia would be a provisional one, that it would fall any day. No one believed that a handful of madmen could subdue the largest country in the world.

THE RUSSIAN GOVERNMENT of Alexander Kerensky (a high-degree Mason) came to power in February 1917 with the abolishment of tsarism, but it was overthrown in October 1917 by the Bolsheviks.

✠

At the beginning of 1917 the Communist Party had but 10,431 members, while the Russian Empire numbered about 130 million inhabitants. By the end of the year, the Communists had gained a further 35,154 members, still but a drop in the ocean that was Russia.

Within two months the Communists had captured virtually the whole part of western Russia, and by February 1918, they had subdued Ukraine. They captured towns with small forces, as the inhabitants were passive and the tsarist soldiers inactive. On entering towns they perpetrated mass crimes, killing thousands, even those who were neutral. Though the Communists captured territory after territory, towns and provinces did not organize defenses, even though their brutal massacres were known of. All trembled with fright, which did not give rise to resistance but to paralysis.

The Czechs, Slovaks, Poles, and Serbs who lived in the Russian Empire were the best organized. They formed their own armies and, without the help of the locals, won battles against the Red Guards. How then can one explain the passivity, the fatalism of the Russians themselves?

In order to clarify this, it is necessary to go back to the Middle Ages, when the Rus appeared on the huge tracts of land in eastern Europe. It was neither a nation nor a country, but a large and religiously diverse

BOLSHEVIK LEAFLET of October 25, 1917, announcing that the revolutionaries had taken control of St. Petersburg.

FEBRUARY REVOLUTION, 1917 Demonstration by workers from the Putilov Mill, St. Petersburg – one of the largest industrial plants in Russia.

STREET CLASHES in St. Petersburg. Fatalities on Nevsky Prospect Street.

131

ICON OF THE DORMITION of Our Most Holy Lady – Kiev Pechersk Lavra.

CHRISTENING OF KIEVAN RUS – probably on January 6, 988.

VLADIMIR THE GREAT – first Christian ruler of Kievan Rus.

Slavonic civilization born of Eastern Christianity. It was not centered around any one place, but many autonomous places such as Pskov, Veliky Novgorod, Tver, Volodymyr-Volynsky, Suzdal, Polotsk, Chernihiv, Halych, and many others. But the most important was Kievan Rus. Its ruler Vladimir the Great accepted the Christianity of the Byzantine Empire (the Eastern Rite), and thus the christening of Kievan Rus. Hence it is no accident that Kiev, established at the beginning of the fifth century, is called the "mother of Russian towns". It was from there that the evangelization of Eastern Slavs was undertaken. It is there that the holiest Christian monuments in Rus are to be found, that is, the Kiev Monastery of the Caves and St. Sophia Cathedral.

In time a great rival to Kiev arose in the north, intent on controlling the whole of Rus. In 1147, Yuri Dolgorukiy, the grand prince of Kiev, ordered the building of a new town, that is, Moscow, which became the capital of the empire. Twenty-five years later, his son Andrei Bogolyubskiy invaded Kiev. The town was plundered and destroyed. Not even the holiest Orthodox places were spared. Kiev has not recovered from that disaster, the first of a series of clashes between Moscow and Kiev that have continued to this day.

GRAND PRINCE OF MOSCOW Vasili III, father of Ivan the Terrible, the first tsar of Russia.

KIEV PECHERSK LAVRA – the oldest monastery in Rus.

The misfortunes of Rus lands lay in the fact that they were located on a large borderland area between steppe and settled civilizations – lands geopolitically unstable, located on boundless plains without natural borders, and constantly invaded by warlike nomad tribes. One of them was the Mongols, which conquered the Duchy of Moscow and ruled there from 1223 to 1380.

The long period of an Asian despotism left an indelible mark on Moscow. It adopted a Mongolian model of state organization, where the exercise of power by the grand prince is more like that of a Tartar khan than a Byzantine emperor. The ruler was not bound by any law, even God's. The ruler's will was law. Grand Prince Vasili III of Russia said bluntly that all his subjects were slaves. Successive Moscow monarchs were wont to show the main royal insignia to their guests, that is, the Monomakh's Cap. They proudly related that it was the headwear of Byzantine emperors, their predecessors. In reality it was a gift Ivan I of Moscow had once received from Uzbeg Khan, the longest-reigning ruler of the Golden Horde.

Under the pressure of Mongolian influences, Moscow began to represent a type of social order that one could call, after Polish

MONOMAKH'S CAP – in reality it was Uzbeg Khan's headwear.

Moscow
Kiev

RUSSIAN EMPIRE

historian Feliks Koneczny, the Turanian civilization, where autocratic government is the source of law and ethics and even stands above them. Subjects knew that total submissiveness was the only way to survive. As a consequence of the continuing influence of Constantinople, Kiev was of the Byzantine civilization. Although also autocratic, Byzantine rulers continued the Roman legal tradition and established codes of law.

Far removed from the West, Russia experienced none of the major developments that shaped modern Europe. As agriculture and commerce improved in the West, a merchant class emerged. The Renaissance, which saw the flowering of humanism, was followed by philosophical and scientific trends that led to political and economic liberalism, and the recognition of individual rights. Meanwhile, Russia remained a largely agricultural and autocratic empire. There were no guilds, no universities, no local governing bodies. Subjects had not the habits of taking initiative or of organizing themselves. When confronted by the motivated and forceful Bolsheviks, they reacted passively.

The Bolsheviks adopted brutal administrative methods that had been proven over the ages. Lenin was well aware that a well-organized and ruthless minority could rule a passive and dependent majority. Hence the Red Terror. He knew that only a merciless dictatorship could guarantee power. The Communists terrorized the

BOLSHEVIK VICTIMS in front of the Soviet secret police building in Kharkiv, Ukraine.

FELIX DZERZHINSKY – malevolent creator of the Soviet secret police.

SOVIET PROPAGANDA
PLACARD
summoning all to
fight the Poles and
Russian counter-
revolutionaries.

BOLSHEVIK
WEEKLY, *Red Terror*,
published by
the secret police
(November 1,
1918). Also
photograph of
destroyed Buddhist
temple and
Orthodox church.

people and murdered political opponents: aristocrats, landowners, government officials, clergy, officers of the tsar's army, judges and public prosecutors, members of political parties and youth organizations, wealthy tradesmen, merchants, landlords, entrepreneurs, and affluent peasants called kulaks. The more ruthlessness, the more obedience. The revolution's bard, Vladimir Mayakovsky, in an enthusiastic verse in honor of Communism, declared that an individual was a nonentity, a nobody.

It is only in this context that one can understand why the new Russian government spread its "errors" throughout the country so easily, encountering little opposition. What is more, since the ruler's will was law, the said "errors" became binding norms. Lenin advocated a new morality: Good was but that which served the victory of the revolution and the rule of Communism, while evil was that which hindered it.

Some of the first victims of Communism were Christians, particularly the Orthodox who constituted the majority of Christians in Russia. Lenin was of the opinion that the more clergy that were shot, the better for the revolution. He and all of the Communist Party leaders were atheists, though not indifferent to religion but at war with it. Lenin was opposed to even questions about God. According to him, it was idiocy to speak of God, and such discussions among party comrades irritated him. In 1908, Lenin flew into a rage when his collaborators Bogdanov, Gorki, and Lunacharsky announced

POEM COVER
The Twelve
by Alexander
Blok.

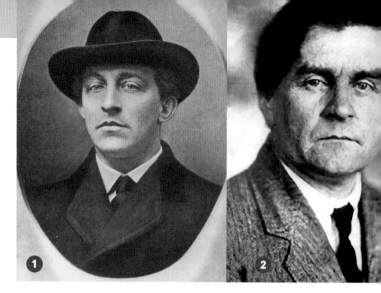

NEW APOSTLES

FROM THE VERY OUTSET, the Bolshevik Revolution had the support of many avant-garde artists (Kazimierz Malewicz, El Lissitzky, Alexander Rodczenko) as well as writers and poets (Isaac Babel, Alexander Blok, Osip Brik, Wladimir Majakowski), who linked the development of contemporary art with the triumph of the new system. They praised Bolshevism and prophesized the triumph of Communism throughout the world.

Alexander Blok's poem *The Twelve*, written in 1918, had a special place in such works. It depicts Bolshevik revolutionaries as contemporary embodiments of the apostles of Jesus. The poet depicts twelve godless Red Guards plunged in darkness, in the middle of a snowstorm, following the faint, distant figure of Christ, the first revolutionary. This is an expression of a new messianism, an allegory that depicts Communism replacing Christianity.

RUSSIAN MASTERS at the service of the system: ❶ Alexander Blok, ❷ Kazimierz Malewicz, ❸ El Lissitzky, ❹ Alexander Rodczenko and Warwara Stiepanowa, ❺ Isaac Babel, ❻ Wladimir Majakowski.

a "God-building" plan, that is, the replacement of the Christian God with a new deity created by progressive social classes. In a letter to Gorki, he wrote that to flirt with God was an inexpressible abomination. He thought that all religious ideas were but flirtations with wickedness and society's most dangerous infection, for they turned the masses' attention away from the most important thing, that is, the class war and the triumph of the proletariat. Hence religion was an enemy that had to be ruthlessly destroyed, its believers wiped out.

Anatoly Lunacharsky, the first minister of education in the Bolshevik government, put it bluntly: All the world's religions were poisonous; the most dangerous was Christianity, as it taught mercy and love of neighbor, whereas in Communism hate was of prime importance, as it was only thanks to hate that the world could be conquered. Hence the aim of Bolshevism was not to reform religion but to wipe it off the face of the earth. Lunacharsky also stated that it was not enough to overthrow temporal powers in order for the revolution to triumph; it was also necessary to kill God.

The Russian temporal power was eliminated in Yekaterinburg in the early hours of July 17, 1918. The Bolsheviks had imprisoned Tsar Nicholas II and his family in the house of Nikolai Ipatiev, a military engineer. About midnight, the prisoners were awoken by a Soviet

SOVIET MINISTER Anatoly Lunacharsky called for the destruction of Christianity.

ATHEISTIC PROPAGANDA PLACARD juxtaposing Orthodox Church services for money with free entertainment in clubs.

137

У ЦЕРКОВНОГО ПОРОГА

БЕЗ ИКОН И БОГА

IPATIEV'S HOUSE, where the tsar and his family were murdered, stood in Yekaterinburg (Sverdlovsk under the Communists) until 1977.

Moscow
Yekaterinburg

RUSSIA 1917

TSAR NICHOLAS II and family – victims of Bolshevik terror.

ALL SAINTS CHURCH (Church on Blood in Honor of All Saints), built in 2003 on the site of Ipatiev's house, which was demolished in 1977.

unit under the command of Yakov Yurovsky, a Chekist. He announced that they were in danger and ordered them to follow him. They all dressed and followed him into the cellar: the tsar (50 years of age); his wife, Alexandra (46); his four daughters, Olga (23), Tatiana (21), Maria (19), Anastasia (17); his son Alexei (14), who suffered from hemophilia; their physician, Dr. Yevgeny Botkin; their cook, Ivan Kharitonov; the butler, Alexei Trupp; and Anna Demidova, the maid. All eleven stood against one side of the cellar wall, while the Bolshevik unit stood on the opposite side. Yurovsky ordered two chairs to be brought for the tsarina Alexandra and the frail tsarevitch. It is not known whether or not the prisoners were aware that they were standing in front of a firing squad. The commanding officer pulled out a document and read the death sentence. He then yanked a revolver out of his holster and aimed it at the tsar. He and his subordinates fired time and again. When the smoke

ORTHODOX CHURCH MARTYRS

WHEN MIKHAIL GORBACHEV, the last leader of the Soviet Union, initiated a plan to restructure the system (*perestroika*) in 1985, a special commission, chaired by Alexander Yakovlev, was appointed to investigate Communist crimes. It established that from 1917 to 1985 the Soviet regime murdered about 200,000 religious of various denominations and arrested a further 300,000. Moreover, a great number (the exact figure is unknown) of lay people perished just for their attachment to the Christian faith. The Russian Orthodox Church suffered the greatest losses, with over 130 of its bishops killed between 1918 and 1939.

The Yakovlev Commission also documented the destruction of 40,000 churches. Also more than half the mosques and synagogues, many of which were priceless historic monuments, were plundered and profaned before being destroyed.

NEW MARTYRS AND CONFESSORS OF THE RUSSIAN CHURCH – victims of Communism.

TIKHON, PATRIARCH OF MOSCOW AND ALL RUSSIA – a political prisoner at the time of Lenin.

METROPOLITAN OF PETROGRAD AND GDOV Benjamin Kazansky – sentenced to death and shot in 1922.

PROTOPRIEST FILOSOF ORNATSKI – arrested and shot with his two sons in 1918, saint and martyr of the Orthodox Church.

VLADIMIR LENIN shortly before his death in Gorki near Moscow.

LENIN'S FIRST PROVISIONAL wooden mausoleum, built in Red Square immediately after his death. A new one was built in 1924. It is of black and red granite, labradorite, marble, and porphyry. It resembles the Pyramid of Djoser in Saqqara, Egypt, and the Tomb of Cyrus the Great in Pasargadae, Iran.

INSTEAD OF AN ORTHODOX empire, which was to lead Christanity ("Moscow is the Third Rome and there will not be a fourth"), an atheistic state arose, the aim of which – to rule the world – is declared on its emblem.

had cleared, Yurovsky approached the victims. The tsarevitch and Tatiana still showed signs of life, so he finished them off with a shot in the back of the head. The bodies were loaded onto a lorry and taken to a forest, where they were stripped bare, cut into quarters, doused with acid, and thrown into an unused mineshaft.

In January 1923 Bolsheviks gathered in the garrison club in Moscow to witness an extraordinary event, a trial attended by, amongst others, party leaders Leon Trotsky and Anatoly Lunacharsky. The prosecutor delivered a sweeping indictment against God Himself, blamed Him for the worst of crimes, and demanded the death penalty. Summoned witnesses also put God in the worst possible light. The defending barrister was unconvincing. After some deliberation the court acceded to the prosecutor's motion and sentenced God to death in absentia. The sentence, announced in a packed hall, was accepted with cries of joy.

Lenin died on January 12, 1924. Towards the end of his life he sat motionless in a wheelchair, his body eaten up by syphilis contracted whilst travelling around Europe over a number of years. Mumbling incomprehensibly, staring so vacantly that his bodyguards did not know whether he could see anything in front of him, he was so unlike the once energetic man who looked alertly and piercingly at his interlocutors, bombarding them with words. After a failed assassination attempt, his health suddenly worsened. On August 30, 1918, when Lenin was getting into his car at the Michelson Hammer and Sickle Factory in Moscow, Fanny Kaplan, a Jewish anarchist, fired three shots at him, two of which struck him: One punctured the upper part of his left lung and lodged near his right collarbone; the other pierced his left shoulder.

Although Lenin was diminishing, Communism was spreading. The Third International, that is, the Comintern of nineteen Communist Parties, absolutely obedient to the Bolsheviks, was established at Lenin's initiative in March 1919 to propagate Marxism and to prepare for a world revolution.

In November 1917, the Bolsheviks were treated with contempt; their government was expected to last but two weeks. Hence

resistance was organized too late. The new government quickly grew in strength, and, thanks to terror, it coerced people into obedience.

At that time civil war broke out in the former Russian Empire. Nations enslaved by Russia fought for independence: Poles, Ukrainians, Finns, Lithuanians, Latvians, Estonians, Georgians, Armenians, Azerbaijanis, and others. Monarchists, constitutional democrats, socialist revolutionaries, and anarchists had their own armed units. Peasant, Cossack, worker, and military insurrections arose. Those opposed to the Communists were scattered, and they were at variance with each other, as the Bolsheviks played them off against each other. Unlike them, the Bolsheviks were better organized, under one high command, and disiplined, with ruthless secret police and effective propaganda. Hence they won the civil war in 1922, crushed the counterrevolution, and proclaimed the rise of a new entity, the Soviet Union, which began its battle to rule the world.

FANNY KAPLAN – a Jewish anarchist who attempted to assassinate Lenin.

141

Das Kapital.

Kritik der politischen Oekonomie.

Von

Karl Marx.

Erster Band.
Buch I: Der Produktionsprocess des Kapitals.

Hamburg
Verlag von Otto Meissner.
1867.
New-York: L. W. Schmidt, 24 Barclay-Street.

Anti-Decalogue

РЕЛИГИЯ-ЯД
БЕРЕГИ РЕБЯТ

ШКОЛА

Moscow

SOVIET PLACARD – "Religion is poison – guard the children." A grandmother, a representative of the decaying old order, trying to force her granddaughter away from school and into the church.

SOVIET RUSSIA

CHAPTER 6

Anti-Decalogue

Fatima was the site of the most important private revelations of the twentieth century, when Our Lady warned against Russia's errors. The danger must have been very great for her to speak of it.

SOVIET PLACARD – "There is no God" as the astronauts did not see Him in outer space.

Communism opposes Christianity. Pope Pius XI called it the greatest heresy of all time, a negation of the Decalogue, or Ten Commandments.

Each of the Ten Commandments that Moses received on Mount Sinai has its opposite in a system that is seen by its advocates as the hope of humanity. John Paul II, in his *Crossing the Threshold of Hope*, wrote that in the modern age there is a war for the world's soul between advocates of the gospel and advocates of the anti-gospel. The latter, according to the pope, have their own resources and programs and oppose the gospel with great determination. He personally experienced and fought such a system, which advocated an anti-Decalogue ideology.

This chapter shows how Communism turned each of the Ten Commandments upside down.

145

I

YOU SHALL NOT HAVE STRANGE GODS BEFORE ME

RED FLAG depicting Lenin, the Bolshevik leader.

BABY LENIN – Pioneer organization badge.

LENIN'S MAUSOLEUM – secular temple of Communism.

Communism, despite loud declarations of its atheism, is a sort of substitute religion. It has a formula akin to a religious belief, wherein providence is replaced by progress. A classless society of the future is the promised paradise on earth, that is, the surrogate of the Kingdom of heaven. Instead of Christian dogmas it has Marxist ones. The Magisterium is replaced by the Central Committee of the Communist Party of the Soviet Union (Bolshevik), which is infallible, like the pope in the Catholic Church or the Orthodox general council. Marx's *Das Kapital* dethrones the Bible. The portraits of Communist leaders are like Orthodox icons, while images of Marx, Engels, and Lenin are akin to a theophany of the Trinity. The cult of the child Lenin recalls the worship of the Child Jesus. The holiest shrine of Communism is Lenin's Mausoleum in Moscow, where a mood of pious silence prevails. God, the supreme lawgiver, has been replaced by man, that is, the Communist Party.

YOU SHALL NOT TAKE THE NAME OF THE LORD YOUR GOD IN VAIN

Communists continually refer to God, not to praise Him but to blaspheme Him. They often particularly mention Jesus, either denying His existence or maintaining that He was but a man about whom we know very little. In 1922 the Soviet authorities established the League of Militant Atheists, an instrument of the forced atheization of society. It advocated Marx's opinion that religion is the opium of the people and Jesus Christ is the main obstacle to a Communist world revolution. That same year it began to issue *Bezbozhnik* (*The Godless*),

a daily newspaper that had a circulation of about two hundred thousand. Apart from that they also published the weeklies *Atheist* and *Antirieligioznik*, which had a circulation of one and a half million.

BEZBOZNIK PRZY PRACY (*Heathen at Work*) – a daily newspaper dedicated to combating religion.

MEMBERSHIP CARD – League of Militant Atheists.

ANTI - Communist caricature published uderground. The founder of the League of Militant Atheists, Yemelyan Yaroslavsky, is depicted as Stalin's watchdog.

III

KEEP HOLY
THE SABBATH DAY

SOVIET CALENDAR with new lay saints.

PLACARD – May I, Communist feast day.

The Communists destroyed Christian churches; ninety-eight Orthodox churches were demolished in Kiev alone. On December 5, 1931, the largest sacral building in Russia, the Cathedral of Christ the Savior in Moscow, built as a votive offering to commemorate the victory over Napoleon, was blown up. The leader of the Bolsheviks, Joseph Stalin, observed the demolition from a window. Many closed churches and Orthodox monasteries were at the disposal of the local authorities. Those that were turned into museums of atheism or concert halls met a somewhat better fate, but the majority became warehouses, factories, shops, bus stations, and even venereal disease hospitals, kennels, or toilets. Not many Orthodox churches, and but a handful of Roman Catholic ones, remained open throughout the country. The authorities prohibited prayers in public as well as the celebration of feast days. Public works were often organized on Sundays, the so-called community activities, in order to prevent people from keeping holy the sabbath day. There were anti-religious carnivals in the larger towns at Christmas and Easter, during which Jesus and Our Lady were derided. The Christmas of 1924 saw twenty blasphemous fancy dress marches in Leningrad alone, some of which ended with the burning of icons. Activists went from door to door terrorizing people, forcing them to sign petitions supporting the closure of churches.

MODEL OF the palace, topped with a statue of Lenin, which was to have been built on the former site of the Cathedral of Christ the Savior in Moscow.

BLOWN UP – the Cathedral of Christ the Savior, Moscow, the largest church in Russia.

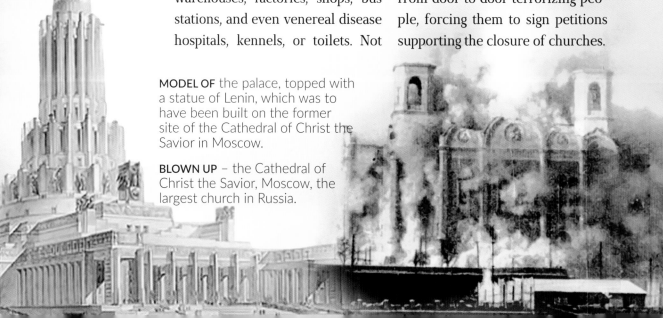

HONOR YOUR FATHER AND YOUR MOTHER

IV

Communist propaganda maintained that fidelity to the party was more important than loyalty to one's parents. An example of such an attitude was Pavlik Morozov, a thirteen-year-old boy from the village of Gerasimovka in the Tobolsk Governorate. He was treated like a hero throughout Russia as he had denounced his own father, who had evaded a compulsory corn levy. His father was arrested, but the juvenile was killed by his own grandfather. Thenceforth, as a Communist martyr, he was to be imitated by the Soviet youth. Portraits of him were displayed in schools. Films and books about him were produced. Maxim Gorky, a writer, admired Morozov as the party was dearer to him than blood ties. Shortly the Betrayal of the Motherland Act of 1934 appeared, making it a punishable offense – including by the death penalty – if someone over twelve years of age did not inform on suspects, even if they were one's own parents.

CHURCHES PLUNDERED by the Bolsheviks.

PAWLIK MOROZOV – hero who betrayed his father.

VICTIMS OF
Communism.

ORTHODOX PRIEST
– to be executed.

LIST OF PEOPLE
killed by the
Bolsheviks.

**COMMUNIST
PROPAGANDA:**
"The Soviet
government does
not punish but
educates."

YOU SHALL NOT KILL

Mass murder was not just a way to gain power, it was also an intrinsic part of the functioning of the Communist system for many years. It was Lenin who established the first Soviet concentration camps, on which the Nazis later modelled their own. Robert Conquest, a British historian, on the basis of archive data, estimated that about forty-two million perished in Soviet forced-labor camps. Another ten to thirty million died during transport to them or from severe exhaustion after being released from such camps. A great famine in Ukraine from 1932 to 1933, artificially created by the Communists, claimed about six or seven million lives. Every so often the party carried out great purges when further millions perished. It did not even spare its own, and even exemplary Communists were sentenced to death at fake show trials, for example, Nikolai Bukharin, Genrikh Yagoda, Nikolai Yezhov, Alexei Rykov, Lev Kamenev, and Grigory Zinoviev.

BACKBREAKING WORK – forced-labor workers building the White Sea–Baltic Canal.

GERMAN PUBLICATION – *Permitting the Destruction of Life Unworthy of Living* (1920) by Karl Binding and Alfred Hoche.

THE RED TERROR

IN OCTOBER 1922 Sergei Petrovich Melgunov, a Russian historian and socialist activist, fled from the Soviet Union. He had gathered accounts and testimonies for five years to inform the world of Communist crimes, publishing a book, *The Red Terror*, in 1924.

Melgunov wrote that every cheka (secret police) unit was known for its own speciality in murdering prisoners, who were crucified or stoned to death in Dnipropetrovsk; tied to planks and burned alive in furnaces in Odessa; impaled in Poltava and Kremenchuk; stripped naked and doused with cold water in freezing weather in Oryol; and in Voronezh, put in barrels filled with nails and then rolled about until dead. The book went unnoticed in the West.

ABORTION

ON NOVEMBER 18, 1920, the Soviet Union was the first country to permit abortion with the full sanction of the law. From then onward it was well-nigh seen as a permissible contraceptive, with some women having as many as 20 to 30 abortions. The Third Reich was the second state to legalize abortion, though only in territories conquered by it. On March 9, 1943, Hans Frank permitted abortion in the Nazi-occupied General Governorate territory in Poland, but only for women of "lower race" nations, mainly Slavs.

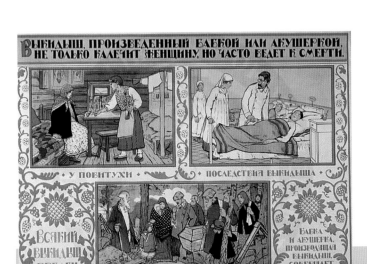

BOLSHEVIK PLACARD encouraging abortion. Juxtaposing illicit abortions by peasant women (resulting in death) with professional abortions in hospitals.

VI

YOU SHALL NOT COMMIT ADULTERY

ALEXANDRA KOLLONTAI
propagator of the Communist sexual revolution.

PROPAGANDA PLACARD
encouraging "free love". The man's reads: "Every male Komsomol [Communist youth organization member] can and should satisfy his sexual needs." The woman's reads: "Every female Komsomol is obliged to meet a man's wishes, otherwise she will be deemed to be bourgeois."

In December 1917, Soviet Russia introduced a law that placed marriage and cohabitation on an equal footing, and made divorce a formality that could be arranged by mail for three roubles, even without informing one's spouse. Alexandra Kollontai called for a sexual revolution. She initiated an educational campaign called Love as a Glass of Water, according to which a sexual relationship is as universal and necessary as quenching one's thirst and replenishing one's bodily fluids.

Bureaus of Free Love were established in many Russian towns, which advocated casual sex. It happened that women were flogged if they refused sex with men designated by such a bureau. In Saratov, the local authorities even issued a directive to "nationalize women", which obliged all females from seventeen to thirty years of age, regardless of marital status, to give their bodies to "male citizens". Every worker who allotted 2 percent of his income to a special fund was guaranteed sex three times a week with a "female citizen" of his own choice.

Komsomols (Communist youth) were placed in communes where everyone lived and had sex together. In 1924, Felix Dzerzhinsky, president of the Commission for the Improvement of the Life

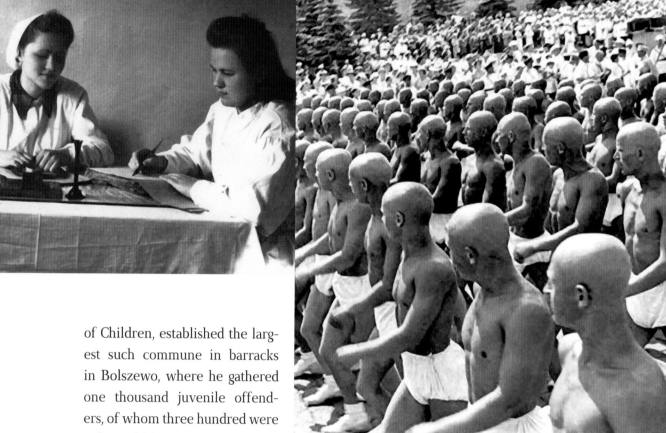

of Children, established the largest such commune in barracks in Bolszewo, where he gathered one thousand juvenile offenders, of whom three hundred were girls aged fifteen to eighteen, who were encouraged to have group sex. The collective coerced people to change partners frquently. The aim of that progressive experiment was to resocialize the youth, and to rear a "Soviet man" (homo sovieticus).

In June 1918 there was a nudist demonstration in St. Petersburg. Several hundred naked men and women marched along the streets carrying banners saying: "Down with Shame!" The world's first gay parade took place in St. Petersburg on December 19, 1918. Sergey Merkurov wrote a textbook, the *Soviet ABC of Eroticism*, for teaching reading and writing; its pornographic drawings were to encourage illiterate boys to learn the alphabet.

The term "sexual revolution" was first introduced into mass circulation by Grigory Batkis, director of the Moscow Institute for Sexual Hygiene, via his pamphlet *The Sexual Revolution in Russia*. He wrote that the bourgeois family, with a husband and a wife, ought to be replaced by the Komsomol commune, where about twenty people had sexual intercourse with one another, as it was only thus possible to reconcile personal feelings with great social tasks. Stalin initiated a move away from the sexual revolution in 1926.

SOVIET PARADE, Red Square, Moscow.

NURSE WRITING an abortion referral.

153

VII

YOU SHALL NOT STEAL

The whole Communist system is based on plunder. One of its basic principles is the elimination of private property, that is, the appropriation of land, factories, warehouses, machinery, and even homes, followed by their nationalization. Not only the rich are subject to expropriation, but also the semiaffluent. During the first stage of the revolution, one of the Communist leaders, "party favorite" Nikolai Bukharin, created a slogan: "Plunder the plunder." That attracted masses of released criminals to the Bolsheviks. Leonid Andreyev, a Russian writer and an eyewiness of the revolution, wrote in 1919 that Lenin became like a magnet that attracted despicable and ruthless individuals. In exchange for fidelity to the party they were permitted to rob the "enemies of the people". In time, when the Communist system was stronger, a new class appeared, Soviet apparatchiks who managed the nationalized, that is, plundered, wealth. They behaved as if they owned the state.

YOU SHALL NOT BEAR FALSE WITNESS AGAINST YOUR NEIGHBOR

Soviet propaganda was in large measure based on lies, false accusations, and slanders. Many people and circles, neutral with regard to Communism, were depicted as enemies of the system. Its opponents, real or alleged, were blamed for thought-up crimes. Catholic priests were depicted as Vatican agents, while high-ranking Red Army officers (during the purges of 1937 to 1939) as Third Reich spies. There were show trials based on fabricated evidence, where the falsely accused often pleaded guilty to imaginary crimes. For example, Lev Kamenev and Grigory Zinoviev admitted to participating in a Fascist plot, for which they were condemned to death.

SECOND MOSCOW trial in 1937 saw 13 prominent Communist Party activists sentenced to death.

ART OF RETOUCHING: Communists not only murdered people, but also tried to efface the memory of them, as evidenced by these photos.
❶ Stalin with Nikolai Yezhov, head of the secret police,
❷ Stalin depicted alone after Yezhov was liquidated.

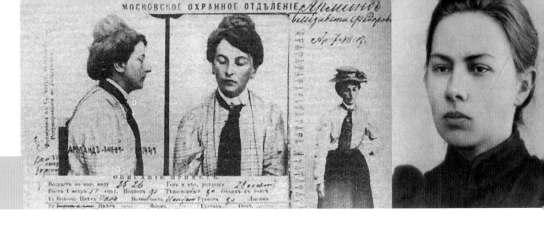

YOU SHALL NOT COVET YOUR NEIGHBOR'S WIFE

TWO OF LENIN'S women: Inessa Armand and Nadezhda Krupskaya.

STALIN'S LOVERS: Vera Davidova, a singer, and Olga Lepeshinskaya, a dancer.

Sexual licentiousness favored the realization of the sexual revolution. Marital fidelity was seen as outdated. This attitude was reflected in decrees and laws, and law – as Aristotle had already noted – creates customs. Hence consent to permissiveness became widespread, and with it the betrayal of wives and husbands. Many Communist leaders are examples in this respect. Lenin was unfaithful to his wife, Nadezhda Krupskaya, over many years, having an affair with Alexander Armand's wife, Inessa. Alexandra Kollontai had relationships with married men. Stalin had many concubines, often the wives of Kremlin dignitaries, for example, Andrey Andreyev's wife, Dora Chazan, whose sexual relationship with the dictator did not save her from death in a forced-labor camp.

YOU SHALL NOT COVET YOUR NEIGHBOR'S GOODS

Marxists claim that one of the basic driving forces of history is class stuggle: the conflict between the exploiters and the exploited, the rich and the poor, the bourgeois and the proletarians, the capitalists and the workers. This historical injustice, they say, cannot be abolished by peaceful reforms – armed revolution is necessary. But the wronged masses are capable of a bloody revolt only when they are inspired by anger and hate. Hence it is necessary to eliminate Christian ideas about peace, mercy, or rewards in the afterlife, which weaken the class struggle and deprive it of its impetus, and replace them with envy towards the rich for their material goods. The only way to realize social justice is to take from the rich and give to the poor. In practice this imperative assumes a brutal form – mass robbery and plunder, linked with violence and murder. Hence it is not surprising that children in elementary schools learned to read and to write using primers with short texts that justify the plunder of other people's private property: "We have the kulaks' houses, their cornfields, their orchards. Get the kulak!"

MARX'S *Das Kapital,* Socialism's bible.

COMMUNIST "HOLY TRINITY": Marx, Engels, and Lenin.

157

Towards Another Catastrophe

Towards Another Catastrophe

It was the beginning of August 1920. Panic had seized the diplomats accredited to Warsaw. They had packed their suitcases and fled to the West. Only two members of the diplomatic corps remained: the Turkish ambassador and the apostolic nuncio. The latter was Achille Ratti, consecrated titular archbishop of Naupactus barely a year earlier in Warsaw.

POLAND
before 1939

POLISH VICTORY over the Bolsheviks at the Battle of Warsaw in 1920 – Polish chapel at the Marian shrine in Loreto, Italy.

160

The Italian heirarch did not flee the capital, though there was daily news from the eastern front that the terrible Red Army, bringing death and wreaking havoc, was approaching. He blessed Polish units about to go to the front. He impressed people by his bravery – he was, after all, a good mountaineer, having climbed Mont Blanc, the Matterhorn, and the eastern wall of Dufourspitze (on Monte Rosa). He was well aware of the gravity of the situation, of what was at stake in the conflict: the fate of Western civilization.

After their victory in Russia, the Bolsheviks intended to spread the flames of revolution throughout the world. Germany was their first target, where a Communist revolution had also broken out.

BATTLE OF WARSAW
– painting by
Wojciech Kossak.

SOVIET POWS
captured by
Poles.

BRIDGE OVER the Niemen blown up during the Polish-Bolshevik War.

POLISH VICTIMS of Soviet murders.

Lenin and Trotsky wanted to join forces with it to conquer Europe together. They counted on the fact that weakened and exhausted by World War I, Europe would not be in a position to defend itself against Communist revolution. But the road to the West was by way of Poland, which had gained independence after one hundred twenty-three years of bondage and which did not intend to yield to the Bolsheviks.

As the Red Army approached Warsaw, Archbishop Achille Ratti knew that he was at the very center of a cyclone, where the fate of Europe was being decided. He observed as the West abandoned Poland. British dockers, French and German railwaymen, influenced by Communist agitation, began mass strikes with but one aim in mind – to prevent aid reaching Poland in time. Hence boxes of arms and ammunition lay in ports and railway sidings, while on the eastern fronts Polish soldiers counted every bullet. The only real aid came from Hungary (August 12, 1920), when the Soviets were

163

JASNA GORA – Chapel of the Miraculous Image.

VENERATED – icon of Our Lady of Czestochowa.

VICTORIOUS DEFENSE of the Jasna Gora Monastery against the Swedes in 1656.

QUEEN OF POLAND

THROUGHOUT HISTORY POLES often made their way to the shrine in Czestochowa to plead for help before the image of Our Lady. Hence in 1929, in the face of a mortal danger, the Polish bishops gathered at the shrine to implore the Blessed Virgin's aid. They entrusted the country to her, and again proclaimed her Queen of Poland.

The Pauline Order, the shrine's custodian, made an appeal: "Our nation is the property of Our Lady, just as the Jewish nation once belonged to God in a special way. Let us learn from them, what the sons of Israel did at difficult times, so that we too might do what is right." The monks advocated the example of the Israelites, who during the Assyrian invasion led by Holofernes, listened to their priest Joakim and began to pray and fast. "Today, according to the Paulines, our beloved Poland has been invaded by a mortal enemy. A contemporary Holofernes-Bolshevik wants to wreak havoc in our country, take our children as loot, defile our women, desecrate our churches, and take our youth into bondage.... From whence aid, whence hope, whence victory and salvation? One has to reply as did Joakim: 'Know ye! Arms, spears and army apart, ye need to fast and pray.' "[24]

COMMANDER-IN-CHIEF JOZEF PILSUDSKI, apostolic nuncio Archbishop Achille Ratti, and auditor of the nunciature Fr. Pellegrini.

but seven miles from Warsaw; the ammunition train that reached Poland from the munitions factory in Budapest was a major factor in Poland's victory over the Bolsheviks.

August 15, 1920, approached, the Feast of the Assumption. That day saw the end of an intercessory-penitential novena for the rescue of Poland, initiated by the bishops assembled at the Czestochowa shrine. That morning articles appeared in the Bolshevik press claiming that the Red Army had already captured Warsaw. But that very day the Polish Army, led by Marshal Jozef Pilsudski, counterattacked and defeated the Soviets. During the following weeks the Red Army was pushed back far to the east. Lord Edgar Vincent D'Abernon, a British diplomat, saw this as the "eighteenth decisive battle in history", known as the Vistula Miracle.

In 1921, when Poles were celebrating the first anniversary of the victory, Achille Ratti was the archbishop of Milan. On February 6, 1922, he was elected pope after the death of Benedict XV, when, like his predecessor eight years earlier, he was the youngest of the hierarchs at the conclave, a cardinal for barely six months. However, he was the only one to have had personal experience of Communism, which the hierarchs saw as the Church's main challenge. Hence they elected Cardinal Ratti, who took the name Pius XI.

165

BENEDICT XV died in 1922, at the age of 67.

LEON TROTSKY, one of the Bolshevik leaders, the actual commander of the victorious Soviet troops during the Russian Revolution.

STALIN AND LENIN – USSR leaders. Two of the most notorious criminals in history.

The Bolsheviks had to revise their plans after the Poles had defeated them. They were not in a position to bring about a world-wide revolution, so they decided to establish Communism in Russia, proclaiming the rise of a new state, the USSR, which, apart from Russia, consisted of countries that they had conquered: Ukraine, Belarus, Armenia, Georgia, Azerbaijan, Kazakhstan, Kyrgyzstan, Uzbekistan, Tajikistan, and Turkmenistan. In 1921 they imposed their system on two Asiatic states, Mongolia and the Tyva Republic. They built an empire based on terror and propaganda, and awaited a convenient time to try again and to impose their system worldwide.

After Lenin's death (1924) it was not clear who would succeed him. Several distinguished Communist Party executive activists came to the fore, the most influential of whom were Leon Trotsky and Joseph Stalin. The latter turned out to be a real master of intrigue, who gradually removed rivals from power. The pupil turned out to be worthy of his master, perfecting administration via the terror initiated by Lenin. Apart from Mao Tse-tung, who would become the Communist leader of China, Stalin was the greatest criminal in human history, ruling via totalitarian methods in an effort to subordinate all spheres of life to Marxist ideology. Even independent thought was a crime.

Stalin did not abandon the Bolshevik desire to conquer Europe. Comintern agents were active in many countries, initiating subversive activities. One of these was the mass murder of mourners at the funeral of Gen. Konstantin Georgiev in Sofia, Bulgaria. On April 14, 1925, at 8:00 p.m., Gen. Georgiev, chief of the Bulgarian Army General Staff, was on his way to an Orthodox church with his granddaughter for the Easter Tuesday liturgy. Atanas Todovichin, a Communist activist, appeared beside him, pulled out a pistol, and killed him. Two days later, at the Cathedral of St. Nedelya in Sofia, there was a solemn funeral attended by the most important people in the country. Explosives planted in the church by Nikola Petrov, a Communist, were detonated, and over one hundred fifty perished on the spot, including fourteen generals, the chief of police, the mayor of Sofia, about fifty state officials, and thirty journalists. Over five hundred people sustained injuries.

When the Bulgarian Communist Party was accused of the bomb attack, Georgi Dimitrov, its leader, said that it was a monstrous capitalist and fascist slander, claiming that the massacre was the work of the police. The Soviet media played along with him, as did the press in many Western countries. The truth did not come out until fifteen

NAZI PLACARDS inspired by Communist ones from the Soviet Union.

ST. NEDELYA
Cathedral in
Sofia, blown up
by Communists in
1925.

JOSEPH STALIN with
his confidant
Georgi Dimitrov,
head of the
Bulgarian
Communist Party.

years later. During the Fifth Congress of the Bulgarian Communist Party in December 1948, Dimitrov himself publicly admitted that members of his own party were behind the terrorist attack.

However, other methods were also used. Soviet military schools and special services academies used Sun Tzu's *The Art of War*, a Chinese strategist's textbook that was written twenty-five centuries ago. Sun Tzu wrote that invaders should gain control of an enemy's territory without an armed struggle, weakening an opponent from within, so that a military attack would be but a formality. Thus Communist Party strategists developed means for weakening the West from the inside, by exploiting the vulnerabilities of its free societies.

Christianity and Communism are worlds apart. Christianity's message is the complete opposite of the ideology and practice of Marxism-Leninism. Instead of hate, Christianity proclaims love. It offers freedom, not enslavement. It rejects the principle that the aim justifies any means. It does not avail itself of murder, lies, and theft, but prayer, fasts, and alms. Its weapons are not bombs and guns, but the Rosary and the Miraculous Medal.

METHODS FOR WEAKENING THE WEST

SUN TZU,
Chinese general,
author of the
oldest textbook
on the art of
war.

1. DISCREDIT all that is good in Western society.

2. LURE representatives of the ruling classes into criminal undertakings.

3. UNDERMINE their good names, and at the appropriate moment leave them at the mercy of the contempt of their compatriots.

4. COLLABORATE with the most base and the most repugnant.

5. DISORGANIZE the activities of Western governments by all possible means.

6. SOW strife and discord among the citizens of the enemy countries.

7. INCITE the young against the old.

8. RIDICULE the traditions of enemy countries.

9. SOW CONFUSION via all possible means at the enemy's rear, its supply lines, and among its soldiers

10. WEAKEN the enemy soldiers' will to fight via sensuous songs and music.

11. SEND them harlots to complete the work of destruction.

12. DO NOT SPARE promises and gifts to get information. Spare no expenses, for money so spent will pay for itself a hundredfold.

13. INFILTRATE spies everywhere.

BAMBOO EDITION – Sun Tzu's *The Art of War*.

JOHN F. KENNEDY was a member of the Blue Army before he became president of the United States.

Stalin, commenting on the significance of the Catholic Church, asked derisively: "How many divisions does the pope have?" He believed in the argument of force, not the force of argument. He was convinced that he was playing the role of the engine driver of history's steam locomotive, that he was history's pointsman, diverting it onto a new track.

But Christians believe that God always has the last word and that He avails Himself of the humble. Lucia dos Santos was one of them. In 1925, she decided to enter the Order of the Sisters of St. Dorothy. At that time the anti-clerical Portuguese authorities prohibited orders to accept new candidates, so the eighteen-year-old was directed to Pontevedra, Spain, to commence her postulancy. There she heard an inner voice informing her that she had been granted an extraordinary grace, a "mystical adoption", that is, that Our Lady had accepted her as her own child.

Lucia had another apparition (December 10, 1925) at the Convent of the Sisters of St. Dorothy in Pontevedra. When she was praying in

STATUE OF the Child Jesus – John F. Kennedy donated it to the convent in Pontevedra, Spain, as evidenced by the brass plaque.

PAINTING DEPICTING Sr. Lucia's apparition on December 10, 1925 – convent chapel in Pontevedra.

the convent chapel, Our Lady appeared with the Child Jesus at her side. She put one hand on the postulant's shoulder and showed her her Heart, encircled by thorns, which she held in her other hand. The Child Jesus said: "Have compassion on the Heart of your most holy Mother, covered with thorns, with which ungrateful men pierce it at every moment, and there is no one to make an act of reparation to remove them."[25]

Then Mary addressed Lucia: "Look, my daughter, at my Heart, surrounded with thorns with which ungrateful men pierce me every moment by their blasphemies and ingratitude. You at least try to console me and say that I promise to assist at the hour of death, with the graces necessary for salvation, all those who, on the first Saturday of five consecutive months, shall confess, receive Holy Communion, recite five decades of the Rosary, and keep me company for fifteen minutes while meditating on the fifteen mysteries of the Rosary, with the intention of making reparation to me."[26]

Lucia recalled what Mary had said during the apparition in Fatima on July 13, 1917: "I shall come to ask for the consecration of Russia to my Immaculate Heart, and Communion of reparation on First Saturdays."[27] Lucia decided to fulfill Our Lady's wishes regarding the devotion. She made her way to her confessor Fr. Jose Aparicio and told him about the apparition. But the Jesuit laid down conditions.

SPAIN

Pontevedra
• Madrid

DOROTHEAN CONVENT garden in Pontevedra, where Sr. Lucia liked to spend time.

SR. LUCIA and other candidates during their novitiate in Tui, Spain.

171
✛

CENTRAL NAVE of the Basilica of Our Lady in Pontevedra, to which Sr. Lucia sent a small boy, who turned out to be Jesus.

He wanted the apparition to be repeated, and he insisted on knowing why the devotion was to be universal in the Church, as many were already observing the First Saturdays worldwide. The disconcerted postulant confided her problem to her superior, who told her that she could not do anything without the consent of her confessor.

Shortly after, in St. Mary's Square in Pontevedra, Lucia chanced on a small boy who had drawn her attention. She asked him if he knew the Hail Mary. He told her that he did, but he was silent when she asked him to recite it. Shen then recited the prayer three times so that he might remember it. When she encouraged him to say it, he became silent again. So Lucia pointed to the nearby Church of St. Mary and told him to go there and pray thus: "Oh my heavenly Mother, give me Your Child Jesus!"

On February 15, 1926, Lucia chanced again on a little boy who seemed to be the boy she had spoken to previously. She inquired whether he had asked Our Blessed Lady for the Child Jesus. He

FRONT WALL of the Dorothean convent in Pontevedra.

SIGN INFORMING that the Sanctuary of Apparitions is to be found in the Dorothean convent.

replied by asking her whether she had spread through the world what Mary had requested of her. At that moment He transformed Himself into a resplendent Child. Lucia realized that she had Christ Himself before her. She told Him of her problems with her confessor and mother superior. Jesus said that many began the devotion of the Five First Saturdays but did not finish it. Those who persevered did so mainly because of the promised graces. But He wanted people to do it fervently in reparation to the Immaculate Heart of Mary, and not indifferently and lukewarmly.

It was only later that Lucia understood why Jesus (the little boy) did not want to say the Hail Mary. Since He was God, He could not pray to His own Mother, but rather the other way round. Christ's words, however, encouraged Lucia. After assuming the habit and commencing her novitiate, she wrote her first letter to her mother general asking for the propagation of the devotion that Jesus had requested.

173

On December 17, 1927, Lucia had another apparition in the convent chapel in Pontevedra. While praying before the tabernacle, Lucia asked Jesus what she could reveal to her superiors if they wanted to know of the origins of the message about the devotion to the Immaculate Heart of Mary. Christ instructed her to reveal the details of the Fatima apparition of July 13, 1917, but not all. She could speak of the vision of hell, the demand to consecrate Russia, and the First Saturdays of the month, but she was to keep the third secret to herself.

At that time Lucia had news from Fatima: A constant stream of pilgrims, some of whom were healed of incurable diseases, kept arriving there. For example, Jose de Oliveira Carvalho, whom doctors had given eight days to live, regained his health after praying and drinking water from a spring; Teresa Jesús Martin, who was in the last phase of tuberculosis was cured; Maria Teixeiria Lopes, who had about five hundred ulcers all over her body, was healed after being blessed with the Blessed Sacrament. Hence it was not surprising that in 1928 the bishop of Leiria had the first cornerstone laid in

THE BASILICA of Our Lady of the Rosary in Cova da Iria began to be built in 1928.

the construction of the Basilica of Our Lady of the Rosary, which became the largest church in Portugal.

As a novice, Lucia was transferred to another St. Dorothy convent in Tui, Spain. She expected Mary to appear to her at any moment to request the consecration of Russia to her Immaculate Heart. This occurred shortly before midnight on June 13, 1929, when she was praying alone before the tabernacle. She recalled:

"Suddenly the whole chapel was illumined by a supernatural light, and above the altar appeared a cross of light, reaching to the ceiling. In a brighter light on the upper part of the cross, could be seen the face of a man and his body as far as the waist; upon his breast was a dove of light; nailed to the cross was the body of another man. A little below the waist, I could see a chalice and a large host suspended in the air, on to which drops of blood were falling from the face of Jesus Crucified and from the wound in His side. These drops ran down on to the host and fell into the chalice. Beneath the right arm of the cross was Our Lady and in her hand was her Immaculate Heart. (It was Our Lady of Fatima, with her Immaculate Heart in her left hand, without sword or roses, but with a crown of thorns and flames.) Under the left arm of the cross, large letters, as if of crystal clear water which ran down upon the altar, formed these words: 'Grace and Mercy'. I understood that it was the Mystery of the Most

APPARITION IN TUI, Spain, during which Sr. Lucia had a vision of the Holy Trinity.

DOROTHEAN CONVENT in Tui – main street entrance.

SPAIN

Tui

Madrid

CONFESSIONAL in the convent in Tui – Sr. Lucia confessed there regularly.

CONVENT CHAPEL in Tui – Sr. Lucia had apparitions there.

Holy Trinity which was shown to me, and I received lights about this mystery which I am not permitted to reveal."[28]

When the vision vanished, Our Lady told Lucia: "The moment has come in which God asks the Holy Father, in union with all the Bishops of the world, to make the consecration of Russia to my Immaculate Heart, promising to save it by this means. There are so many souls whom the Justice of God condemns for sins committed against me, that I have come to ask reparation: sacrifice yourself for this intention and pray."[29]

Lucia told her confessor, Fr. Jose Bernardo Goncalves, about the apparition. The Jesuit, however, did not understand why the prayer of reparation for the affronts to Our Lady was to be said for five Saturdays. Lucia could not explain this. But she shortly received the answer. She thus explained it in a letter to the inquisitive priest:

"My daughter, the motive is simple: there are five ways in which people offend and blaspheme against the Immaculate Heart of Mary:

MARIAN SHRINE on the convent wall in Tui.

DOROTHEAN CONVENT in Tui from the garden.

177

(1) Blasphemies against the Immaculate Conception; (2) Blasphemies against her Perpetual Virginity; (3) Blasphemies against her Divine Maternity and at the same time the refusal to recognize her as the Mother of all mankind; (4) Blasphemies of those who seek openly to foster in the hearts of children indifference or contempt and even hatred for this Immaculate Mother; (5) The offenses of those who directly outrage her in her holy images."[30]

During the same apparition Jesus disclosed that sins against His Mother offended God Himself most gravely. Yet Mary was solicitous about the salvation of these sinners, requesting acts of reparation to save them from eternal damnation. Christ also asked Lucia to pray and to make spiritual sacrifices for mercy for these sinners. He added that if the faithful could not participate in the First Saturdays devotion, they could practice it on First Sundays.

During the apparitions Our Lady told Lucia that there would be another world war, famines, many armed conflicts, and persecutions of Christians unless people were converted and regretted their sins; that such misfortunes could be avoided by people entrusting themselves to the Immaculate Heart of Mary and practicing the Five First Saturdays devotion.

After the apparitions, Lucia was certain that she had to inform the pope that he could prevent a war by consecrating Russia to the Immaculate Heart of Mary. On October 13, 1930, Bishop of Leiria Jose Alves Correia da Silva acknowledged the authenticity of the Fatima revelations, which enhanced Lucia's credibility. Yet, Pius XI, who was aware of Our Lady's wishes, did not comply with the request.

Why? It has never been fully explained. Various explanations are circulating on this matter. One version is that Achille Ratti was always distrustful of private revelations. During his pontificate, for example, Padre Pio was burdened with severe limitations. Another

BISHOP OF LEIRIA
Jose Alves Correia da Silva. In 1930 he confirmed the authenticity of the Fatima apparitions.

SICK PILGRIMS
in Fatima.

version maintains that Communist agents were active in the Vatican, and they did not want Russia consecrated to Our Lady. But on the other hand, in 1929, Pius XI handed out pictures of Our Lady of Fatima to a Portuguese delegation and blessed a statue of her. A year later he permitted pilgrimages to Fatima and introduced special indulgences connected with them.

The Portuguese bishops, however, took Lucia's requests to heart, and on May 13, 1931 (the anniversary of the Fatima apparitions), they collectively consecrated Portugal to the Immaculate Heart of Mary. The bishops were very worried because the Communists were causing disturbances in the country, fuelling a revolutionary mood. The apostolic nuncio in Lisbon, Archbishop Giovanni Beda Cardinale, noticed that while left-wing propaganda kindled divisions in society, Our Lady of Fatima was a great unitive force.

The devotion of the Immaculate Heart of Mary also developed dynamically in Poland. In 1927, Maximilian Kolbe established a small monastery complex near Warsaw. He called it Niepokalanow

CELEBRATIONS IN FATIMA on May 13, 1932, the fifteenth anniversary of the apparitions.

PORTUGUESE EPISCOPATE consecrated the country to the Immaculate Heart of Mary.

POPE PIUS XI during the opening of Vatican Radio on February 12, 1931. On the left: Secretary of State Cardinal Eugenio Pacelli, later Pope Pius XII.

FR. MAXIMILIAN Kolbe and seminarians from the minor seminary in Niepokalanow, Poland.

THE KNIGHT OF THE IMMACULATE was the world's most widely read magazine before World War II.

(Immaculate) in honor of Our Lady, and it became the largest Catholic monastery in the world, with as many as seven hundred monks in 1939. Its printing house issued books and magazines, one of which was the monthly *The Knight of the Immaculate* magazine, initially edited by the charismatic Franciscan, which was the most widely read magazine in the world, reaching a circulation of one million copies, while its *Maly Dziennik* newspaper had a circulation of three hundred thousand. The monastery had a radio station, as well as a television station, which broadcasted the first experimental programs (before World War II). Kolbe's motto: "All to the greater glory of the Immaculate."

It was only after many years that the Franciscans discovered an extraordinary coincidence. The year 1917 saw the Bolshevik Revolution and the beginning of the most bloody and anti-Christian system in history. That same year there were two reactions to that danger: one from above, the other from below. The one from heaven, the Fatima apparitions, the one from earth, the knighthood established

by Maximilian Kolbe. The essence of both responses was the same, that is, that the way to God was via the Immaculate Heart of Mary.

Meanwhile world events developed as foretold in Sr. Lucia's apparitions. In 1920, Stalin ousted all his rivals from power and assumed complete control of the goverment. He introduced such a rule of terror that even his closest collaborators could not be sure of the day or the hour. The head of Soviet diplomacy Vyacheslav Molotov – though totally faithful to him – expected to be arrested at any moment and condemned at a show trial. He was unable to save his wife, who was sentenced to five years in a labor camp on the basis of false testimonies. Those suspected of any dis- obedience whatsover were severely punished.

THE PRINTING HOUSE in Niepokalanow was one of the most modern in Europe in the interwar period.

Niepokalanow
Warsaw

POLAND
before 1939

BASILICA OF OUR LADY Mediatrix of All Graces – Niepokalanow

FR. MAXIMILIAN KOLBE even established a fire brigade in Niepokalanow.

FR. MAXIMILIAN KOLBE among some Franciscans in Japan.

FRANCISCAN SEMINARY in Nagasaki – founded by Fr. Kolbe.

THE EDITOR-IN-CHIEF of *The Knight of the Immaculate* corresponded with readers.

The persecution of Christians recommenced. Evangelization, called "religious propaganda", was categorized in the constitution as a crime against the state. Religious and their families were deprived of their civil rights, and Christian churches were destroyed.

Fr. Maximilian Maria Kolbe appeared in Moscow at a time when the Soviet machinery of terror was crushing the followers of Christ. The Franciscan was returning to Poland from Japan on the Trans-Siberian Railway. The train stopped in Moscow for several hours. Kolbe, dressed in civilian clothes, visited the city to see what the land of universal equality looked like for himself. He saw glaring inequality. On returning to Poland he told his fellow monks that a time would come when a statue of the Immaculate would be seen in Moscow.

Meanwhile Stalin ordered a long-term industrialization plan. He was aware that heavy industries had to be developed in order to build a military power to conquer the world. Large financial out-lays were necessary to carry out the so-called Five-Year Plan, and to bring about an "industrial leap". The main source of funds was exporting grain, especially from Ukraine, the breadbasket of the Soviet Union. The government imposed unreasonable grain quotas

on Ukraine for the benefit of the state. When their realization was in doubt, Stalin ordered the complete collectivization of the countryside, that is, the elimination of private farms and the establishment of government-owned ones. In order to meet the compulsory quotas, army and militia brigades forcibly took all that the peasants possessed, including their seed for sowing. One of the Soviet leaders, Lazar Kaganovich, boasted that nearly all the grain in Ukraine had been appropriated by the state. That led to a great famine, during which the USSR exported grain.

The great famine of 1932–1933 was not a natural disaster caused by a crop failure, a drought, or a flood, but an artificially created catastrophe. Historians and demographers are still arguing over the number of victims that the genocide claimed; it is most often reckoned to be from six to twelve million.

Yet most people in the West did not know about this great crime. The most renowned authority among the foreign correspondents in Moscow at the time was Walter Duranty, a *New York Times*

SOVIET UNION

Moscow

UKRAINE

THE GREAT famine in Ukraine – people as well as animals suffered.

TOWN STREETS in Ukraine were strewn with the victims of the famine.

183

✥

THE GREAT FAMINE of 1932–1933 decimated the population in Ukraine.

MALCOLM MUGGERIDGE was one of the few Western journalists who wrote the truth about the famine.

IN 1933 THE WORLD MASS MEDIA informed the world of the 6 million victims of the Great Ukrainian Famine.

journalist, a Pulitzer Prize winner for his "objective reports and explanatory interpretations of events". But he denied the existence of the famine even when the Ukranian countryside was littered with the corpses of victims who had been reduced to skin and bones. (In the spring and summer of 1933, Ukranian peasants were dying at the rate of twenty-five thousand a day, that is, seventeen every minute.) Duranty did not write about the disaster, but of food surpluses record crops, plump babies, and market stalls that sagged under the weight of meat, vegetables, and fruit. Simultaneously, he claimed that Stalin was being wronged, a victim of false accusations. He compared those who accused the Bolsheviks of bringing about an artificial famine to Nero stirring up Rome against the Christians or Hitler causing a fire in the Reichstag.

Malcolm Muggeridge was another Western journalist in Moscow, a *Manchester Guardian* correspondent who, disguised as a worker, managed to visit Ukraine without permission from the Soviet authorities. He saw depopulated towns and children dying in the torment of hunger on the streets. When he wrote about it, his editors refused to publish his article as they thought that nobody would believe him. On returning to Great Britain, he related what he saw, but his family

SIX MILLION PERISH IN SOVIET FAMINE

PEASANTS' CROPS SEIZED, THEY AND THEIR ANIMALS STARVE

"USEFUL IDIOTS"

COMMUNIST AGENTS won over to their ideology many Westerners, particularly intellectuals fascinated by the pioneering social experiment in the Soviet Union. Lenin once called them "useful idiots" as they aided and abetted Communists who would eventually turn on them. They went on "pilgrimages" to the Soviet Union, where they saw institutions set up for naïve guests from abroad, while special guides made sure that they did not come into contact with ordinary people and learn of their miserable lot.

In 1932, over 100 outstanding Western intellectuals who had visited the Soviet Union published articles during the widespread famine in Ukraine. They included well-known writers, for example: Noble Prize winners Anatole France, Romain Rolland, George Bernard Shaw, and Upton Sinclair, as well as Henri Barbusse, Heinrich Mann, Gerhart Hauptmann, John Dos Passos, Herbert George Wells, Theodore Dreiser, Egon Erwin Kisch, and Andre Maurois. They all described Stalin's state as if it were a paradise on earth – as the only place where true social justice prevailed.

WESTERN AUTHORS fooled by the criminal system: ❶ George Bernard Shaw, ❷ Herbert George Wells, ❸ Egon Erwin Kisch, ❹ Theodore Dreiser, ❺ Romain Rolland, ❻ Henri Barbusse.

STATUE OF MARY
in the Sardao
College garden,
before which
Lucia liked to
pray.

SARDAO COLLEGE
in Vila Nova de
Gaia, near Porto.

ANTONIO SALAZAR
ruled Portugal
autocratically for
36 years, from
1932 to 1968.

thought that had gone out of his mind and wondered if he needed psychiatric treatment.

In 1932, Antonio de Oliveira Salazar became the prime minister of Portugal. In 1933, he initiated an authoritarian government and proclaimed the rise of a New State (Estado Novo). He introduced a corporate system based on solidarity, inspired by Catholic social teaching. He disbanded all the political parties except one, the National Union, and fought against left-wing opposition. Hard-line government and shrewd diplomacy helped Portugal to avoid Spain's fate, the Civil War of 1936–1939, in which six hundred thousand perished. The Red Terror reaped a bloody harvest, particularly among Catholics. Antonio Montero Moreno, a historian, documented 6,832 cases of Catholic religious (including 283 nuns) who perished at the hands of Communists and Anarchists who fought on the Republican side. All in all, 12 percent of the Spanish clergy perished in the Civil War, though in some places occupied by the left it was as many as 80 percent. Lucia and some other nuns left Tui for the College of the Sacred Heart of Jesus, near Porto, Portugal.

Meanwhile the situation in Europe was ever worse. In 1933 the National Socialists came to power in Germany. To Adolf Hitler, their leader, Bolshevism was the greatest enemy. On the one hand, he hated Communists, but on the other, he was fascinated by their effectiveness and their ability to mobilize the masses. He called Stalin a beast, but one of considerable stature, and saw him as one of the most extraordinary figures in history. With a touch of jealousy, he observed how in the Soviet Union the wills of thousands of people were embodied in one individual – the leader. He imitated Marxist ideology, changing but the object of deification – race and nation instead of the proletariat – and also imitated Leninist models, establishing a one-party system, as well as concentration camps.

On October 3, 1934, Sr. Lucia dos Santos professed her perpetual vows at the Dorothean convent. She was one of the second choir sisters, that is, nuns assigned to physical work. At that time she was in Spain, either at the convent in Tui or in Pontevedra. It was in Spain that she received some unusual news, that is, that a special grave had been prepared for Francisco and Jacinta at the rural cemetery in Fatima. Hence on September 12, 1935, Jacinta's body was transferred from Vila Nova de Ourem to Fatima. During the exhumation, it was

EXHUMATION of Francisco and Jacinta.

REV. DR. FISCHER examined Jacinta's body in September 1935. Her body had not decomposed though 15 years had passed since her death.

SARDAO COLLEGE CHAPEL. Balcony where Sr. Lucia prayed.

ARTICLE in the weekly *Digane* about the Holy Grail from Valencia being hidden from the Republicans during the Civil War in Spain.

SPANISH MARTYRS raised to the altar – victims of the Civil War from 1936 to 1939.

discovered that her body had not decomposed, though she had been dead for fifteen years. Bishop Correia da Silva sent a photo of Jacinta to Lucia and asked her to write a profile of her cousin, which she did in December. Thus arose the first account of the Fatima appatitions. Two years later, in November 1937, the bishop of Leiria asked her to write down the facts once again, including the events that she had omitted earlier. Thus arose her second memoir.

During her stay in Spain, Sr. Lucia had further revelations, reminding her of the consecration of Russia to the Immaculate Heart of Mary. Her superiors strived to inform the Holy See about it, but did not receive an answer. During one of the visions she heard Jesus' voice: "They did not wish to heed my request. Like the King

FIRING SQUAD shooting at a statue of Jesus in Madrid.

FRENCH MYSTIC
St. Margaret Mary
Alacoque.

"SUN KING" Louis XIV
did not venerate
the Sacred Heart of
Jesus.

DEATH of Louis XVI –
guillotined.

THE DISREGARDED REQUEST FROM HEAVEN

IN 1689, Margaret Mary Alacoque, a French mystic, conveyed a message to King Louis XIV, which she had received from the Lord Jesus during one of her visions. The Lord promised the king that He would assure him of His blessing on earth, victory over his enemies, and eternal salvation if the king fulfilled four conditions regarding the Sacred Heart of Jesus. Firstly, that he embroider the Lord's Heart on his standards. Secondly, that he build a royal chapel in His honor. Thirdly, that he personally entrust himself to Him. And fourthly, that he request the pope to say Holy Mass in honor of the Sacred Heart of Jesus. But the Sun King disregarded the requests.

One hundred years later, the French Revolution led to the arrest of Louis XVI. In 1792, the imprisoned king pledged that he would fulfill Christ's wishes, which his predecessor had diregarded. But it was too late. The king and his wife were guillotined, France was seized by an anti-Catholic fury, while Europe saw a period of wars which did not end until 1815.

Christ's requests were not carried out by French bishops until 1871. But a church in honor of the Sacred Heart of Jesus was built, financed by lay Catholics – the Sacre-Cœur Basilica in Paris.

ROYAL ARMY of Vendee flag depicting the Sacred Heart of Jesus.

SACRE-CŒUR BASILICA, Montmartre, Paris.

FRANCE

Paris

SPIRITUAL WEAPON advocated by Our Lady in Fatima, that is, the Rosary.

ST. FAUSTINA Kowalska prayed and offered her suffering for Russia.

of France, they will repent and do it, but it will be late. Russia will have already spread her errors throughout the world, provoking wars, and persecutions of the Church; the Holy Father will have much to suffer."[31]

Lucia's request met with a lively response from the Portuguese episcopate once again. The mystic's credibility was confirmed by further Fatima miracles. Between May 1926 and December 1937, the Bureau of Medical Invesigations recorded as many as 14,725 cures in Fatima. Hence, when the Spanish Civil War broke out, Portuguese bishops assembled in Fatima and pledged that they would solemnly renew the consecration of Portugal to the Immaculate Heart of Mary if the country was saved from fratricidal conflict.

They kept their word. On May 13, 1938, twenty archbishops and bishops, as well as one thousand priests, participated in the consecration. They were accompanied by as many as half a million people present at the consecration and thousands more in parishes throughout the country, who spiritually united themselves with them. A great many took the Fatima message seriously, fasting and reciting the Rosary regularly. That same day, the episcopate dispatched a letter to Pius XI, which stressed that Mary had saved Portugal from Communism.

During one of her discussions with Jesus, Sr. Lucia asked Him why He would not convert Russia without it being consecrated by the Holy Father. Christ told her that He wanted the whole Church to see it as the triumph of the Immaculate Heart of Mary, which would contribute to the spread of devotion to her. Christ also requested perseverance in prayer for the Holy Father. He told her that the pope would consecrate Russia, but it would be too late. Nevertheless, He assured her that Russia would eventually be saved by Our Lady.

Hence it is not surprising that in her letters to Fr. Goncalves, her confessor, Sr. Lucia frequently referred to the consecration, pointing out that a war would thus be avoided. Urged on by her, the bishop of Leiria sent a letter to the Vatican once again, but he again did not receive a reply.

There were people in Europe, however, who, unaware of the Fatima message, prayed as if they knew about it. On December 16,

Bischof von Speyer.

An die ehrwürdigen Brüder Erzbischöfe
und Bischöfe Deutschlands
und die anderen Oberhirten
die in Frieden und Gemeinschaft
mit dem Apostolischen Stuhle leben

über die Lage der Katholischen Kirche
im Deutschen Reich

Papst Pius XI.

Ehrwürdige Brüder

Gruß und Apostolischen Segen!

Mit brennender Sorge und steigendem Befremden beobachten Wir
seit geraumer Zeit den Leidensweg der Kirche, die wachsende Bedräng=
nis der ihr in Gesinnung und Tat treubleibenden Bekenner und Be=
kennerinnen inmitten des Landes und des Volkes, dem St. Bonifatius
einst die Licht= und Frohbotschaft von Christus und dem Reiche Gottes
gebracht hat.

Diese Unsere Sorge ist nicht vermindert worden durch das, was die
Uns an Unserem Krankenlager besuchenden Vertreter des hochwürdig=
sten Episkopats wahrheits= und pflichtgemäß berichtet haben. Neben
viel Tröstlichem und Erhebendem aus dem Bekennerkampf ihrer Gläu=

1936, Sr. Faustina Kowalska wrote in her *Diary*: "I have offered this day for Russia. I have offered all my sufferings and prayers for that poor country. After Holy Communion, Jesus said to me, 'I cannot suffer that country any longer. Do not tie my hands, My daughter.' I understood that if it had not been for the prayers of souls that are pleasing to God, that whole nation would have already been reduced to nothingness. Oh, how I suffer for that nation which has banished God from its borders!"[32]

From the very outset, Pius XI discerned that both Communism and Nazism were demonic. As they expanded, he decided to speak out. In 1937 he published two encyclicals. The first, *Divini Redemptoris*, condemned Communism; the second, *Mit brennender Sorge*, condemned National Socialism. The pope explicitly stated that both ideologies could not be reconciled with Christianity in any way.

SR. LUCIA and a statue of the Immaculate Heart of Mary.

PIUS XI ENCYCLICAL *Mit brennender Sorge* (1937) condemned National Socialism.

191

PIUS XI AGAINST COMMUNISM

IN HIS ENCYCLICAL *Divini Redemptoris*, Pope Pius XI referred to the Second Letter to the Thessalonians (2:4), where St. Paul describes the signs prior to Jesus' second coming. According to Pius XI, "For the first time in history we are witnessing a struggle, cold-blooded in purpose and mapped out to the least detail, between man and 'all that is called God.'"[33]

The Russian system, according to Pius XI, is based on a false ideology, and so it cannot yield good fruit. The pope also noted that Communism is a child of atheistic Liberalism, which prepared the way for this terrible system.

POPE PIUS XI was a severe critic of totalitarian systems.

THE ENCYCLICAL, *Divini Redemptoris* (1937), condemned Communism.

Pius XI stated that people were attracted to the Bolshevik system primarily by empty promises and insidious propaganda, effectively aided by a conspiracy of silence in the Western press, which did not mention Communist crimes, particularly the persecution of Christians. He mentioned three countries that were responsible for massacres in the name of a godless ideology, that is, Russia, Mexico, and Spain.

The pope also stated that the Communist system is evil in itself, and that one could not cooperate with it in any field if one wanted to save Christian civilization and social order from disintegration.

Writing about the spread of Russia's errors through propaganda, the pope had no idea of the excellent methods that the followers of a utopian ideology would develop in the future. Marxist philosopher and cofounder of the Italian Communist Party Antonio Gramsci died in Rome about a month after the publication of *Divini Redemptoris*. His death went virtually unnoticed, apart from in Italy, where Fascism prevailed. On departing this world he was unaware that he had lit the fuse of a bomb meant to destroy Christian civilization.

Gramsci was perturbed as to why the proletariat in Europe did not support Bolshevism. He concluded that the working masses had a false consciousness, as it had been infected by Christianity, the most serious obstacle to worldwide Communism. According to him, the working masses were unable to recognize their real class interests, as their souls had imbibed ideas from the Gospels. Hence the assumption of power would not solve the problem, as politicians were not in control of human souls. Therefore a cultural hegemony was necessary. It would be accomplished via a "long march through the institutions" to take over and transform schools, colleges, magazines, newspapers, theaters, cinemas, and art. It was necessary to control opinion-forming centers to change the prevailing culture, but primarily to eliminate Christian influences. It was necessary to shape

ANTONIO GRAMSCI, leader of the Italian Communist Party, was an advocate of cultural Marxism and the author of the "long march through the institutions" plan.

AURORA BOREALIS STARTLES EUROPE:

PEOPLE FLEE IN FEAR, CALL FIREMEN

BRITONS THOUGHT WINDSOR CASTLE ABRAZE

SCOTS SEE ILL OMEN- SNOW CLADS SWISS ALPS

GLOW .... SHORT-WAVE RADIO HALTS

WORLD NEWS AGENCIES on the extraordinary aurora over the Northern Hemisphere on January 26, 1938.

appropriate trends, fashions, customs, sympathies, interests, phobias. Thus formed, the new man of the future would accept Communist postulates as his own, without state coercion.

Gramsci died a forgotten philosopher. But after World War II his works became akin to revelations to Marxists in many countries, books that indicated the way forward. In Italy at that time, the priest Ernesto Buonaiuti published his works concerning the history of religion. He was then excommunicated for spreading the modernist heresy, which claimed that religion is largely a matter of subjective experience and historical trends and that the Church needed to update her dogmas. While Gramsci hated Christianity, and wanted to destroy it, Buonaiuti dreamt of a subtle transformation of Catholicism. The ultimate victory would be, according to him, a modernist pope.

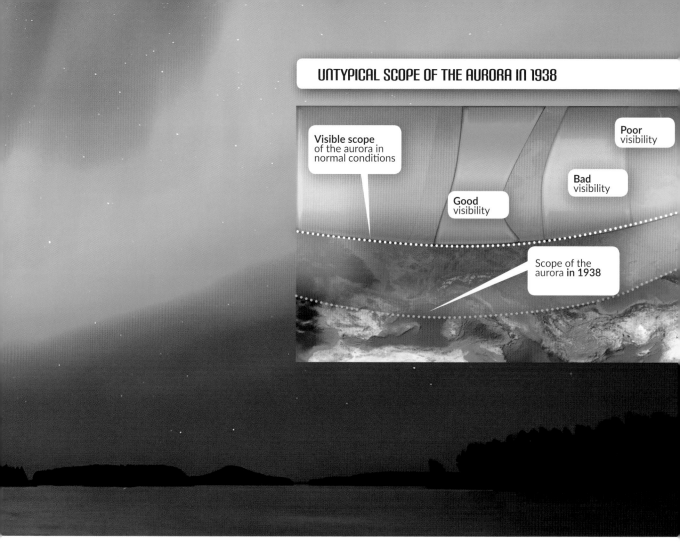

UNTYPICAL SCOPE OF THE AURORA IN 1938

Visible scope of the aurora in normal conditions

Good visibility

Poor visibility

Bad visibility

Scope of the aurora **in 1938**

Meanwhile events were quickly unfolding. On the night of January 25, 1938, an extraordinary aurora appeared over Europe and parts of North America. From 8:15 p.m. onwards, people observed an enormous, colorful glow that shimmered from the southeast to the northwest for several hours. Lucia knew that it was the sign that Our Lady had spoken about.

In March 1938, Nazi Germany invaded Austria. The Third Reich occupied the whole country with little resistance. About six months later, Germany, with the approval of the Western powers, partitioned Czechoslovakia. Lucia was convinced that the war Mary had spoken about had begun. On February 10, 1939, Pius XI died in Rome. He was eighty-two. He had not responded in any public way to the Fatima message.

TOWARDS THE END of December 1938, newspapers throughout the world wrote at length about an extraordinary phenomenon – a multicolored polar light over Europe and North America. It was the sign that was spoken of in Fatima.

Between Two
Totalitarianisms

CHAPTER 8

Between Two Totalitarianisms

The conclave that began on March 2, 1939, ended that same day. The hierarchs were aware that Europe was not only endangered by Communism, but also by National Socialism. They sensed that the new pope ought to be an experienced diplomat, as well as an expert on Germany. Cardinal Eugenio Pacelli was such a man.

POPE PIUS XII – Pius XI's successor to the throne of St. Peter.

As it happened, Pacelli's sixty-third birthday was on March 2. He was elected pope in the third vote and took the name Pius XII. In the past he had been a long-standing papal nuncio in Bavaria, Germany, and later secretary of state at the Vatican. In 1933 he negotiated a concordat with Nazi Germany. After the Kristallnacht (Crystal Night) in 1938, he appealed to the representatives of sixty churches in the world to help to obtain two hundred thousand visas for German citizens of Jewish origin who wanted to leave the Third Reich.

Hitler continued his policy of territorial conquests in Europe. In March 1939, Czechoslovakia was occupied without a shot being fired, and Slovakia was turned into puppet state, totally subordinated to Berlin. Poland became the next target of the aggressive National Socialist policy. Germany demanded territorial concessions and

SHOP WINDOWS smashed by terrorists – Jewish shops in Magdeburg, Germany.

JEWISH SYNAGOGUE in Berlin – destroyed during Kristallnacht in 1938.

199

Poland's accession to the Anti-Comintern Pact initiated by Germany. In response, Jozef Beck, minister of foreign affairs, delivered an address in the Sejm on May 5, 1939, saying that Poles would not sue for peace at all costs, nor yield to dictates. Hence war was a foregone conclusion.

Yet Lucia thought that war was not at all certain. On June 20, 1939, she wrote of the Five First Saturdays devotion: "Our Lady promised to postpone the scourge of war if this devotion is spread and practiced. We see her putting off this chastisement in the measure that efforts are being made to spread it. But I am afraid that we are not doing all that we are able to, and that God, in no way satisfied, may raise the arm of His mercy and let the world be ravaged by this punishment, which will be as never has been, horrible, horrible!"[34]

In another letter about the same time, she again wrote of the First Saturdays devotion: "I want to spread it, but, first and foremost, it is the wish of Our Good Lord

THIRD REICH and USSR heads of diplomacy signing the Molotov–Ribbentrop Pact in Moscow, which instigated World War II.

BATTLEFIELD IN POLAND on the outskirts of Lviv, where on the night of September 16, 1939, the Poles defeated the SS-Germania regiment.

and Our Lady…. Peace on earth depends on the First Saturdays devotion…. War or peace on earth depends on the practice of this devotion as well as on consecrations to the Immaculate Heart of Mary."[35]

On August 23, 1939, the Third Reich came to an understanding with the Soviet Union. That day the head of German diplomacy Joachim von Ribbentrop flew to Moscow, and he and the Soviet foreign affairs minister Vyacheslav Molotov signed a nonaggression pact between the two states. A secret protocol was attached to the document, wherein the two states divided areas of influence in Central Europe between themselves. That alliance of two Socialisms, national and international, Nazi and Communist, opened the way to World War II.

Lucia recalled that Our Lady told her that a great war would begin during the pontificate of Pius XI, whereas the beginning of the conflict is acknowledged to be September 1, 1939, when Pius

SR. LUCIA was of the opinion that World War II started with the annexation of Austria in 1938.

CHAPEL IN PONTEVEDRA, where Sr. Lucia often spent long hours in prayer.

201

XII was the pope. In the visionaries opinion, the dawn of World War II was the Third Reich's occupation of Austria and the partition of Czechoslovakia in 1938.

Poland was the first victim of military aggression, attacked by Germany on September 1, 1939, and by the Soviet Union seventeen days later. Great Britain and France, despite written guarantees, did not come to its aid, and Poland was partitioned between the two aggressors. Thus Communism expanded once again, encompassing eastern Poland. For hundreds of thousands of people that meant transportations to forced-labor camps, for others death sentences, like the twenty-two thousand Polish prisoners of war murdered (despite the Geneva Convention) in Katyn and other places.

MASS TRANSPORTATIONS of Poles to Siberia in cattle wagons.

After the onset of World War II, Bishop of Leiria Correia da Silva, seeing that the Fatima prophecy about a great armed conflict was coming true, decided to act. On September 13, 1939, he endorsed the First Saturdays devotion in his diocese. Later, similar decisions were taken by bishops throughout the world.

Another attempt to expand Communism came on November 30, 1939. That day the Soviet Union, without declaring war, attacked Finland, for which it was expelled from the League of Nations. To the world's amazement, the Red Army, despite an overwhelming advantage, was defeated. The Finns succeeded in defending their independence.

But Stalin was not discouraged by the defeat. In June 1949, he annexed further territories. In accord with the secret protocol of the Molotov–Ribbentrop Pact, he occupied the Baltic republics of Lithuania, Latvia, and Estonia, and part of Romania, that is, Moldova and Northern Bukovina. Everywhere he imposed the Communist order, marked by murder, intimidation, and expropriation.

Stalin's ally Adolf Hitler also took over more countries. On April 9, 1940, he quickly occupied Denmark and attacked Norway, which he eventually defeated on June 10. But the very rapid conquest of France, achieved between May 10 and June 22, was a shock to all Europe. A state hitherto regarded as a world power collapsed like a house of cards under the tracks of German tanks within two weeks. The Germans also occupied Belgium, Holland, and Luxembourg.

In April 1940, Pius XII received a letter from Sr. Lucia. The pope nurtured a great devotion to Our Lady of Fatima as he was consecrated bishop on May 13, 1917, the very day of the first apparition at the Cova da Iria. Hence he carefully read the letter, wherein the nun requested him to fulfill the Most Blessed Virgin's request concerning the consecration of Russia – by the pope and the bishops throughout the world – to the Immaculate Heart of Mary, whereby the war would end earlier, and the persecutions of the Church would be shortened.

About the same time the pope received other signals from Portugal. The mystic Alexandrina Maria da Costa from Balazar, on

MADDONA AND CHILD, the work of Polish exiles in Siberia – made of tins.

203

BLESSED ALEXANDRINA

ALEXANDRINA MARIA DA COSTA was born into a poor peasant family in 1904. When she was 14, three men attempted to rape her. To save herself, she jumped out of a window and was paralyzed by the fall. Confined to bed for the rest of her life, she had many visions and mystical states, for example, she bodily experienced Christ's suffering during the Passion. She was a so-called breatharian, not eating or drinking for 14 years, consuming but Holy Communion, which was confirmed by two independent medical commissions.

Apart from Sr. Lucia, she was the most recognizable figure in Portuguese Catholicism. People from all over the world – 15,000 people in 1953 alone – visited her to ask for spiritual advice. She died in 1955 and was beatified by John Paul II in 2004.

PORTUGUESE MYSTIC
Bl. Alexandrina Maria da Costa asked Pius XII to consecrate the world to the Immaculate Heart of Mary.

PORTUGAL

Balazar

Lisbon

THE MYSTIC'S ROOM in Balazar, Portugal.

SOVIET POWS captured by the Germans in 1941.

ROAD SIGNS erected by German soldiers in Eastern Europe.

the outskirts of Porto, had visions of Jesus beginning in 1934. She sent letters to the Vatican conveying Christ's request that the pope consecrate the world to the Blessed Virgin Mary.

Meanwhile Hitler was enjoying great triumphs on successive fronts. In October 1940, Fascist Italy, Germany's ally, attacked Greece. The attack was repelled, but when Germany entered the fray in April 1941 Greece capitulated in but seventeen days. That same month Germany also conquered Yugoslavia, in barely eleven days.

The pope's advisers urged him to consecrate the whole world to Mary rather than just Russia. The geopolitical situation inclined the pope to do just that. On June 22, 1921, however, Germany attacked the Soviet Union, and Stalin sided with the Allies. So the consecration of Russia would have created serious problems for the Vatican.

MEDIEVAL CASTLE,
Leiria, Portugal.

MARIAN SHRINE,
Leiria.

Firstly, it would have provoked the displeasure of the United States in the anti-Nazi coalition, and the papacy would have been accused of not having thus condemned Nazi Germany. Secondly, such an act might well have been publicized by the Nazis themselves as a public gesture of support for Germany policies. Thirdly, the Holy See would have been accused of abandoning neutrality, of taking sides in the war. This could well have ocassioned an invasion of the Vatican by Germany and the pope's subsequent deportation. In any case, such a scenario was seriously considered by Hitler.

As the twenty-fifth anniversary of the Fatima apparitions approached, Bishop Correia de Silva planned to publish a book that would describe the events of 1917 as accurately as possible. The main heroine was to be Jacinta. With this in mind, he asked Lucia for the third time to write down her memoirs. She set to work in July and August 1941. This time she wrote more than before, seeing that it would not be possible to portray adequately her cousin without depicting her reactions to Our Lady's message. Hence she decided to reveal two of the Fatima secrets. Hitherto she had written about Russia's consecration and the First Saturdays solely in internal Church correspondence to the Vatican, stressing that she could not reveal the third secret to anyone.

After reading the text, the bishop was somewhat dissatisfied as it did not contain enough information about Francisco. Hence he sent her certain questions, on the basis of which she wrote her fourth memoirs in December 1941.

On May 13, 1942, the first and second Fatima secrets were publically revealed for the first time, the Vatican publishing Fr. Gonzaga da Fonseca's book, *Meraviglie di Fatima*. Fr. da Fonseca was a Portuguese Jesuit professor at the Pontifical Biblical Institute. Despite having an imprimatur, his book was a censored version of the second secret; as the war was in progress, with the Soviet Union siding with the Allies, the Holy See did not want to strain its relations with Moscow.

During the Fatima apparitions, Our Lady said: "If my requests are heeded, Russia will be converted, and there will be peace; if not, she will spread her errors throughout the world, causing wars and persecutions of the Church."[36] But in the 1942 book the word "Russia" was replaced by "godless propaganda", which could also have meant the Third Reich's National Socialism, and "consecration of the world" replaced "consecration of Russia". Fr. da Fonseca consented to the changes as – in his opinion – prudence prescribed one to avoid offending any of the conflicting sides. That same month, Fr. Luigi Moresco published *La Madonna di Fatima*, which also contained a censored version of the second secret.

It was not until October 13, 1942, that, at the initiative of the Portuguese episcopate, the uncensored contents of the said secret were revealed. That same day a book about Jacinta Marto was

PORTUGAL

Leiria
• Fatima
Lisbon

LEIRIA CATHEDRAL – seat of the diocesan bishop. The diocese includes Fatima.

ROAD TO THE BISHOP'S PALACE in Leiria, where the third Fatima secret was kept from 1944 to 1957.

GENERALGOUVERNEMENT
DISTRIKT RADOM
Stadt-Kommissar der Stadt Ostrowiec
[Kreishauptmannschaft Opatów]

BEKANNTMACHUNG

Es ist wiederholt festgestellt, dass geflüchtete
juden von Polen aufgenommen sind. Ich mache
auf die 3. Verordnung über Aufenthaltsbeschränkung
im Generalgouvernement vom 15. 10. 1941. VO. Bl.
GG. S. 595 aufmerksam. Danach werden diejeni-
gen Polen, die den geflüchteten Juden Unterschlupf
der Beköstigung gewähren oder ihnen Nahrungs-
mittel verkaufen, mit dem Tode bestraft. Ich weise
darauf letztmalig hin.

Ostrowiec, den 28. September 1942.

Der Stadtkommissar

(gez.) Motschall

Komisarz Miasta ... Ostrowiec
Starostwo Powiatowe w Opatowie

OGŁOSZENIE

Stwierdzono powtarzające się wypadki ukry-
wania się żydów uchodźców u polaków. Zwracam
uwagę na 3 rozporządzenie z dnia 15. 10. 1941
(VO. Bl. GG. str. 595) w sprawie ograniczenia
pobytu na terenie Generalnego Gubernatorstwa
pouczam, że kto udziela żydom uchodźcom po-
mieszczenia i żywności lub sprzedaje żydom środ-
ki żywnościowe, będzie karany śmiercią. Pouczenie
jest ostateczne.

Ostrowiec, dnia 28 września 1942 r.

Komisarz Miasta

(—) Motschall

NAZI ANNOUNCEMENT from World War II threatening Poles with the death penalty for helping Jews.

published. Its author was Fr. José Galamba de Oliveira. Manuel Goncalves Cerejeira, the archbishop of Lisbon, wrote the introduction, while Bishop of Leiria José Alves Correia da Silva wrote the prologue. This publication contains direct warnings against "Russia's errors" as well as the request to "consecrate Russia".

News of the first two secrets spread quickly around Europe. The book by Fr. Gonzaga da Fonseca appeared in Slovakia in 1942 and made a great impression on Pavol Hnilica, a tweny-one-year-old Jesuit seminarian. On December 8, he heard a sermon on the Immaculate Conception of the Blessed Virgin Mary during Mass in Ruzomberok and was overwhelmed by a great love for Our Lady and a desire to pray for Russia's conversion. He decided to be true to that mission to the end of his life.

After attacking the Soviet Union, the Germans decided to speed up the "Final Solution of the Jewish Question". Jews were forced into ghettoes and murdered at the very outset of the war, but not on a mass scale. Later, the genocide was akin to a factory process, with extermination camps filled with Jews from all over Europe. The Nazis, in accord with their racist ideology, saw them as subhuman, to be eradicated like insects. Poring over maps, German planners decided that, for logistic reasons, occupied Poland was the most convenient place for the genocide. Gas chambers and crematoria were built in Auschwitz, Stutthof, Chelmno nad Nerem, Treblinka, Sobibor, and Belzec.

About 140,000 people of Polish nationality ended up in the Auschwitz concentration camp. One of them was Fr. Maximilian Kolbe. When a prisoner escaped on September 2, 1941, the Germans retaliated. Ten Poles were condemned to death by starvation, victims of a collective responsibility policy, one of whom was forty-year-old Franciszek Gajowniczek, father of a large family. Fr. Kolbe offered to take Gajowniczek's place, and he was locked up with nine other victims in a starvation bunker, where he kept up their spirits until their deaths. On August 14, only Fr. Kolbe was still alive, and he was finished off with a lethal injection.

The Third Reich was victorious on many fronts. The year 1942 seemed to see the apogee of its successes. Gen. Erwin Rommel led a triumphant campaign in North Africa, while in the East the Germans conquered Crimea, occupied Caucasia, and got as far as the Volga. Europe was losing hope in Hitler's defeat.

There was no war in Portugal. The majority of the Portuguese ascribed that to Our Lady of Fatima. On the twenty-fifth anniversary of the apparitions, the Portuguese episcopate issued a pastoral letter that listed all the graces and blessings that God had granted to Portugal over the last twenty-five years: no war, civil peace, religious freedom, a fourfold increase in religious vocations in barely ten years, all of which, according to the bishops, was due to the intercession of Our Lady of Fatima.

After much thought, Pius XII eventually decided to consecrate the world (not Russia specifically) to the Immaculate Heart of Mary. On October 22, 1942, Lucia had a vision, in which Jesus told her that the consecration would not fulfill the Fatima requests, but would bring a certain, very limited grace, that is, it would shorten the war. Nine days later, October 31, Pius XII carried out the consecration in Rome, which was transmitted over the

ENTRANCE TO AUSCHWITZ-BIRKENAU – German extermination camp.

ICON OF A MARTYR from Auschwitz – St. Maximilian Kolbe.

CREMATORIUM in Dachau.

LETTER *P* on a striped uniform signified a Polish concentration camp prisoner.

SPAIN

PORTUGAL

Tui

Valença

• Madrid

• Fatima

• Lisbon

FONSECA ORPHANAGE in Valença where Sr. Lucia gave the third Fatima secret to the bishop of Leiria.

BRIDGE on the River Minho, between Spain and Portugal, links Tui with Valença.

radio. Only the Portuguese bishops, assembled in the cathedral in Lisbon, united with him in prayer. The pope repeated the consecration on December 8 of that year in St. Peter's Basilica in the presence of forty thousand believers, of which there were but several heirarchs.

After October 31, 1942, something started to jam in the well-oiled German war machine. The Nazis suffered successive defeats, beginning with the Battle of El Alamein in Egypt, on November 4, when the Allies destroyed the hitherto invincible Afrika Korps commanded by Erwin Rommel, which sought to capture the Suez Canal. The Battle of Stalingrad in February 1943 was the crucial defeat, in which seven hundred fifty thousand Germans perished and over ninety thousand (including Field Marshal Friedrich Paulus, the commanding officer) were captured. Thenceforth the Germans were always forced to retreat.

In June 1943, Sr. Lucia contracted pleurisy. The illness lasted for months as treatment only created complications. In September,

Bishop Jose Alves Correia da Silva asked the mystic to write down the third Fatima secret as he was afraid that she would take it with her to her grave. Sr. Lucia hesitated as it was not an order but just a request. Hence, in the middle of October, the bishop ordered her to do it. But she was still uncertain. Her dilemma was solved on January 2, 1944, when Our Lady appeared at the convent infirmary and instructed her to comply with the bishop's request. The next day, Sr. Lucia wrote down the third secret on one page of lined paper (folded so as to make four pages). On January 9, 1944, she sent a letter to the bishop informing him that her text was ready.

On June 17, 1944, Bishop Jose Alves Correia da Silva's emissary, Bishop Manuel Maria Ferreira da Silva, arrived in Valenca, Portugal, a town on the River Minho, near the Spanish border. Sr. Lucia, who lived in Tui on the other side of the river, crossed the frontier by way of an iron bridge and headed for Fonseca orphanage in Valenca, where she had arranged to meet the emissary. She gave him a sealed envelope with the text about the third secret, and he left for the bishop of Braga's country residence in Quinta da Formigueira that same day and passed on the text to Bishop Jose Correia da Silva. There was a note on the envelope saying that

CATHOLIC ORPHANAGE
chapel in Valenca.

211

PIUS XII'S CONSECRATION OF THE WORLD TO THE IMMACULATE HEART OF MARY

OCTOBER 31, 1942

Queen of the Holy Rosary, Help of Christians, Refuge of the human race, winning all the battles of God! We prostrate ourselves before your throne, to implore mercy and graces and to receive appropriate help and defense in this time of disaster, not because of our merits, which we presume not, but only for the abundant goodness of your motherly heart.

To you, to your Immaculate Heart, in this tragic hour of human history, we entrust and consecrate ourselves, not only in union with the Holy Church, the mystical body of your Jesus, who suffers and bleeds in so many parts and in many tribulations, but also with the whole world torn by fierce discord, consumed in a fire of hatred, the victim of its own iniquity.

Look with compassion on the many material and moral injuries; the great pain and anxiety of fathers and mothers, spouses, brothers, innocent children; the many lives cut short in the bloom of youth; the many bodies torn to pieces in brutal slaughter; the many tortured and dying souls, many in danger of being lost forever!

You, O Mother of Mercy, obtain peace for us from God! Obtain first of all those graces that can in an instant convert human hearts, those graces that prepare, establish, and ensure peace! Queen of Peace, pray for us and give to the world at war the peace for which the peoples long, peace in the truth, the justice and the charity of Christ. Give them peace at arms and peace of souls, so that in the tranquility of order the Kingdom of God may expand.

Turn your protection to unbelievers and to those who still lie in the shadow of death; grant them peace and let the Sun of Truth rise for them, so they can, together with us, say to the only Savior of the world: Glory to God in the highest, and on earth peace to men of good will! (Lk 2: 14).

Give peace to those separated by error or discord, and especially to those who profess to you singular devotion, and among whom there is no home without a place of honor for your venerable icons (today perhaps hidden and stored for better days); gather them together in the one fold of Christ, under the one true Shepherd.

Obtain peace and complete liberty for the Holy Church of God; stop the rampant flood of neo-paganism; foment in the faithful a love of purity, the practice of Christian life and apostolic zeal, so that the people who serve God will increase in merit and in number.

Lastly, just as to the Heart of your Jesus were consecrated the Church and the whole human race, because, putting all hope in Him, He was for them a sign and pledge of victory and salvation; so also we in perpetuity consecrate ourselves to you, to your Immaculate Heart, our Mother and Queen of the world: that your love and patronage hasten the triumph of the Kingdom of God, and that all nations, reconciled with each other and with God, proclaim you blessed, and sing with you, from one end of the earth to the other, the eternal Magnificat of glory, love, and gratitude to the Heart of Jesus, in which alone they find Truth, Life, and Peace.[37]

PIUS XII'S PONTIFICATE lasted almost two decades, from 1939 to 1958.

BISHOP OF Leiria Jose Alves Correia da Silva with an envelope containg the third Fatima secret.

SOVIET SOLDIERS in Berlin in May 1945 – the Brandenburg Gate in the background.

the secret was not to be publically revealed until after 1960. Only the bishop of Leiria, the archbishop of Lisbon, and the Holy Father had the right to familiarize themselves with it earlier.

On returning to his diocese, Bishop Correia da Silva put the sealed envelope into his safe. He never read the text, though he took the envelope out several times to show it to trusted friends. He once consented to being photographed with it on a table in front of him – the photo was published in *Life* magazine on January 3, 1949.

Sr. Lucia's apparitions, however, were questioned by people within the Church. In 1944, Fr. Edouard Dhanis, a Flemish Jesuit, published two works that undermined the authenticity of the visions. He divided them into two groups, false and true, claiming that the visions were but a product of an unbridled imagination. Our Lady's requests regarding the First Saturdays devotion and the consecration of Russia seemed particularly incredible to him. He saw them as offensive to Russians. Hence he wrote a letter to Pius XII stating that the consecration was impossible without

the consent of the Moscow authorities and the Orthodox Church. Later, some Catholic theologians accepted the critic's arguments.

The pope, however, had great trust in the Fatima apparitions. On May 4, 1944, he established a new feast day in honor of the Immaculate Heart of Mary. It was as if a response to what Our Lady had told the visionaries in July 1917, that is, that people who had a special devotion to the Immaculate Heart of Mary would go to heaven.

The fortunes of war tipped in favor of the anti-Nazi coalition. Stalin, hitherto seen as a criminal, Hitler's ally, became the key player on the international scene, a friend tenderly known as Uncle Joe. It was largely due to him, who treated the Red Army as cannon fodder, that the Germans were defeated. On May 2, 1945, the Soviet Army captured Berlin. The Third Reich fell, and Hitler committed suicide.

TWO SOLDIERS – American and Russian – allies during World War II.

DISARMING of German soldiers after Germany's surrender.

215

The March of Communism

SR. LUCIA – Valinhos, 1946 – identifying the place of the fourth Marian apparition.

THE "BIG THREE" – Winston Churchill, Franklin D. Roosevelt, and Joseph Stalin – deciding on Europe's fate after World War II.

CHAPTER 9

The March of Communism

On May 8, 1945, Germany surrendered to the Allies, and Europe was freed from National Socialism. Victory, however, did not bring liberation to some nations on the Old Continent, but a new enslavement – Communism.

The allied victors came to an understanding as to the post-war order in the world. Of key importance were two meetings of the "Big Three" – US President Franklin D. Roosevelt, UK Prime Minister Winston Churchill, and USSR Premier Joseph Stalin – who met in Tehran in 1943 and in Yalta in 1945. The Allies agreed that Central Europe, occupied by the Soviet Union, would remain in Moscow's sphere of influence.

Hence Communism was imposed on Poland, Czechoslovakia, Hungary, Romania, Bulgaria, and East Germany (GDR from 1949), as well as Yugoslavia and Albania, though the vast majority of people in those countries were against the system. The new power established a bloody reign of terror. Nations lost

219

CRUCIFIX and statue of the Immaculate Heart of Mary – convent chapel, Pontevedra.

WAR HERO Witold Pilecki – Polish cavalry captain, Auschwitz prisoner, sentenced to death at a Communist show trial. Beside him in the dock: Maria Szelagowska and Tadeusz Pluzanski, both also sentenced to death.

their sovereignty, and people lost their freedom of speech, conscience, and association.

Anti-Communist partisans were active in most of the countries that were enslaved by the Soviet Union. But those soldiers had little chance against a totalitarian machine, perishing in skirmishes or shot in prisons. On May 25, 1948, a Polish cavalry captain, Witold Pilecki, was executed by the Communist state – a bullet in the back of the head. During World War II he allowed himself to be imprisoned in Auschwitz (for two and a half years), whereupon he provided the Allies with information about the Nazi genocide. Before his death, he said that Auschwitz was child's play compared with what the Communist secret police had done to him.

Wherever Communism assumed power, the Christian religion became a particular object of persecution: Churches were closed, the clergy murdered, believers arrested, while the least

sign of attachment to the Faith disqualified one from promotion at work. Schools and the mass media oozed atheistic propaganda. In Western Ukraine the Greek Catholic Church was banned altogether, with eighteen bishops (of whom only one survived – Josyf Slipyj) murdered or sent to Siberian forced-labor camps. In Romania and Bulgaria, the Orthodox Church suffered bloody repressions.

On December 26, 1948, the Hungarian security services arrested Cardinal Jozsef Mindszenty, who found himself in the dock two months later. During the trial, the cardinal was evidently not himself – unintelligible, eyes vacant, wandering about the courtroom – while he listened to successive absurd allegations, which he confirmed apathetically. Later, it came to light that he had been not only tortured, but also forced to down stupefying drugs by the handful. He was eventually sentenced to life imprisonment for high treason.

In 1950 the Communist authorities in Budapest issued a decree that dispossessed the Church of all her schools, apart from eight that were of historical importance to the country. Shortly after, religious orders were banned, their property nationalized, and their members sent to isolated places. The

221

A MODEL OF STATE ATHEISM

ALBANIA SAW a particular social experiment. Its dictator Enver Hodza, a Montpellier University and Sorbonne graduate, dreamed of establishing the world's first thoroughly atheistic state (he even added such a regulation to the constitution in 1967). The Communists murdered five of the six Catholic bishops, 115 of the 200 priests, and sent the rest to concentration camps. About 2,500 churches were closed, and bulldozers destroyed crosses in cemeteries throughout the country. All signs of religious life were to be eliminated once and for all. The secret police searched homes for Bibles, prayer books, rosaries, and crucifixes, possession of which could have meant the death penalty. Christian first names were prohibited, while those who already had such names had to change them. Historians estimate that 100,000 Albanians perished because of their faith, while 500,000 were imprisoned.

ORTHODOX CHURCH
in Labova, Albania.

ALBANIAN COMMUNIST
Army entering Tirana on November 20, 1944.

BUNKER
in the Albanian mountains.

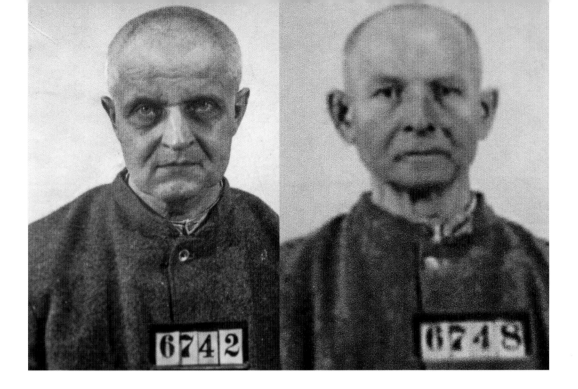

Hungarian Church authorities accepted far-reaching compromises, yielding to the regime in order to survive. Some of the religious went underground and carried on with their pastoral work. Others became "peace priests", who collaborated with the government, dividing the Church from within. Not all did so of their own free will. Miklos Beresztoczy, one of the leaders of that faction, was imprisoned and tortured, his finger and toe nails pulled out before he finally agreed to cooperate.

In Czechoslovakia the authorities set up their own structures within the Church. Fr. Josef Plojhar, one of the organizers of such structures, was excommunicated by Josef Beran, the archbishop of Prague. In response, the Communists arrested the primate and detained him in various prisons until 1963, not daring to subject him to a staged show trial. During the war he had been imprisoned in a Nazi concentration camp in Terezin.

The night of April 13, 1950, the secret police appeared at all the male monasteries in Czechoslovakia. The religious were divided into several groups and sent to concentration monasteries, that is, forced-labor camps for priests, while their property was taken over by the army. The Jachymov camp was the most oppressive, located near a uranium mine where many priests died from radiation sickness.

PRISONERS OF CONSCIENCE of the Communist regime – Slovak bishops Pavel Gojdic (beatified by John Paul II in 2001), and Jan Vojtassak.

PAVOL HNILICA
mementoes
– Bible and
Sr. Faustina's
Diary.

Pavol Hnilica, a twenty-nine-year-old seminarian, was arrested. According to his memoirs police with rifles forced their way into the Jesuit seminary in Trnava at about midnight, dragged the seminarians out of their cells, and loaded them into buses. Hnilica had a Bible on him, hidden in his pocket. He opened it at random: "Was it not necessary that the Christ should suffer these things and enter into his glory?" (Lk 24:26). Those words of Jesus raised his spirits.

After being in several labor camps, he was eventually assigned to auxiliary military service, during which he

JESUIT SEMINARIAN
Pavol Hnilica with
Joseph, a co-
seminarian, during
a visit to his home
in Ruzomberok
in 1941. Also
his grandmother
Anna, his young
brother, Jan,
and his mother,
Katarina.

PAVOL HNILICA'S
winter shoes.

PAVOL HNILICA as a
young priest.

Prague

Rozniawa ✠

Bratislava

CZECHOSLOVAKIA

decided to fulfill his greatest desire, that is, become a priest. At that time all the bishops in Czechoslovakia had been imprisoned or were under special supervision. The secret police followed their every step so as not to allow them to ordain new priests. Thus the Communists hoped that within one generation all the priests in the country would have died off.

On obtaining a pass on September 29, 1950, Hnilica sneaked into the hospital in Roznava. At that time the local bishop, Robert Pobozny, with two secret police officers in close attendance, was having medical tests at the hospital. While the police smoked cigarettes in the corridor, not suspecting anything, the young Jesuit was ordained in the hospital chapel. Afterward he sent a coded telegram to his friends: "Operation successful, patient is well, come and visit."

CATHEDRAL OF the Assumption, Roznava, Slovakia.

PAVOL HNILICA was secretly ordained while he was away on a military pass.

THE BISHOP of Roznava Robert Pobozny secretly ordained Pavol Hnilica and later consecrated him bishop.

On February 2, 1951, Bishop Pobozny and Fr. Pavol Hnilica met at the Roznava hospital again as the bishop had an appointment for further tests. Though two plainclothes officers were nearby, a doctor managed to take the bishop to the cellar, where the young Jesuit awaited him, excited as never before, incredulous as to what was about to happen. He had become a priest but four months earlier, yet he was about to become a bishop. He had resisted the promotion at first, but his provincial told him to accept the consecration out of obedience. Hence Fr. Hnilica became the world's youngest Catholic bishop, at barely thirty years of age. On August 24, 1951, he secretly consecrated Jan Chryzostom Korec, a Jesuit who was even younger than he was. Later, Bishop Korec led the underground Church in Czechoslovakia for over four decades, virtually a quarter of which he spent in various prisons. When freed, he was forced to work as, for example, a street cleaner in Bratislava.

In time, the authorities learnt that the bishop was active underground. He was forced into hiding, escaping to Austria in December 1952 and eventually reaching Rome.

PIUS XII'S MIRACLE OF THE SUN

PAPAL LEGATE Cardinal Federico Tedeschini arrived in Fatima on October 13, 1951, to conclude the Pope Pius XII Jubilee Year. This tradition arose in Western Christianity in 1300, when Pope Boniface VIII invoked a holy year. One could then obtain indulgences, hence pilgrimages to holy places increased.

The Jubilee Year proclaimed by Pius XII was from December 24, 1949, to October 13, 1951, when there was an extraordinary event in the life of the Church. On November 1, 1950, the Holy Father announced a new dogma: the Assumption of the Blessed Virgin Mary. The Assumption had always been a Catholic belief, but the pope declared it to be official Church teaching.

During his homily in Fatima, in the presence of one million pilgrims, Cardinal Tedeschini said that Pius XII had witnessed a "miracle of the sun", similar to the Fatima one, in the Vatican gardens on October 30 and 31, and December 1 and 4, 1950. The Holy Father saw it as a sign that heaven had accepted the dogma.

Vatican

ITALIAN WEEKLY *La Domenica del Corriere* – front page depicting Pius XII's "miracle of the sun".

VATICAN GARDENS, where the four miracles of the sun were to haven taken place.

SR. LUCIA throughout almost six decades of convent life carried on a copious correspondence with people throughout the world, replying to every letter that she received.

COIMBRA, the former capital of Portugal, where Sr. Lucia spent 57 years.

CARMELITE CHURCH in Coimbra, where Sr. Lucia participated in daily Mass.

The Church does not look on idly when Catholics are persecuted. However, she has little influence on states with which she has no diplomatic relations. On July 1, 1949, the Holy Office issued a decree that excommunicated Catholics who voluntarily cooperated with Communists. The decree states: "Communism is materialistic and anti-Christian. Although Communist leaders sometimes declare in words that they do not attack religion, they demonstrate through either their doctrine or actions that they are hostile to God, the true religion, and the Church of Christ."[38]

At that time there were great changes in Lucia's life. In 1946, she returned to Portugal – a convent near Porto – after twenty

THE CONSECRATION of the Basilica of Our Lady of the Rosary in Fatima took place in 1953, 25 years after the construction had begun.

years in Spain. She increasingly felt that God was calling her to a more contemplative kind of religious life. Apart from that, she was weary of the constant pestering of curious people avidly seeking phenomena, continually asking for details concerning the apparitions.

Hence on March 25, 1948, she entered the Discalced Carmelite Order and settled at the convent in Coimbra. Subject to the rule of a cloistered order, she did not appear in Fatima for the exhumations of Francisco and Jacinta on March 1, 1951. It turned out that their bodies were still intact, thirty-one years after their deaths. They were transferred to the basilica in Cova de Iria, which was consecrated on October 7, 1953, twenty-five years after it was built.

Meanwhile the Blue Army grew ever more quickly. Its beginnings are connected with the three hundredth anniversary of the consecration of Portugal to Our Immaculate Lady by King John IV in 1646. A procession with a statue of Our Lady of the Immaculate Conception set off for Lisbon, enthusiastically welcomed everywhere. Three white doves accompanied the statue

PORTUGAL

Porto

Coimbra

Lisbon

PEN AND INK bottle – used by Sr. Lucia.

229

THREE STATUES OF MARY

THREE DIFFERENT STATUES of Our Lady of Fatima are being popularized throughout the world. All of them were the work of Jose Ferreira Thedim, a Portuguese sculptor.

One, Our Lady of Fatima Capelinha, in the Chapel of Apparitions in Fatima, was carved in 1920 according to that which Lucia had related about the apparitions at the Cova da Iria.

The second is the Immaculate Heart of Mary, carved after Lucia had revealed (1941) more details about the apparition in July 1917 (including the first two secrets), when Mary pointed to her Immaculate Heart. The statue is now at the Carmel in Coimbra.

The third is the Pilgrim Virgin. It was made in 1947, when Thedim asked Lucia for a more exact description of Our Lady. Twelve copies of this statue are presently circulating around the world.

STATUE OF OUR LADY – held by Fr. Krzysztof Czaple (left), director of the Fatima Secretariat in Poland, and Fr. Marian Mucha, custodian of the Shrine of Our Lady of Fatima in Zakopane, Poland.

JOSE FERREIRA THEDIM sculpted three statues of Our Lady of Fatima: ❶ Capelinha, ❷ the Immaculate Heart of Mary, ❸ the Pilgrim Virgin.

all the way to the capital. Believers saw the birds as a sign from heaven. Miraculous cures and many conversions occurred during the procession.

Initially, the Portuguese episcopate planned to have but one procession. However, as numerous places were keen on hosting the statue, Bishop Correia da Silva blessed five Pilgrim Virgin statues to circulate around Portugal. In time there were requests from all over the world, hence statues of Our Lady began spreading the Fatima message on all the continents.

One of the statues reached the United States. Fr. Harold V. Colgan, a seriously ill parish priest from Plainfield, New Jersey,

Plainfield
New Jersey

USA

BLUE ARMY cadet banner – the organization promotes the Fatima message.

CHURCH IN PLAINFIELD, the statue of the Pilgrim Virgin ended up there after World War II.

231
✚

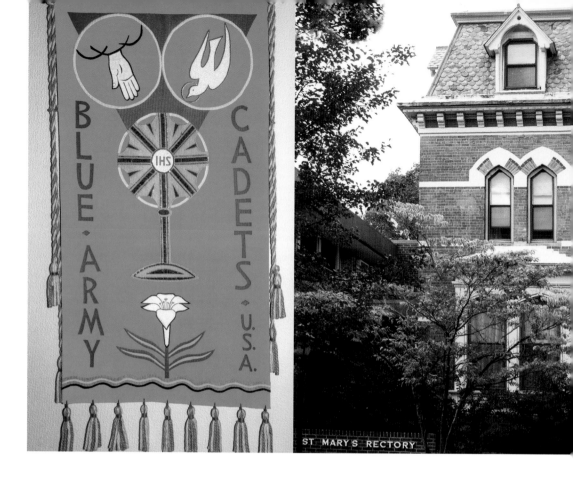

ST MARY'S RECTORY

RECTORY IN PLAINFIELD, New Jersey, where the Blue Army was founded.

BLUE ARMY banners.

prayed before it and was inexplicably cured. Convinced that he was healed at Our Lady's intercession, he decided to devote his life to spreading the devotion in her honor.

Eventually, Fr. Colgan and John Haffert, a writer, established the Blue Army of Our Lady of Fatima, the aim of which was to spread the Fatima message throughout the world, particularly the practice of the Five First Saturdays. The new organization received the blessing of Pius XII, who was aware that spiritual weapons were the most effective in the struggle against Communism. In 1950 the Blue Army had one million members, and barely three years later as many as five million. As a result, from 1947 to 1960 the following countries were consecrated to the Immaculate Heart of Mary: Austria, Hungary, Spain, Italy, and Switzerland, as well as Bavaria.

In May 1952, Sr. Lucia had another apparition. Our Lady urged Lucia to remind the pope about her request to consecrate Russia to the Immaculate Heart of Mary. She told her that without being consecrated, Russia would not be converted, and the world would

know no peace. Hence Sr. Lucia sent another letter to the Vatican, and there was a response.

On July 7, 1952, an apostolic letter, *Sacro Vergente anno*, was published, wherein all the nations under Russian rule were consecrated to the Immaculate Heart of Mary. Later, Sr. Lucia said that the consecration did not fulfill the Fatima request, as it was not done in unity with all the Catholic bishops, but that it might well lead to beneficial results for Christians.

The Soviet Union, meanwhile, was preparing to attack Western Europe in order to impose Communism on the whole continent. But Stalin died on March 5, 1953. Hence an unpredictable despotism came to an end, as did the plans for a quick conquest of Europe.

The Catholic Church's situation in Poland was better than in any other country under Communist rule. Marian piety prevailed, and the primate Cardinal August Hlond took the Fatima message very seriously, for which there was a simple explanation. An exile in Rome during World War II, he witnessed Pius XII consecrate the

world to Mary in 1942, and he took to heart the pope's call for other bishops to do the same. Hence he decided to do just that whenever he returned to Poland.

Poland, after Portugal, was the first country to practice the First Saturdays devotion and to be consecrated to the Immaculate Heart of Mary. The Polish episcopate decided on the consecration during Advent of 1946. The consecration was in three stages: all Poland's parishes simultaneously (July 7); all the bishops in their own dioceses (August 15); and the Polish episcopate, assembled in Czestochowa, in the presence of pilgrims from all over Poland (September 8). The fact that over one million had gathered in Czestochowa attested to the strength of the Church, which shocked the Communists.

From 1945 to 1948, when the Communist system was as yet not firmly established, many Catholic booklets and leaflets on

POLAND

THE FIRST BROCHURE that promoted the Fatima devotion (apart from those in Portugal) appeared in Poland after World War II.

PRIMATE HLOND'S VISION

AUGUST HLOND, the primate of Poland, had no doubts that the victory over Communism would come thanks to the Immaculate Heart of Mary, as did Cardinal Stefan Wyszynski, his successor, who witnessed the death of his predecessor, which he described in his memoirs:

"The last hours of Cardinal Hlond's life passed in some sort of extraordinary state of spiritual stress, as if he had had a prophetic vision.... He kept repeating: 'Pray! Difficult times are coming, difficult times. Never cease praying. Call out! Victory, when it comes, will be the victory of Our Blessed Mother'.... He saw a frightful confusion in the skies, as St. John the Evangelist once did on the island of Patmos, when he wrote of a shocking scene, a Woman battling with a dragon, lying in wait for her Child, to whom she was about to give birth.... No doubt he then, seeing her victory, encouraged those that he was about to leave, those who were to continue the battle against the fiery dragon."[39]

POLISH PRIMATE, Cardinal August Hlond (left), at Jasna Gora during the consecration of Poland to the Immaculate Heart of Mary in 1946.

CARDINAL HLOND, a great devotee of Our Lady.

WHEN IN ROME, Cardinal Hlond witnessed Pius XII's consecration of the world to the Immaculate Heart of Mary, which he decided to repeat in Poland.

the Fatima apparitions appeared in Poland. But later, distributing these became impossible. The very mention of Russia's errors or its conversion infuriated the Communists. The name of Fatima was censored in all publications. Hence the message was spread secretly, via Church channels, by priests, religious, and other believers.

On December 20, 1948, three Franciscans were arrested in Niepokalanow: Fr. Zbyslaw Niebrzydowski, Br. Innocenty Wojcik, and Br. Symeon Blacha, accused of subversive, anti-state activities. Their one fault was that they produced and distributed materials on the Fatima apparitions among their acquaintances.

On July 19, 1949, they were tried in Warsaw. The prosecutor accused them of sabotage, conspiracy, and high treason, and demanded life imprisonment for Fr. Niebrzydowski and ten years for the brothers. Eventually, the sentence was, in those circumstances, a lenient one, that is, two years imprisonment. An article with pictures of the religious appeared in a Communist newspaper, *Gazeta Robotnicza,* which read: "They Wanted War – They Have Peace".

While imprisoned, the Franciscans were intimidated, beaten, and urged to cooperate with the secret police, to inform on their fellow brothers. They all refused.

One night Br. Symeon, lying on his cell floor after having been beaten up, feeling abandoned, despairingly cried out to God, to Our Lady, and to St. Joseph, his patron. Suddenly, St. Joseph appeared. Br. Symeon knew that it was not an illusion. St. Joseph sat down beside him and said: "As you love Our Lady and bravely speak of her, I have come to strengthen you. You will not die in prison. You will die an old monk. Do not worry, you will not betray anybody. At the moment of your death she and I shall come to you. And because you love the Church and her priests, seven priests will be at your bedside."

Br. Blacha died in Niepokalanow over half a century later. As he was dying, Fr. Derylo was walking in the monastery garden when he suddenly heard an inner voice: "Hurry to Br. Symeon."

CRUCIFIX
in St. Dorothy's Church, Lichen, Poland, which was shot at by Bertha Bauer, a Nazi youth leader, when the church housed a Hitler Youth school. In the background, a painting of 108 martyrs of World War II.

237

As he entered his cell, he saw six priests standing beside the bed of Br. Symeon, who was semiconscious. Fr. Derylo knelt down beside him and asked: "Are Our Lady and St. Joseph here? If so, move your hand." Br. Symeon moved the fingers of his left hand. Fr. Derylo said, "Pass on my greetings to them in heaven, and pray for me." Br. Symeon suddenly opened his eyes, which were very bright. He looked around and smiled at everyone, and then he died.

Cardinal Stefan Wyszynski became the primate of Poland in 1948. The authorities in Warsaw were keen to arrest him and stage a show trial, but Stalin himself advised against it. He thought that it would make a martyr of him, and thereby strengthen the Church rather than weaken her. Stalin suggested

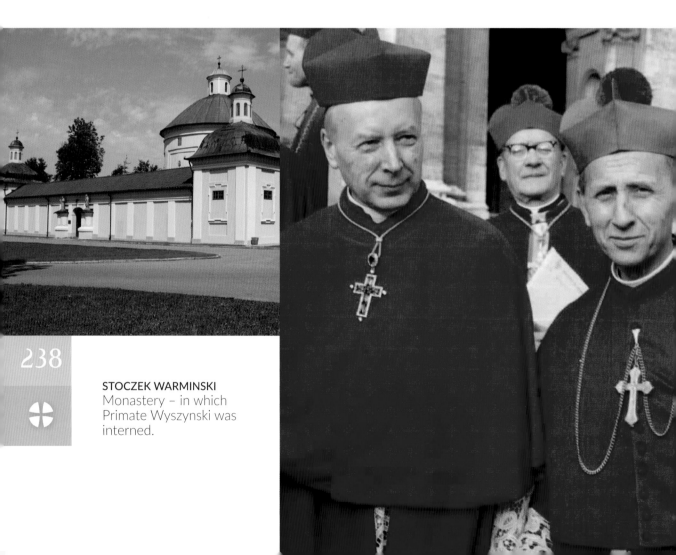

238

STOCZEK WARMINSKI
Monastery – in which
Primate Wyszynski was
interned.

another method: destruction of the Church from within. He himself did not eliminate the Russian Orthodox Church but totally subordinated her to him. He even personally chose two Russian Orthodox Church patriarchs: Sergius I, installed in 1943, and Alexy, in 1945.

The Communists in Poland likewise attempted to control the Church. After the death of Stalin, and that of Lavrentiy Beria, chief of the Soviet security and secret police apparatus (NKVD), they arrested Cardinal Wyszynski in October 1953. The secret police also arrested his secretary, Fr. Antoni Baraniak, who was tortured for months to force him to incriminate the primate with false allegations and thus pave the way for a show trial. He was interrogated 145 times over a period of two years, frequently several hours at a time. Fifty of the interrogations ended in him being taken to a hospital. His fingernails were pulled out, his flesh burned, and his kidneys pummeled. But Fr. Baraniak stubbornly remained silent. Thanks to the priest's steadfastness, the primate's imprisonment did not end with a show trial.

TWO PRISONERS – Cardinal Stefan Wyszynski and Archbishop Antoni Baraniak – arrested on the same day.

The period after 1945 saw the Cold War between two geopolitical and military blocks, the capitalist West (NATO) and the socialist East (Warsaw Pact). There were military clashes at times, for example, in Korea (1950–1953) and Vietnam (1962–1975), but Communism expanded, particularly outside Europe: China, North Korea, Laos, Cuba, Vietnam, Cambodia, and Ethiopia. Its expansion went hand in hand with mass murders, committed by the likes of Mao Tse-tung, Kim Il-sung, Pol Pot, and Mengistu Haile Mariam.

The Cold War did not change into a hot war because of, for example, the nuclear balance of power. In 1945, America developed atom bombs and dropped them on Hiroshima and Nagasaki in Japan, which caused so much destruction that Japan capitulated. In 1949, the Soviet Union tested its own atomic bomb in Semipalatinsk. Thus began the arms race between the Soviet Union and the United States. In 1952, the United States tested a hydrogen bomb, followed by the Soviet Union a year later.

239

COMMUNISM IN ASIA

COMMUNISM TOOK on a most ominous face in Asian countries, where the number of the Red Terror victims was much higher than in Europe. It is estimated that about 50 to 60 million were murdered in China alone, while one-third of Cambodia's population was exterminated by the Khmer Rouge.

The repressions by Asiatic Communism were facilitated by local religious beliefs, particulary that of the transmigration of souls. Reincarnation undermines man's uniqueness as it is understood in the West. A personalistic understanding of man, the concept of person, not known at all in Asia, developed within the Christian civilization. According to Boethius' classical definition, a person is the individual substance of a rational nature who can distinguish between good and evil, and make free decisions.

Reincarnation wrecks such a conception of person: man is not free, as he is determined by his actions in his previous lives, and he is not an individual substance, as the link between body and soul is of an incidental nature, for the same soul might well abide in an animal or even a stone. Hu Nim, a minister in the Khmer Rouge governments, put it bluntly, as he was wont to say that he was not a human being but an animal.

If the human person does not exist, then individual rights make no sense. According to Christian anthropology,

we were made in the image and likeness of God. So every attack on the dignity of man is equivalent to a sin, that is, an offense against God Himself. But if man shares in divinity on the same grounds as animals or plants, if man is but a pollen grain circulating in an eternal cycle of beings, embodiments of a rational nature in some, irrational in others, then how could one demonstrate the uniqueness of man, his dignity? We could then hold all creation in high esteem, but man's ontological status would be identical to that of a fly or a cockroach.

MAO TSE-TUNG – successor of Marx, Engels, Lenin, and Stalin.

BUDDHIST STATUES destroyed by Chinese Communists during the Cultural Revolution.

CHINESE BALLET – watched by US President Richard Nixon during his visit to Peking in 1972.

GENOCIDE VICTIMS of the Khmer Rouge in Cambodia.

TANKS IN Poznan, Poland, June 1956.

POZNAN 1956 protests – workers from the Joseph Stalin Metal Works.

The world's two greatest powers blackmailed each other with their nuclear capabilities, accumulating enough bombs to destroy life on earth several times over. That awareness served as a deterrent, a global balance of power based on mutual intimidation. Mankind was as if asleep on a barrel of gunpowder that could well have exploded at any moment. A human error or a systems failure could have occasioned the launching of rockets that would have entailed further chain reactions.

Communist governments brutally suppressed any protests against them. On June 16, 1953, strikes broke out in East Germany against the government's policies. The following day, the strikes turned into workers' uprisings, and the Soviet Army and the police entered the fray. Bloody violence ensued, with the loss of over three hundred lives.

Three years later, on June 28, 1956, Polish workers at the Stalin Metal Works in Poznan organized a strike that turned into a

general protest against Stalinism. The uprising was suppressed with the loss of fifty-eight lives. Prime Minister Jozef Cyrankiewicz turned up in Poznan and threatened that if one raised one's hand against the state it would be chopped off.

Several months later, in October 1956, there was an anti-Communist uprising in Budapest, which the Hungarian authorities, including Prime Minister Imre Nagy, supported. One-party rule was ended, and Cardinal Mindszenty was released from prison. But Soviet intervention brutally put an end to the uprising: About 2,500 were killed, and about 200,000 fled as refugees.

After the Soviets put down the uprising, they arrested and executed those who had instigated the revolt. The youngest of these was sixteen-year-old Peter Mansfield, who was kept in a cell until he came of age and was executed eleven days after his eighteenth birthday.

An extraordinary event occurred between the East Berlin (1953) and the Budapest (1956) uprisings. In 1955, the Soviet Union voluntarily withdrew from Austria without a shot being fired. It was the

HUNGARIAN FLAG with its red star cut out – symbol of the Budapest anti-Communist uprising in October 1956.

RUSSIAN ARMED intervention in November 1956 put down the Hungarian uprising.

243

HUNGARIAN GOLGOTHA

THE FAILURE of the 1956 anti-Soviet uprising in Hungary occasioned 200,000 to flee the country. Many emigrants believed that the fall of Communism would not be possible until the requests of Our Lady of Fatima were fulfilled. One of the best-known propagators of the Fatima message was a Hungarian priest of the Society of the Divine Word, Fr. Lajos Kondor, who had to flee his country because of anti-Catholic persecutions in 1948. Four years later he settled in Fatima, and was appointed vice postulator for the causes of Jacinta and Francisco Marto. After the suppression of the 1956 uprising, Hungarian emigrants from all over the world, at the initiative of Fr. Kondor, raised funds to build the Stations of the Cross in Fatima, called the Hungarian Golgotha.

PORTUGAL

Fatima

●Lisbon

THE STATIONS of the Cross in Fatima ends on a hill with the Hungarian Golgotha.

FR. LUIS KONDOR – vice postulator of Francisco's and Jacinta's beatification process.

first time it had surrendered an occupied country without a fight. Why? Chancellor of Austria Julius Raab had no doubt that it was thanks to Mary.

In order to understand why the Austrian leader so thought, we have to go back to August 1944, when a Wehrmacht orderly, forty-two-year-old Petrus Pavlicek, was captured in France by the Americans. He was actually an Austrian Franciscan – as a civilian he was known as Otto – who had been forced into the German Army. He had led a stormy life: a half orphan, a graduate of the Academy of Fine Arts in Wroclaw, an artist (who had given up painting, his last work being the *Resurrection of Lazarus*, and who had wandered around Europe), and a divorcee who had returned to the Catholic Church, which he had abandoned as a youth in December 1935.

Petrus Pavlicek felt a calling to the religious life. Not knowing whether or not, as an apostate and divorcee, he was worthy to be a

FR. BENNO MIKOCKI, who replaced Fr. Pavlicek as head of the Holy Rosary Crusade of Reparation, interviewed by Grzegorz Gorny.

245

JOHN PAUL II, Fr. Petrus Pavlicek, and Fr. Benno Mikocki in the Vatican on May 7, 1981, six days prior to the assassination attempt. Fr. Pavlicek then asked the pope to devote himself to propagating the Fatima message.

PROCESSION OF LIGHT – Vienna, Austria.

FR. PETRUS PAVLICEK – charismatic Franciscan who believed that prayer could save his country.

religious, he made his way to Konnersreuth in Bavaria, Germany, to seek the advice of Therese Neumann, a famous stigmatic. On entering her room, he was about to speak, but she anticipated him, telling him it was high time that he became a priest. She promised to pray for him and offer up sacrifices for his sake. He then went to a nearby Franciscan church. While praying he became certain that he was to enter the Franciscan Order, and no other. He was accepted in Prague at the third attempt, the Vienna and Tyrol provinces having rejected him. On entering the order he had no possessions whatsoever, having given eveything to the poor. In December 1941, he was ordained and took the name Petrus. Six months later he was arrested by the Gestapo for refusing to do military service, and after five months he was forced into the German Army as an orderly.

Captured by the Americans, he ended up in a POW camp in Cherbourg, France, where he became a chaplain. He came across a booklet on the Fatima apparitions that changed his life, as he began to understand the significance of the events of the last twenty-five years.

He had no doubt that Our Lady was the key to understanding history and man's vocation. On being released, he made his way to the basilica in Mariazell, the most important Marian shrine in Austria. While praying before image of the *Magna Mater Austria*, he heard an inner voice: "Do as I ask and you will have peace!" He later learnt that the three Fatima visionaries had heard the same thing.

After World War II Austria and its capital, Vienna, were divided into four zones: American, British, French, and Soviet. There was a similar situation in Germany, which led to the rise of two mutually hostile states, that is, Soviet-controlled East Germany (GDR) and free West Germany (FRG). Berlin, the former capital of Germany, was also divided into East and West. Austria was determined to avoid a similar scenario, horrified at the thought of a new Communist state from

CARRIED on a sedan chair, a statue of Our Lady of Fatima is the center of all Vienna's Rosary processions.

247

Burgenland (lower Austria) to north of the Danube (upper Austria).

Studying the contents and the history of the Fatima apparitions, Fr. Pavlicek came to the conclusion that only a good spiritual force, emanating from an entrustment to God and Our Lady, could overcome Communism, primarily a spiritual evil. Hence in 1947 he initiated the Holy Rosary Crusade of Reparation, the aim of which was to fulfill the Fatima message by calling Austrians to penance, prayer, and conversion. He initiated the mission in numerous towns. His Masses were attended by great numbers, and on one occasion he heard confessions without even a brief respite for seventy-two hours.

In 1950 this charismatic Franciscan decided to organize a Procession of Light for the withdrawal of the occupying forces from Austria. He had a meeting with Chancellor Leopold Figl, who said

SOVIET WAR MEMORIAL commemorating the Red Army, which liberated Vienna from the Germans in 1945 – Schwarzenberg Square, Vienna.

Vienna

AUSTRIA

GOTHIC CATHEDRAL – St. Stephen's, Vienna, the city's most beautiful church.

FR. PETRUS PAVLICEK and Leopold Figl, the Austrian chancellor, during the Procession of Light on September 11, 1950, when 15,000 participated.

that even if but two soldiers were to go it was worth doing. The procession, which set out in the evening from the Votive Church in Vienna and ended at the Franciscan monastery, attracted tens of thousands. It was headed by the chancellor and Fr. Petrus, followed by a statue of Our Lady of Fatima carried on a sedan chair.

There were more processions, the largest of which was on December 8, 1954, the hundredth anniversary of the announcement of the Immaculate Conception dogma, and attracted eighty thousand people in Vienna and half a million in Austria as a whole. Fr. Pavlicek convinced the government to declare the day a public holiday, which it had been before the Anschluss (the German annexation prior to World War II). Hence the feast day was restored.

Austrian politicians made as many as three hundred attempts to come to an agreement with the Kremlin regarding the withdrawal of its troops, but all ended in a fiasco, as was the case

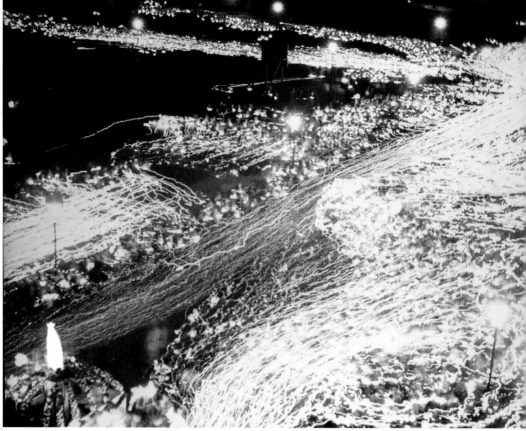

WORLD'S LARGEST PROCESSION – December 8, 1954, Vienna, when 80,000 participated.

PROCESSION with 14 crosses, symbolizing the 14 countries that were enslaved by Communism.

in December 1954, when Soviet Minister of Foreign Affairs Vyacheslav Molotov categorically refused. Fr. Pavlicek, however, informed Chancellor Julius Raab that it was possible to bring about the Soviet withdrawal through prayer, through Our Lady's intercession.

After Easter 1955, when another delegation had set off for Moscow, Raab asked Fr. Petrus for the members of the crusade to pray for the success of the negotiations, as he realized that only a miracle could liberate Austria. Leopold Figl, the then chief of diplomacy, concurred. Hence during the negotiations in Russia, the churches in Austria were filled with people.

On April 13, 1955, the Russians suddenly changed their stance. That morning, Julius Raab recalled, he recited a short prayer to Our Lady, beseeching her to obtain a favor for Austria. That evening the negotiations ended successfully. In May – a Marian month – a pact regarding the withdrawl of troops from Austria was signed, while in October – another Marian month – the last Soviet troops left the country.

PRESENTATION of the Austrian Independence Treaty of May 15, 1955, which saw the occupational forces withdraw from Austria. On the Belvedere balcony in Vienna, the ministers of foreign affairs: Dulles (USA), Macmillan (GB), Pinay (France), and Molotov (USSR). In the center, Leopold Figl, the Austrian chancellor, presenting the treaty.

On September 12, 1955, there were celebrations in Vienna – the feast day of the Most Holy Name of Mary. The thanksgiving prayers were personally led by Chancellor Julius Raab, during which someone cried out: "We are free! Thanks to you, Mary!" The Austrian leader foresaw that the events of 1955 would be interpreted in a completely different way, in geopolitical terms. But he himself had no doubt that prayer was Austria's main weapon. He publicly thanked Fr. Petrus, seeing him as one of the prime movers of Austria's liberation

After Stalin's death, Nikita Khrushchev, the leader of the Communist Party, succeeded him. At the beginning of 1956 he initiated the process of de-Stalinization. The totalitarian regime mellowed: Insubordination that once ended with a death sentence, ended with imprisonment; that which once ended in twenty-five years in a forced-labor camp, ended in a several-year stretch. There was a general amnesty, and millions of prisoners were vindicated.

In Poland, Cardinal Wyszynski was released in October 1956. Earlier, an important event occurred. The primate was an adherent of the biblical conception of nation, that is, a pilgrim community with which God had sealed a covenant. Cardinal Wyszynski was of the opinion that at that difficult time in history Poland ought to renew its covenant with God through Our Lady. Hence he drew up what is called the Jasna Gora Oath of the Polish Nation, which was

FRANCISCAN CHURCH, Vienna. Statue of Our Lady of Fatima that was carried during the Procession of Light.

252

AUSTRIAN CATHOLICS pray before Fr. Petrus Pavlicek's tomb.

smuggled out of Komancza (where he was under house arrest) by habitless nuns, and then read out on August 26, 1956, at Jasna Gora, where one million took the oath.

In 1955 Cardinal Alfredo Ottaviani, prefect of the Holy Office, went to Fatima to talk to Sr. Lucia about the third secret, the text of which was in the safe of the bishop of Leiria. She told him that only the local bishop and the pope were to familiarize themselves with it before 1960, and only after that was it to be revealed to the public. Bishop Correia da Silva refused to familiarize himself with the secret, as he did not want to burden himself with an additional responsibility. Being paralysed, he had to move about in a wheelchair. Joao Perreira Venancio, his

POLAND

PRIMATE WYSZYNSKI
– Marian feast
day celebrations
– Jasna Gora,
Czestochowa.

PORTRAIT of
Pius XII.

personal secretary, auxiliary bishop since 1954, often accompanied him on walks. One day the infirm ordinary said: "Let's take the Virgin Mary to Moscow." The auxiliary bishop saw that as a prophecy.

At the beginning of 1957, the Holy Office asked the bishop of Leiria to send the text of the third secret, which was enclosed in a sealed envelope that had *Secretum Sancti Officii* written on it, to the Vatican. Bishop Joao Perreira Venancio took it to the nunciature in Barcelona, from whence the nuncio, the later cardinal, Fernando Cento took it to Rome. On April 4, it ended up in a small wooden safe in the papal apartments. Pius XII also did not want to read it, leaving that to his successor.

On May 14, 1958, French journalist Robert Serrou was allowed to take photographs of the papal rooms in the Vatican. He was shown around by the German nun Sr. Pasqualina Lehnert, Pius XII's secretary. At a certain moment, the press photographer, pointing to the wooden safe, asked her what was inside, and was told that it was the third Fatima secret. On October 18, a photo of the safe appeared in the weekly *Paris Match*, which fuelled curiosty throughout the world regarding the secret.

That same year, Sr. Lucia had meetings with Fr. Augustin Fuentes, the postulator of Francisco's and Jacinta's beatification processes, with whom she corresponded. She wrote, amongst other things, that people would draw down punishment on themselves if they did not pray, do penance, and be converted, that godless nations would be God's scourge, that Jesus suffered most because of those priests and monks who had abandoned the religious life and had taken many souls to perdition with them, and that God had provided humanity with an extraordinary weapon to stave off Satan, that is, the Rosary. Sr. Lucia urged all not to wait for the pope to act, but to be converted, and to listen to Mary's appeals. She pointed out that political, national, or international activities were beyond the reach of most people, but each person could recite the Rosary and thereby have some influence regarding the fortunes of the world.

PIUS XII'S SAFE, where he kept confidential documents, including an envelope that contained the third Fatima secret. The safe stood on a desk where the pope signed fourteen encyclicals and the dogma of the Assumption. On the desk there is a statue of Ignatius Loyola before which Pius XII often prayed.

Pope Pius XII died on October 9, 1958. During his pontificate he consecrated the world to the Immaculate Heart of Mary in 1942 and 1952, but he did not fulfill her conditions. The task fell to the next pope. Meanwhile Russia continued to spread her errors throughout the world.

Neither Anathema nor Condemnation

ST. PETER'S BASILICA, Rome, during the inauguration of Vatican II in 1962.

POPE JOHN XIII unexpectedly summoned the Council.

CHAPTER 10

Neither Anathema nor Condemnation

Cardinal Giovanni Roncalli, a seventy-eight-year-old with cancer, became pope on October 28, 1958. Vatican watchers said his would be an "interim pontificate" that would not result in anything new. But John XXIII surprised everyone. Barely five days after his election, he noted in his diary the idea of summoning a council, which he officially announced on December 25, 1959. The Second Vatican Council would be the most important event of his papacy and would affect the fulfillment of the Fatima message.

Rome

ITALY

In August 1959, the new pope familiarized himself with the third Fatima secret, which he decided not to reveal publicly. He also familiarized several clergy with the contents, for example, Cardinal Alfredo Ottaviani and Loris Capovilla, his personal secretary. But he was not convinced of the authenticity of the Fatima apparitions. Hence he ordered Sr. Lucia to be silent about the third secret, an order that remained in force until near the end of her life. Isolated from the world in the

259

WARSAW AIRPORT, Poles greet the Our Lady of Fatima Statue in 1995.

Warsaw

Zakopane

POLAND

enclosed convent, she could not speak to anyone about it without the express permission of the Holy Office, while those who were allowed to come into contact with the mystic were not to ask her any questions on the subject.

The Holy See did not issue an official communique as to the nondisclosure of the secret. On February 8, 1960, the Portuguese News Agency – citing very reliable Vatican sources – claimed that the third Fatima secret would probably never be revealed: "In view of the pressure exerted on the Vatican, the same sources stated that – since some are demanding the disclosure of the secret to the whole world, while others, on the assumption that the secret contains alarming prophecies, are against its publication – the Vatican has decided that Sr. Lucia's text will not be revealed, and will stay a close secret."[40]

The Holy See's decision disappointed many Catholic circles throughout the world. Members of the Blue Army were particularly disappointed, as they had led an extensive media campaign claiming that the secret would be made public after 1960. In October, Pope John XXIII publicly confirmed that it would not be revealed.

OUR LADY
OF FATIMA
Shrine,
Zakopane,
Poland.

SHRINE IN ZAKOPANE
– Poland's main
center of devotion
to Our Lady of
Fatima.

ICON OF MARY –
shrine in Zakopane.

In 1960, Bishop of Leiria Joao Pereira Venancio sent two statues of Our Lady of Fatima to Cardinal Stefan Wyszynski. To avoid their being confiscated by the Communists, the statues ("dolls" on the shipping list) were first sent to Holland, and then by sea to Gdynia. The Polish primate sent one of them to the Warsaw Theological Seminary, the other to the Pallottine Order in Zakopane, where it was received by Bishop of Krakow Karol Wojtyla in 1961.

In their chapel, the Pallottines established the first Polish center of devotion to Our Lady of Fatima, which they spread by taking the statute in a suitcase from parish to parish. They were monitored by the secret police, hence they had to propagate the devotion in a discreet manner. They avoided mentioning Fatima in their communications, and they called their initiative the Family Rosary Retreat.

Meanwhile Pope John XXIII did not consecrate Russia to the Immaculate Heart of Mary, though Vatican II afforded him a splendid opportunity to do so. After all, 108 cardinals, 5 patriarchs, 9 primates, 543 archbishops, and 2,171 bishops, representing 141 nations, had gathered in Rome for the Council. But also present were representatives of the Russian Orthodox Church, which was subordinated

to the Soviet Communist Party; the majority of Russian Orthodox bishops were KGB officers or agents. Hence John XXIII did not want to offend Moscow by a public consecration that might have been seen as a condemnation of Communism. Instead, the pope ordered behind-the-scenes talks with the Kremlin. Thus began the Vatican's Ostpolitik era.

In the middle of September 1962, there was a meeting in a monastery on the outskirts of Metz, France. Cardinal Eugene Tisserant, the former long-standing secretary of the Congregation for the Oriental Churches, but then chairman of the Central Preparatory Commission for the Council, met Nikodim, the Russian Orthodox metropolitan of Leningrad, a KGB agent, whose pseudonym was "Adamant". Cardinal Tisserant assured Nikodim that the Council Fathers would refrain from making any comments about Communism, and thus facilitated the attendance of his representatives at the Council as observers. Nikodim requested that a guarantee to that effect be delivered to him in person by a papal envoy.

Hence Cardinal Johannes Willebrands, president of the Pontifical Council for Promoting Christian Unity, flew to Moscow on September 27 and stayed there until October 2. The Soviet authorities did not even pretend that the Russian Orthodox Church was independent. Those that negotiated with the Vatican envoy were not representatives of the patriarch (Aleksy – a KGB agent, pseudonym "Drozdow") but officials responsible for the state's religious policy. Cardinal Willebrands promised that the issue of Communism would not be raised during Vatican II, and he agreed to two Russian Orthodox clerics as observers.

Six days after Cardinal Willebrand's departure from Moscow, the Council of Constantinople was inaugurated. It was led by Patriarch Athenagoras I, seen as *primus inter pares* in the Orthodox world – the most important dignitary in the Eastern Church – and long regarded as an advocate of reconciliation with Catholicism, was in favor of participating in Vatican II. But news reached the Orthodox hierarchs, who acknowledged the titular supremacy of Constantinople, that representatives of the Soviet Union were to be at Vatican II. That was a shock to them. They had no doubts that

DUTCH CARDINAL Johannes Willebrands – negotiated the participation of Moscow observers at Vatican II.

THE PATRIARCH of **MOSCOW** and all Rus Alexy I was nominated by Stalin in 1945.

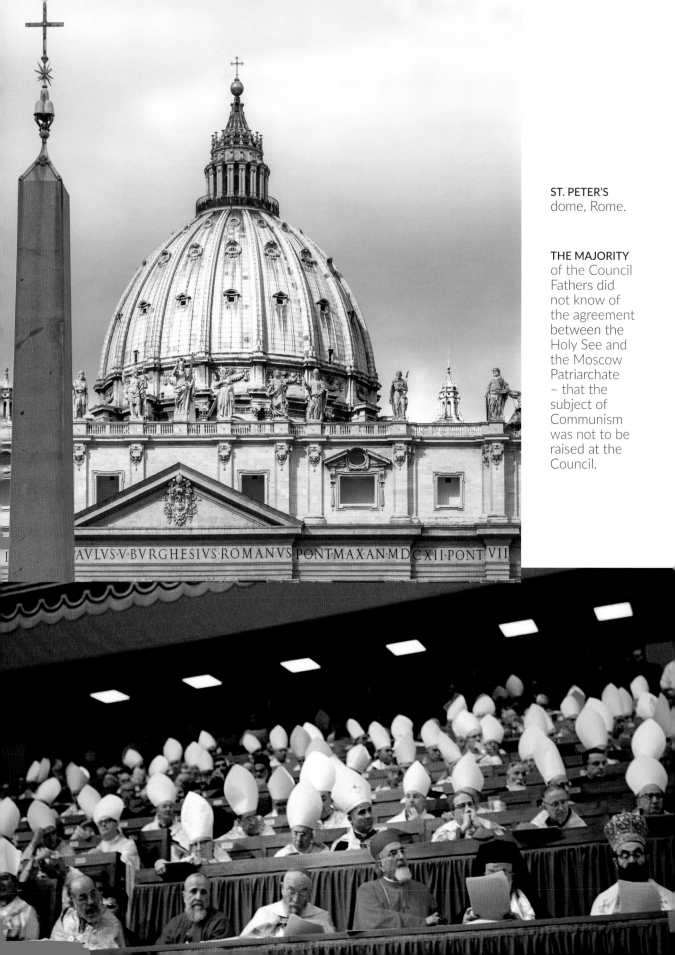

ST. PETER'S dome, Rome.

THE MAJORITY of the Council Fathers did not know of the agreement between the Holy See and the Moscow Patriarchate – that the subject of Communism was not to be raised at the Council.

VATICAN II had 3,058 participants, representing 141 nations. It was the most important event in the Catholic Church during the 20th century.

the Moscow Patriarchate was a Kremlin puppet. Hence the council, including Athenagoras, unanimously decided that the Constantinople Patriarchate would not send observers to Vatican II. John XXIII hoped that the Council would be ecumenical, but no representatives from the numerous Orthodox churches throughout the world turned up, apart from the ones from Russia.

The aim of the negotiations had been achieved. On October 12, 1962, the day after the inauguration of Vatican II, Archpriest Vitaly Borovog and Archimandrite Vladimir Kotlyarov, representatives of the Moscow Patriarchate, arrived in Rome. As secretly agreed, Communism was not to be mentioned during Vatican II. The Soviet media praised the Vatican for seeking, together with the forces of progress, to preserve world peace.

While the Soviet Union officially announced further peace initiatives at international conventions, it simultaneously located

medium-range ballistic missiles in Cuba, where Communists led by Fidel Castro took power in 1959.

Four days after the inauguration of Vatican II, the Cuban Missile Crisis arose. The Americans demanded the removal of the missiles in Cuba and blockaded the island to prevent the arrival of Soviet ships loaded with more armaments. Neither of the two superpowers wanted to give way; the world was on the verge of a global nuclear conflict. Eventually US President John F. Kennedy won the war of nerves. On October 28, 1962, Soviet Premier Nikita Khrushchev agreed to turn the ships back and to remove the Cuban missiles, while the Americans agreed to withdraw their missiles from Turkey so that Khrushchev might not lose face.

The danger of an atomic war and the refusal of the Vatican to reveal the third Fatima secret occasioned all sorts of conspiracy theories and apocalyptic speculations. In October 1963 the German

MONUMENT OF John XXIII, Wroclaw. The world's only statue of a pope in a Communist country that was not financed by a Church institution or by donations from the faithful, but wholly by the Communist authorities.

SOVIET ROCKET launcher in Cuba – US spy plane photo of October 14, 1962.

PRESIDENT John F. Kennedy – he opposed Soviet rocket installations near US borders.

TWO COMMUNIST leaders – Fidel Castro (Cuba) and Nikita Khrushchev (USSR).

magazine *Neues Europa* published an article by its editor Louis Emrich, author of *The Third World War* (published in 1948). In his article Emrich included what he called "an extract" of the third Fatima secret, which he claimed came from Vatican insiders and was circulating among political leaders throughout the world. In the quoted "extract", Mary warns of another world war in the second half of the twentieth century, which will evaporate the oceans and kill millions of people. Those who survive will envy the dead, and Satan will rule the earth.[41]

The article was an international sensation. In Communist countries, typed or handwritten copies were passed from person to person. In time, copyists added new elements. The Polish Mariologist Wincenty Laszewski recalled that the text was characterized by an extraordinary dynamism: "When, for example, the Fatima secret, copied for the umpteenth time, reached a woman from Lublin, who took it to the cathedral parish priest, he read the list of towns that had been saved and called out: 'Lublin is not here! Please add Lublin!' After some years, someone gave him another version of the Fatima secret, and to his amazement Lublin was one of the towns that would not be destroyed."[42]

Emrich's piece was very popular as it was in accord with the fears of millions of people as to an atomic war. There were also rumors that the Cuban Missile Crisis had been resolved by John XXIII, who had allegedly revealed the third Fatima secret to President Kennedy, Premier Krushchev, and British Prime Minister Harold Macmillan. Terrified by the apocalyptic vision, the rumors erroneously claimed, they gave up the idea of escalating the conflict.

John XXIII died on June 3, 1963. Shortly afterward, his personal secretary, Cardinal Loris Capovilla, revealed why the Vatican had changed its policy regarding the Soviet regime. According to him, the pope realized that criticism and anathemas were ineffective.

HEAD OF USSR diplomacy Andrei Gromyko and President John F. Kennedy.

AMERICAN DIPLOMATS showing photos of Soviet rocket launchers in Cuba during a United Nations Security Council session.

US NAVY patrol plane above a Soviet ship sailing to Cuba with military equipment.

THE BERLIN WALL

JOHN XXII'S pontificate saw another escalation of the Cold War, this time centered on Germany, which was divided into two states after World War II, that is, East and West Germany. Wherever Communism was imposed, there was not only terror, but also economic inefficiency and a lack of basic goods.

Masses of East Germans fled to West Germany. From 1949 to 1961 as many as 600,000 abandoned their work and homes and entered West Germany illegally. In the first two weeks of August 1961, over 47,000 fled, leaving East Germany in danger of depopulation.

During the night of August 12, 1961, East German soldiers and police began to build a wall that eventually divided free Berlin from Communist Berlin. The two states were also divided by the "death strip", a barbed wire fence of a few hundred miles in length, minefields, and 1,600 guard towers with machine guns. The Berlin Wall became a symbol of the Iron Curtain, the tragic division of Europe into an enslaved East and a free West.

BERLIN WALL – GDR's best-known construction, built in 1961.

EAST GERMANY (GDR)

West Berlin   East Berlin (capital of the GDR)

US PRESIDENT John Kennedy during his famous speech in West Berlin, when he said: "Ich bin ein Berliner."

BRANDENBURG GATE, Berlin – it was inside East Berlin during the Cold War.

POPE PAUL VI, elected in 1963 – continued Vatican II, summoned by his predecessor, John XXIII.

VATICAN COUNCIL II lasted three years, 1962–1965.

He thought that openness, moderation, and kindness was the only way forward. Cardinal Capovilla also thought that a tempered policy regarding socialist regimes would reduce the number of repressions in Communist states. Vatican officials thought that dialogue with Russia and its satellite states was justified in order to save the "substance of the Church" in those countries.

Archbishop of Milan Giovanni Battista Montini became pope on June 21, 1963, took the name Paul VI, and continued John XXIII's line regarding the Soviet Union. Vatican II lasted for another two and half years under his patronage, during which a petition appeared that condemned "godless Communism". The pope rejected it, even though it had been signed by 450 bishops, including Polish Primate Stefan Wyszynski.

Pavel Hnilica arrived in Rome during Vatican II. After escaping from Czechoslovakia, he remained a clandestine bishop, forbidden by successive popes to reveal the fact that he had been consecrated. He travelled extensively, organizing material and spiritual support for Christians under Communist rule, working closely with Fr. Werenfried van Straaten, founder of Aid to the Church in Need. He

SLOVAKIAN BISHOPS Pavol Hnilica and Jan Chryzostom Korec during an audience with Paul VI.

BISHOP HNILICA was a great friend of Mother Teresa of Calcutta.

also frequently visited India, where he became a friend of Mother Teresa. Additionally he was involved with the Focolare movement, assisting its founder, Chiara Lubich. Eventually, on May 17, 1964, Paul VI announced that Pavel Hnilica had been a bishop for thirteen years – hence he could participate in Vatican II.

During the fourth session of the Council, on September 26, 1965, Bishop Hnilica declared that he was speaking on behalf of all his countrymen – bishops, priests, religious, and laity – who were being persecuted for fidelity to God and Church – and depicted Communism as "Satan's false mystical body", which was waging war against the true Mystical Body of Christ, that is, the Church. A few minutes later, another Czechoslovakian bishop, Michael Rusnak, who had also fled from behind the Iron Curtain, took up the same theme, demanding that the Council occupy itself with an assessment of Communism. Both bishops were heartily applauded, yet their stance was not taken into consideration when the final documents were drawn up.

During Vatican II, Bishop Hnilica befriended Karol Wojtyla, the metropolitan of Krakow. At that time an unusual letter from Fr. Dolindo Ruotolo to Count Witold Laskowski arrived at the bishop's Rome address. The bishop did not then associate the contents

CONVERSION OF SALVADOR DALI

IN 1961, JOHN HAFFERT, the director of the World Apostolate of Fatima, commissioned Salvador Dali, an outstanding Catalonian painter, to paint a vision of hell as depicted to the three visionaries at the Cova da Iria in 1917. The artist approached the commission very seriously. He studied all the documents on the subject, had numerous talks with theologians, and even acquired permission to meet Sr. Lucia, all of which occasioned his conversion. It is true that he was a Catholic, but he had not taken the Faith seriously. But from that time on he began to pray and to participate in Mass regularly.

His painting, in the "nuclear mysticism" style, was unknown for a long time as it lay forgotten at the World Apostolate of Fatima in Washington Township, New Jersey, for almost 40 years. It was exhibited in Fatima in 2014.

VISION OF HELL painted by Salvador Dali on the basis of the Fatima apparitions.

SALVADOR DALI, one of the best-known painters of the 20th century.

Sac. Dolindo Ruotolo

nato a Napoli il 6.10.1882
iniziato la comunità di Santità il 19.11.1970

«Se piacchierete sul mio sepolcro io dirò ancora: "Confido in
Confido in Dio sia gloria a Te o mio Dio, e Te solo nella mia ...

of the letter with his new friend from Poland. The situation was out of the ordinary and worth a closer look. Fr. Ruotolo, a Franciscan tertiary, a mystic who was frequently compared with Padre Pio, lived in Naples. Witold Laskowski, a Polish aristocrat in exile in Rome, wanted to meet Fr. Ruotolo to request prayers for his oppressed country. The letter from Fr. Ruotolo to Count Laskowski said that the priest did not know Count Laskowski's address but knew that Laskowski worked with Bishop Hnilica in the Pro Fratibus movement. Hence the letter to the bishop was to be passed on to the count, whom Fr. Ruotolo had neither met nor hitherto known about.

The letter of July 2, 1965, contained this prophetic utterance from Mary: "The world is in decline, but Poland, thanks to the devotion of my Immaculate Heart, will liberate the world from the terrible tyranny of Communism, as at the time of Sobieski, when he delivered Europe from the tyranny of the Turks with but twenty thousand knights. A new John shall arise in Poland, who, after a heroic struggle will break the fetters of the Communist tyranny beyond its borders. Remember this. I bless Poland!"[43] Bishop Hnilica recalled the letter thirteen years later, after the conclave in October 1978 that elected John Paul II.

During the Council, the idea of consecrating the world to the Blessed Virgin Mary was supported by Paul VI, who on November 21, 1964, at the Basilica of Santa Maria Maggiore, Rome, renewed Pius XII's consecration of 1942. But he did it alone, not in union with the bishops, even though he had an exceptionally good opportunity to do so as hundreds of hierarchs from all over the world were in Rome for the Council. Sr. Lucia stated later that the consecration did not fulfill the conditions that were specified in the Fatima message.

On February 11, 1967, Cardinal Alfredo Ottaviani, prefect of the Holy Office, gave a lecture during a Mariology symposium in Rome, wherein he recalled his visit of May 1955 to the Carmel in Coimbra to meet Sr. Lucia. He then asked her why she had not wanted the third secret revealed until 1960. She said that it would then be better understood. The cardinal commented as follows: "I concluded from this that the message was of a prophetic nature, as prophecies in Holy Scripture are shrouded in mystery. They are not expressed in a univocal language, clear and understandable to all."[44]

On March 27, 1967, Paul VI familiarized himself with the third secret. But like John XXII he returned it to the Holy Office archives. Shortly after, on May 13, the pope was in Fatima for the fiftieth anniversary of the apparitions. During his homily he stood up for Christians deprived of freedom of religion in states where the official ideology negated the existence of God. He also announced the issue of an apostolic exhortation, *Signum Magnum*, wherein he calls for individual people, dioceses, and nations personally or collectively to consecrate themselves to the Immaculate Heart of Mary. But that once again did not meet Our Lady's conditions, as laid down in the apparitions of 1917.

Paul VI was the first pope to converse with Sr. Lucia for any length of time. She requested a face-to-face meeting, which the pope initially refused. They did indeed meet, though they but courteously exchanged views. According to Jean Guitton, a friend of the Holy

SOME OF the Vatican II dignitaries wanted the world to be consecrated to the Immaculate Heart of Mary.

FR. DOLINDO Ruotolo, an Italian mystic, was compared with Padre Pio.

ITALIAN CARDINAL Alfredo Ottaviani, prefect of the Holy Office from 1959 to 1968. The Holy Office was renamed as the Congregation for the Doctrine of the Faith in 1966.

POPE PAUL VI
before the statue
of Our Lady of
Fatima during
his pilgrimage to
Portugal in 1967.

SR. LUCIA beside
Paul VI in Fatima.
Bishop Pavol Hnilica
is behind her.

PORTUGAL

Fatima

● Lisbon

Father, Paul VI harbored a certain aversion to visionaries, thinking that their visions were unneccesarily given an exaggerated significance, while the whole of Christian revelation had already been
communicated in Holy Scripture.

During his stay in Portugal, Paul VI blessed forty-five statues of
Our Lady of Fatima. Each one was meant for countries that were
particularly endangered by war or Communism. One was meant for
Poland. When the Communist authorities learnt of this, they tight-
ened border controls. The statue remained in Fatima for two years,
and then, in 1969, it was smuggled into Poland via Paris by a priest
from the United States. It eventually ended up in Niepokalanow.

Bishop Hnilica accompanied Paul VI as a papal legate to Fatima,
where he befriended Bishop of Leiria Joao Pereira Venancio. After
two days of talks, the bishop stated that he had not met anyone who
had grasped the meaning of the Fatima secrets so profoundly. He

supposed that only someone who had personally experienced Communism could adequately respond to Our Lady's requests.

Statues of the Pilgrim Virgin circulated around the world, including in Islamic countries where they were warmly welcomed because Fatima was Muhammad's beloved daughter. According to Muslim tradition, Fatima is, after Mary, the most blessed of all women. A surah is dedicated to her in the Koran. During processions with the Our Lady of Fatima statue in Mozambique, numerous Muslims were converted to Christianity.

Meanwhile Russia continued spreading her errors throughout the world and prevented countries from breaking free of her control. In 1968, the Communist government in Czechoslovakia began reforms, the aim of which were "Socialism with a human face", but these ended with the invasion of Czechoslovakia by Warsaw Pact forces.

ONE OF THE STATUES of Our Lady of Fatima, blessed by Paul VI in 1967, ended up in Niepokalanow, Poland.

STATUE of Our Lady of Fatima – Franciscan monastery, Niepokalanow.

275

SOVIET FORCED-LABOR camps were largely deserted after 1956 on account of general rehabilitations and amnesties.

WARSAW PACT military intervention in Czechoslovakia, 1968.

In December 1970, Polish workers protested in Gdansk, Gdynia, Szczecin, and Elblag. The Polish Army fired on the protesters, killing forty people and wounding a thousand. There were further protests in 1976 in Radom and Ursus, which were also quashed.

Yet Communism still had many followers throughout the world. They maintained that after Stalin's death the "era of errors and perversions" in the Soviet Union had gone forever; after all, millions of prisoners had been released from forced-labor camps. Hence the catchphrase "Socialism – yes, perversions – no" was staggeringly successful. Its promoters claimed that the Communist system was a good one, but that it had been distorted by the negative traits of Stalin's character. The era of a true realization of the system was approaching, they said, one that would bring humanity social justice.

But that optimistic view had its opponents who noted that the Soviet dictatorship was more lenient simply because it had destroyed old principles and norms. They compared the birth of the Communist system to establishing a lawn – the "dirty work", that is, preparing the ground, is followed by tending to the seedbed and mowing the grass. At the present stage the "dirty work", that is, the

use of terror, was unnecessary as society was so enslaved that there was no longer any need of mass force. An awareness that it could well return was sufficient to control people. Other methods had replaced large-scale violence: the loss of dissenters' jobs, arrests, beatings, and one or two assassinations.

Forms of coercion changed, but the essence of the system remained. The priority was the battle against Christianity. It was true that Khrushchev did not have clergy and religious murdered, but he ordered monasteries and churches to be demolished, and he intensified the campaign to create an atheistic society. In 1961 he declared that in ten years he would present the last Christian in the Soviet Union on television for all to see.

Ten years later Christians still existed, but Khrushchev had gone. He died in 1971, seven years after being overthrown by a coup. But the system did not change. The next USSR leader, Leonid Brezhnev, continued the war against religion, and the Soviet Union was still intent on conquering Europe, on continuing the arms race. Exploiting the 1970's economic and political crisis in the West, the Soviet Union extended its area of influence in the world. The Soviet Army's general staff prepared a plan to attack NATO states. Kremlin leaders believed that they could shift the balance of power between NATO and the Warsaw Pact in their favor.

WORKERS IN GDYNIA, December 1970, carrying Zbyszek Godlewski, an 18-year-old youth who had been shot by soldiers.

BLACK THURSDAY location – the film is about the massacre of Polish workers on the Baltic coast in 1970.

277

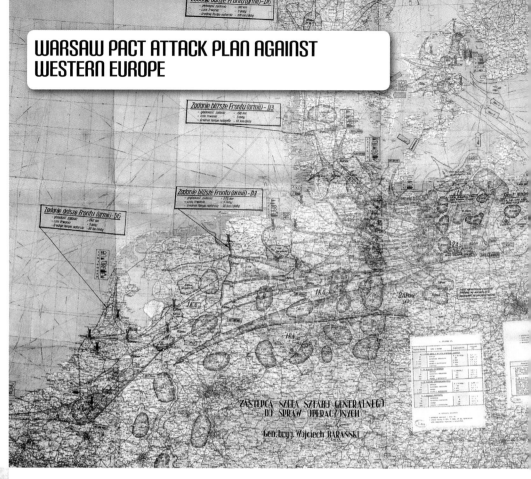

WARSAW PACT ATTACK PLAN AGAINST WESTERN EUROPE

TOP SECRET offensive military operations on the Polish front depicting the Warsaw Pact attack against Western Europe, which was approved by Gen. Wojciech Jaruzelski on February 25, 1970.

RYSZARD KUKLINSKI, a Polish Army colonel, the most valuable spy in CIA history.

In 1970 Col. Ryszard Kuklinski, chief of a military strategic command planning division of the Polish Army, discovered the Soviet Union's intentions. He was one of the few in the whole Communist bloc who had access to the Soviet Army's most secret plans. Hence he knew that Moscow's peace initiatives were but a mere pretence.

The Communist offensive included a missile attack against NATO states in Western Europe. In but a moment atom bombs, one thousand times more powerful than the one dropped on Hiroshima, would have destroyed many European cities. Soldiers from the Soviet Union, East Germany, Poland, and Czechoslovakia would then have attacked West Germany, Belgium, Holland, and Denmark. The Moscow planners assumed that over half of their eight hundred thousand soldiers would perish in the offensive. Victory was to come via an attack by a two-million-strong Soviet Army, the main strength of which lay in its

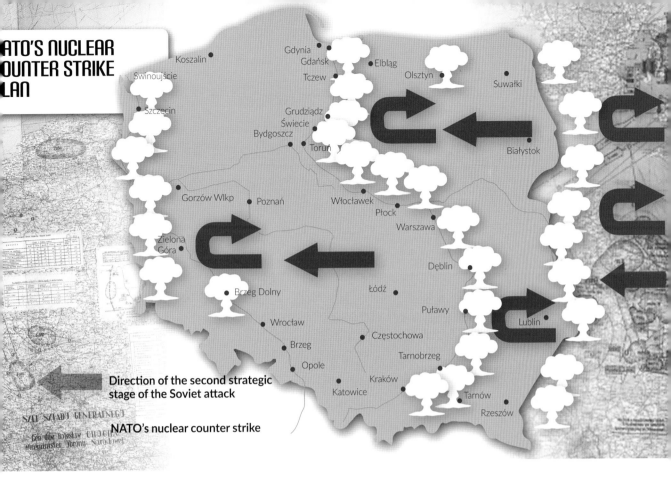

NATO'S NUCLEAR COUNTER STRIKE PLAN

Koszalin
Gdynia
Gdańsk
Elbląg
Olsztyn
Suwałki
Swinoujście
Tczew
Szczecin
Grudziądz
Świecie
Bydgoszcz
Toruń
Białystok
Gorzów Wlkp
Poznań
Włocławek
Płock
Warszawa
Zielona Góra
Dęblin
Brzeg Dolny
Łódź
Puławy
Wrocław
Częstochowa
Lublin
Brzeg
Tarnobrzeg
Opole
Kraków
Katowice
Tarnów
Rzeszów

Direction of the second strategic stage of the Soviet attack

SZU SZTABU GENERALNEGO

Gen dyw Bolesła ...
...minister Obrony Naro ...

NATO's nuclear counter strike

armored units. The Russian marshals and generals were aware that NATO would not be passive. Hence they assumed that four to six hundred atom bombs would have to fall on Poland, as it was the Warsaw Pacts's main military corridor. That would have meant that the whole country would have become a deserted, radioactive wasteland.

Col. Kuklinski, horrified that his superiors, including Gen. Jaruzelski, were going along with the Soviet plans without batting an eyelid, saw Poland being wiped off the face of the earth. Hence he decided to pass on the Warsaw Pact's secret files to the Americans, copying top secret military documents over a period of ten years. In sum, he passed on forty thousand pages of top secret documents, mainly Soviet, to the Pentagon and is seen as the most important spy in CIA history. His materials allowed the Americans to neutralize effectively the Soviet Union's plans without the Kremlin knowing anything about it.

MAP OF POLAND depicting nuclear attacks if the Soviet offensive would have been realized.

279

SYNTHETIC DRUGS
– ecstasy pills.

RAF SYMBOL
– Red Army
Faction.

Meanwhile, Communists were weakening and destabilizing enemy countries from within: They financed and trained terrorist organizations that carried out attacks, for example, the Red Army Faction and the Palestine Liberation Organization; the Soviet, Cuban, Lao, and Bulgarian special services smuggled narcotics into North America and Western Europe, while the Soviet Union and its satellite states sponsored liberation theology, which undermined the identity and unity of the Catholic Church.

Cultural Marxism developed in Western intellectual circles, particulary among the elite, in accord with Antonio Gramsci's premises. The new left accepted the old Marxist patterns of thought, but translated them into concepts from the world of culture. Thus the ideology that once formed Lenin and his comrades became the foundation of the new currents germinating in Western universities: It fostered the sexual revolution and lies at the roots of radical feminism, gender ideology, gay rights, and radical environmentalism.

There was but one permanent factor amidst all the changes, that is, the further undermining of the Christian foundations of Western civilization, blamed for the contemporary world's greatest evils: imperialism, racism, Nazism, fascism, anti-Semitism, sexism, xenophobia, homophobia, and other social plagues. In the dock we have Christianity, as a source of exclusion; the patriarchal family, as a place for forming authoritarian personalities; tradition, as a cause of backwardness; morality, as an obstacle to self-realization; patriotism, as a seedbed of intolerance.

In 1968, the Portuguese dictator Antonio Salazar, who had ruled authoritatively for thirty-six years, had a brain hemorrhage

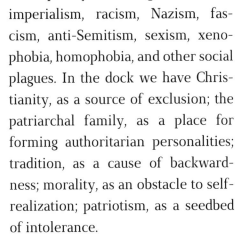

ULRIKE MEINHOF, a West German journalist who was fascinated by Communist ideas, eventually became a terrorist.

THE CHE GUEVARA MYTH

PROOF OF THE EFFECTIVENESS
of Antonio Gramsci's strategy is the permeation of Marxism into mass culture, an example of which is the extraordinary popularity – particularly among the youth – of Che Guevara, based on a romantic myth that depicts the Argentine revolutionary as a noble fighter for justice. Apart from those of Christ, Guevara's images are the most popular male images in the world.

In actual fact, Guevara was a sadist and a criminal. He stated that hate was an inseparable element of war, hence one had to fuel it within oneself unto a liberating convulsion, to be free of human limitations, and thus become a cold and effective killing machine. This was not a mere theory. During the Cuban campaign, Guevara was famous for exceptional cruelty, killing a young boy, for example, for stealing some food. Humberto Fontova, a historian, called him a childkiller.

In January 1959, after the victory of Communism in Cuba, Guevara became the governor of a prison in La Cabana, where he condemned several hundred people to death without trial. Later, he began establishing a system of concentration camps on the island. Historians see him as responsible for about 10,000 executions, some of which he personally carried out.

COMMUNIST CRIMINAL, Che Guevara, still seen by the world's youth as a romantic fighter for justice.

WIRE OUTLINE of a statue of Our Lady of Fatima. It was made by some Franciscans in 1978 and circulated around Poland.

and died two years later. His successor was Marcelo Caetano, whose political activities, particularly those related to the colonial wars, aroused increasing dissatisfaction. On April 25, 1974, that autocrat was overthrown by a bloodless military coup called the Carnation Revolution, which was primarily led by the Armed Forces Movement (MFA). A power struggle ensued. In the fourth interim government, the well-organized and disciplined MFA and the Portuguese Communist Party gained the upperhand. Thus there was a real threat that a Soviet-inspired system would be imposed.

Seeing such a great danger on the horizon, a group of Portuguese women founded the National Rosary Crusade to save the country from Communism. In time, it had over one million members. Parliamentary elections were called in 1975 and, unexpectedly, the radical left was defeated: The MFA gained but 12.5 percent of the votes, and the Communists but 4.1 percent. On November 20, the defeated parties staged a coup d'état that ended in failure. In February 1976, a parliamentary majority removed a regulation from the constitution preamble concerning the establishment of a socialist system. The organizers of the prayer crusade were certain that the success was thanks to Our Lady of Fatima, though they thought that the danger could well return at any moment. Hence they decided to continue the crusade, which has been active without a break to this day.

On the one hand, Communists speak disparagingly of religion, while on the other, they fear its influence on people. Of all the forms of Catholic piety, it is devotion to Our Lady of Fatima that arouses their anger most. In May 1978, when the statue of the Pilgrim Virgin, which was circulating around the world, reached Warsaw, it was detained at the airport, the security men watching over it as if it were a threat to the state. Meanwhile, believers in numerous parishes awaited its arrival. The Franciscans came up with an unusual idea. They made a wire outline of the statue and commenced the pilgrimage around the country. The mere wire frame was welcomed everywhere by crowds of people praying that Russia might cease to spread its errors throughout the world.

In 1978 Communism seemed to be at the height of its power, ruling in twenty-three countries, where almost a quarter of the world's population lived. Many Western intellectuals thought that naught could prevent the victory of the system. Such was to be the allegedly inexorable historical necessity. Others thought that the system would fail to conquer the whole world, but that it would be a permanent element of the international order for a long time to come. And it is just then that Karol Wojtyla unexpectedly became pope.

PORTUGUESE MURAL commemorating the Carnation Revolution in 1974.

ALVARO CUNHAL, leader of the Portuguese Communist Party from 1961 to 1992. He was in exile from 1960 to 1974, but returned to Portugal after the Carnation Revolution and became a minister without portfolio. He left the government in the hope of staging a coup, but it failed.

PORTUGAL

Fatima

Lisbon

283

HABEMUS PAPAM
IOANNEM PAULUM I

Kardynał Karol Wojtyła
Następcą Świętego Piotra

SŁOWO
powszechne

KAROL WOJTYŁA

Imię Polski
na ustach Rzymian

Życiorys
Ojca świętego
Jana Pawła II
zamieszczamy
na stronie 2

Polish Pope Throws Down the Gauntlet

NIKODEM, METROPLITAN of Leningrad, died in John Paul I's arms.

JOHN PAUL I's pontificate lasted but 33 days.

JOHN PAUL II during a Mass in Victory Square, Warsaw, on June 2, 1979. The Holy Father then said the following prophetic words: "Let your Spirit descend! Let your Spirit descend! And renew the face of the earth. The face of this land!"

CHAPTER 11

Polish Pope Throws Down the Gauntlet

On September 28, 1978, the Catholic world was completely stunned as John Paul I had died of a heart attack. The pontificate, on which great hopes were pinned for a spiritual renewal of the Church, lasted barely thirty-three days.

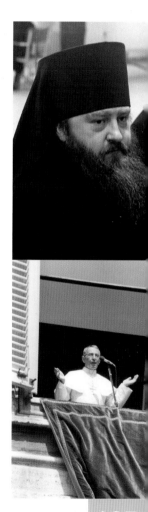

Cardinals, who but several weeks earlier had elected a pope, asked themselves what God wanted to tell them through his death. Another conclave in such a short time was seen as an urgent need for a new solution.

Nobody was surprised when Paul VI died on August 6, 1978, as he was over eighty years of age and had been seriously ill for some time. But the ultra-quick election of Albino Luciani, the patriarch of Venice – on the very first day of the conclave – was a great surprise. In honor of his two predecessors, he took the name John Paul I.

Shortly afterwards, an extraordinary event occurred: On September 5, Orthodox Metropolitan Nikodem (a KGB agent – pseudonym "Adamant") had a heart attack immediately after a private audience with the new pope, who managed to administer extreme unction before he died. Not much later, when John Paul I was dying, there were rumors that his ill health was caused by his reading the

INFLUENTIAL CARDINALS
– participants in the
conclave of October
1978: ❶ Giuseppe Siri,
❷ Giovanni Benelli,
❸ Bernardus Johannes
Alfrink, ❹ Sebastiano
Baggio.

"HABEMUS
PAPAM!" –
announcement
of a new pope.

horrifying third Fatima secret, which was untrue, as he had not read it.

The cardinals, assembled in Rome once again, wondered whether the next pope ought to be an Italian. It seemed that the opinion of the Dutch primate Bernardus Johannes Alfrink would prevail, for many cardinals thought that even the worst Italian would be better than the best from any other country. The course of the first votes confirmed this, as the favorites were Cardinal Giuseppe Siri and Cardinal Giovanni Benelli, but neither had a decisive advantage. Hence another candidate was necessary. A fifty-eight-year–old Pole, Karol Wojtyla, thus became the focus of attention. He became pope on October 16, 1978, and took the name John Paul II. He was the first pope in 455 years who was not an Italian and the first Slav pope.

The conclave participants were well aware that the Church faced two threats, one from the West, the other from the East. The former was secularization combined with consumerism and hedonism, which occasioned people to live as if God did not exist. The churches were becoming empty, while a large number of Catholics rejected the teaching of the Church. The latter, Communism, not only persecuted Christians, but even began to encroach on the Church in the form of liberation theology, which combined the Christian religion with Marxist ideology to depict Christ as a revolutionary with a rifle over His shoulder, not a cross.

JOHN PAUL II
– first non-
Italian bishop
of Rome in
455 years.

289

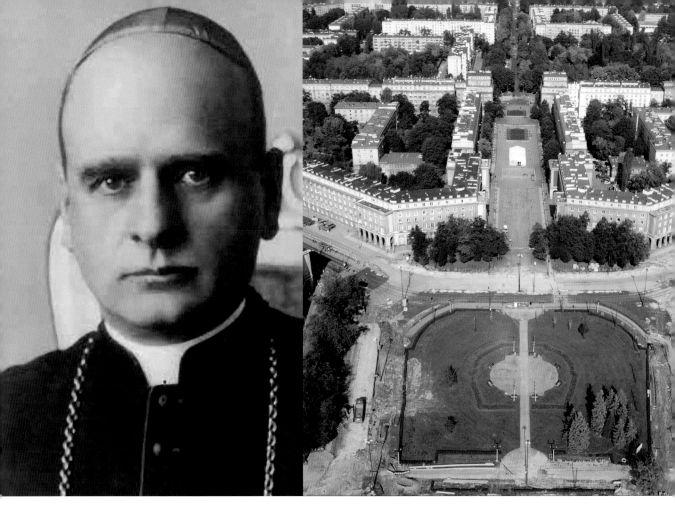

METROPOLITAN OF Krakow Archbishop Eugeniusz Baziak – initiated the consecration of Karol Wojtyla as bishop.

NOWA HUTA – "a town without God", a Communist flagship project.

Karol Wojtyla had experience of both dangers, which he successfully confronted. In the Krakow Archdiocese, he imparted a new impetus to evangelization, realizing a postconciliar renewal, avoiding the confusion and the abuses that were common in Western countries. Hence Poland stood out among other countries – churches were full, and the vast majority were faithful to the Church – a great contrast to the Communist East, which succumbed to a forced atheization, and to the capitalist West, which voluntarily gave way to secularization.

The metropolitan of Krakow also had confrontations with the Communist system, which were connected with his unexpected consecration in 1958. It was then that Archbishop Eugeniusz Baziak decided that his auxiliary bishop in Krakow was to be a little-known thirty-eight-year-old, Fr. Karol Wojtyla, who had been a priest for but twelve years. The curia personnel were unhappy with the decision as they preferred to have an older bishop with curial experience.

Hence they put forward distinguished candidates – prelates, canons, and monsignors. Archbishop Baziak made it clear that he wanted someone who could meet the challege in Nowa Huta. This silenced opponents, as nobody felt that they were up to the task.

Nowa Huta, near Krakow, was a flagship Communist project, "a town without God", without churches, the first in Polish history, built between 1949 and 1951. It was thought up as a workers' counterbalance to Krakow's intellectual circles and was to see the rise of "a new man" – homo sovieticus.

In but several years the demoralization in Nowa Huta was appalling. Alcoholism, prostitution, and veneral diseases were commonplace, a situation that was a challenge to the Church. But it was difficult to do pastoral work without parishes.

Bishop Wojtyla had an asset that no other priest had. During World War II he worked in quarries and in a chemical factory, hence he was familiar with the

KAROL WOJTYLA – auxiliary bishop of Krakow Archdiocese.

QUARRIES – young Karol Wojtyla worked in quarries during the German occupation of Poland.

NOWA HUTA
– the cross over which the workers fought in 1960.

LORD'S ARK – the Nowa Huta church that was consecrated by Cardinal Karol Wojtyla in 1977.

working class from the inside, and he knew that priests ought to be in close contact with the faithful. So he often visited Nowa Huta and celebrated open-air midnight Masses at Easter and Christmas, even in freezing weather. Religious life was concentrated around a cross that had been put up by the inhabitants. There was something symbolic in the fact that the cross stood at the intersection of Marx Street, named for Communism's main ideologist, and Majakowski Street, in honor of the most famous Bolshevik poet.

There were mass riots in April 1960, when the Communists attemped to get rid of the cross. Many were injured or arrested during street clashes. But the cross remained.

Despite harassment on the part of the authorities, pastoral work developed in a small provisional wooden chapel, which reminded

Warsaw

Krakow

POLAND

one of a storehouse for tools. Priests went from house to house rais-
ing people's spirits, telling them that a human person was not merely
an animal whose end was but a grave, but a spiritual being in the
image and likeness of God, with an immortal soul and endowed with
dignity. At that time Cardinal Wojtyla was in dispute with the authorities over the building of a church. He eventually consecrated the
Lord's Ark (1977), the first church in Nowa Huta.

Karol Wojtyla completely changed the face of Nowa Huta. In 1980
it became one of the most important anti-Communist bastions in the
country, boasting the strongest Solidarity groups in southern Poland,
concentrated in the newly established parish.

When the news of Karol Wojtyla's election as pope reached
Warsaw, Edward Gierek, the first secretary of the Polish United

OUR LADY OF THE ROSARY –
the statue that was brought
to Nowa Huta by Fr. Jozef
Gorzelany in 1965 – in the
Lord's Ark Church.

293

TOTUS TUUS

EGO SUM ET OMNIA MEA TUA SUNT
ACCIPIO TE IN MEA OMNIA
PRAEBE MIHI COR TUUM. MARIA

TOTUS TUUS

KAROL WOJTYLA had felt a very strong bond with Our Lady ever since his childhood. St. Louis-Marie Grignion de Montfort's *True Devotion to Mary* was one of the greatest discoveries of his life. It accompanied him during the difficult years of the Nazi occupation of Poland, and it helped him to decide on becoming a priest.

When he became a bishop, he chose "Totus Tuus" as his motto, which referred to Our Lady; his coat of arms included the letter *M* (for Mary), which was under a cross. Hence on becoming pope he brought his own brand of Marian piety to the papal ministry.

"TOTUS TUUS" –
Karol Wojtyla's
motto. Inscriptions
in Krakow and
Zakopane.

EDWARD GIEREK,
leader of the
Polish United
Workers' Party,
was shocked to
hear of the result
of the conclave.

*SLOWO
POWSZECHNE*
newspaper on the
election of John
Paul II.

COUNCIL OF CONSTANCE 1414–1418. The Polish delegation defended the "faith is not to be coerced" principle.

Workers' Party, exclaimed: "Jesus and Mary!" That exclamation perfectly reflected the national character of Poles. Though covered by a layer of anti-clerical varnish, there is, according to a Tertullian term, *anima naturaliter christiana*, a soul of a Christian nature.

Karol Wojtyla was formed by the spiritual experiences of Poland, a country that received Christianity in 966. A feature of his Catholicism was an evangelical radicalism that avoided coercive means, based on a respect for freedom, but at the same time dynamic and missionary. During the Council of Constance (1414–1418), the Polish delegation helped to rediscover the principle that "faith is not to be coerced." Pawel Wlodkowic, rector of the Krakow Academy, came into conflict with the Teutonic Knights and convinced Pope Martin V and the Council Fathers that one should not convert pagans by force. The Poles had to engage in heated discussions on the matter, and they almost to a man opposed the burning of Jan Hus though they were in the minority and were threatened by John of Falkenberg, the grand inquisitor, with being burnt at the stake.

PAWEL
WLODKOWIC,
rector of
the Krakow
Academy, a
great advocate
of religious
freedom in the
15th century.

295

GRAND-CHANCELLOR OF THE CROWN
Jan Zamoyski, advocate of religious toleration.

KING OF POLAND, Casimir III, "the Great", welcomed Jews who had been expelled from Western Europe and granted them privileges. Painting by Wojciech Gerson.

Religious toleration was a consequence of the historical experiences of Poles. In 1341 King Casimir III, "the Great", assured the Orthodox Church of complete religious freedom, so too the Armenians, who were Monophysites (1356), and he opened the border to Jews who had been expelled from Western Europe. Even the Tartars, that is, Muslims, who came in 1396, enjoyed complete religious freedom for centuries.

From the fourteenth century on, Poland did not develop on the basis of military conquests, but on the basis of peaceful methods, that is, by forming unions. It attracted other nations by its interesting civilizational and cultural propositions. Hence the Polish-Lithuanian Union, thanks to which the largest state in Europe arose, the Polish-Lithuanian Commonwealth (or Republic of Both Nations) – which German countries joined, for example, Prussia in 1454 and Livonia in 1561.

While the West was plunged in religious conflicts, symbolized by the bloody St. Bartholomew's Day Massacre (1572), Poland was forming permanent political guidelines for toleration, an expression of which was the Warsaw Confederation of 1574, which officially advocated freedom of religion. At a time when Western Europe accepted the barbarian principle, that is, *cuius regio, eius religio*, which violated people's consciences, King Sigismund II Augustus declared that he was not the master of the consciences of his subjects. Jan Zamoyski told infidels in the Polish Sejm (fifty years before Voltaire) that he would have his hand cut off for their conversion, but he would give his other hand were they to be forced. Yet he was not religiously indifferent, as he patronized the establishment of Jesuit colleges, which became lively centers of evangelization. It was not by accident that sixteenth–century Poland was famous as a *paradisus Judeorum* (a paradise for Jews), as well as a *paradisus haereticorum* (a paradise for heretics), as infidels and those that were persecuted could find shelter there.

FORMATION of the Polish–Lithuanian Union, Lublin, 1564. Hence Europe's largest state, the Polish–Lithuanian Commonwealth (or Republic of Both Nations). Painting by Jan Matejko.

297

QUEEN OF POLAND

IN NAPLES, ON AUGUST 14, 1608, Fr. Giulio Mancinelli had a vision of Our Lady, who said: "Why do you not call me Queen of Poland? I greatly cherish that kingdom, and intend great things for it, as its sons burn with a singular love for me."[45]

The missionary made his way to Poland, where he had another revelation in 1610: "I am Queen of Poland. I am the Mother of that nation, which is very dear to me." The then 80-year-old priest had a third vision in 1617, similar to the one in Naples.

Fr. Mancinelli became a zealous propagator of the Marian message, and he won over many influential Poles. But the consent of the king was necessary to crown Our Lady. This occurred in 1656, as the successful defense of the monastery in Czestochowa against the Swedes convinced King John II Casimir that the victory was thanks to Our Lady.

On April 1, 1656, King John II Casimir, kneeling beside Cardinal Pietro Vidoni in the cathedral in Lviv, declared Our Lady Queen of Poland: "Today I elect you as my patron and queen of my states." That was a state declaration of the highest order, confirmed by the king of Poland in the presence of the papal nuncio, a declaration that has never been revoked to this day.

GRACIOUS MOTHER OF GOD – image before which King John II Casimir made his declarations.

JOHN II CASIMIR declaring Our Lady Queen of Poland – Lviv, 1656.

Karol Wojtyla, enamored of Polish history, referred to this intellectual and spiritual tradition. He was one of the leading figures of Vatican II, seen as the main architect of the Declaration on Religious Freedom, *Dignitatis humanae*, wherein there is a profound and wise statement that corresponds to the Polish religious tradition: "The truth cannot impose itself except by virtue of its own truth, as it makes its entrance into the mind at once quietly and with power."[46]

The election of Karol Wojtyla was like a bolt out of the blue to the leaders of the Communist bloc, causing panic and horror. They were aware that the new pope, who came from behind the Iron Curtain, knew socialism's weaknesses well. Yuri Andropov, head of the KGB, ordered a special report on how a Pole had become pope. It concluded that it was the result of a plot hatched in Washington to first weaken and then break-up the Warsaw Pact. According to the report, the main originator and organizer of the plot was Zbigniew Brzezinski, an American politician of Polish decent and President Jimmy Carter's national security advisor. Moscow feared that Pope John II's pontificate would revive and activate Catholic circles in Communist countries including the Soviet Union, which would undermine the

CHESS GAME at Camp David between Israeli Prime Minister Menachem Begin and US National Security Advisor Zbigniew Brzezinski. They conversed in Polish.

WHITE HOUSE, Washington, DC.

JOHN PAUL II offering Our Lady of Częstochowa a gold rose in 1979.

DURING HIS PILGRIMAGE to Poland in 1979, John Paul II visited the Jasna Gora monastery, where according to the pope, if one strains one's ear, one can hear Poland's heartbeat.

300

Communist system. Andropov ordered an increase in KGB spying activities in the Vatican.

John Paul II's first two pilgrimages abroad were connected with Communism. At that time the Church in Latin America was in danger of breaking up, as liberation theology – a mixture of Christianity and Marxism – was enjoying great success. It even led some Catholic priests into becoming leftist partisans or members of Communist governments. In Nicaragua, for example, some Catholics saw the class struggle as the only way to eliminate social inequality and to bring human happiness.

John Paul II's first pilgrimage abroad was to Mexico. In 1979 he participated in the general assembly of the Latin American Episcopal Council in Puebla, where he spoke of liberation theology, which had an influence on almost half of all the Catholics in the world.

The pope appealed to the Latin American hierarchs to teach the truth about Christ. He shattered the image of Christ as the revolutionary, telling them that Christ was not a political activist Who fought against Roman domination, nor did He engage in the class struggle. He warned against instrumentalizing religion and the use of force, pointing out that the battle was primarily a spiritual one – Christ with a cross over His shoulder, not a rifle.

John Paul II contrasted Marx's liberation with Christ's, achieved through truth, love for one's neighbor, and forgiveness and reconciliation, not through force. The testing ground for the papal strategy was Poland.

In Mexico, the pope addressed poor Indians in Culiacan. He passionately told them, denouncing the injustice that was ruining the lives of the Latin poor, that he wanted to be the voice of those who had no voice or who were not listened to.

It was likewise in Poland, where the pope arrived in June 1979. As one who had spent all his priestly life fighting for religious freedom, he spoke for millions who were under the yoke of Communism, for those who had been deprived of a voice. During a homily in Gniezno, on seeing a placard in Czech: "Holy Father, do not forget your Czech children", he suddenly stopped reading his text and assured the Czech nation, and all those who were not listened to, that he would never forget them.

During his homily in Gniezno, the pope questioned the Yalta Conference division of Europe. The pope, at a time when the Berlin Wall and the Iron Curtain were absolute certitudes to virtually all the world's leaders, was the first to break the conspiracy of silence as to that matter. He knew Communism inside and out, that it was a colossus with clay feet. He agreed with the poet T. S. Eliot, that politics was a function of culture, while religion was the heart of culture. Hence to him spiritual strength was greater than military strength; fervent prayer could crumble empires.

Papal biographer George Weigel saw John Paul II's pilgrimage to Poland (June 2–10, 1979) as "nine days that changed the world", in that he imparted Poles with a sense of individual dignity and collective strength, thanks to which their fears and sense of hopelessness were dispelled. The pilgrimage was the prime factor in later events, particulary the rise of Solidarity.

Strikes broke out in Poland in August 1980. Television viewers throughout the world were surprised to see a large sign – Lenin

JOHN PAUL II talking to youth from a window.

301

Shipyard – above a gate in Gdansk, as well as an image of Our Lady of Czestochowa. The Communist system, though officially pro-workers, was opposed by them, and not just in their own interests, political or economic. They established the Independent Self-governing Trade Union – Solidarity – motivated by, as stated in the first two chapters of their program, a concern for "justice, democracy, truth, law and order, human dignity, freedom of convictions, reform of the Republic, and not just bread and butter. All the elementary values have been so badly neglected that it is difficult to believe that anything will change for the better without a return to them. An economic protest must be a social protest at the same time; a social protest must be simultaneously a moral protest."[47]

Thus arose Solidarity, the first mass organization between the Elbe and Vladivostok that was completely independent of the Communists. In a short time, ten million of a population of thirty-eight million became members, which was indeed a real catastrophe for the Communists.

Information on Moscow's preparations for armed intervention in Poland to suppress Solidarity reached Washington in December 1980. On hearing of it, John Paul II wrote a letter to Leonid Brezhnev, the

SOLIDARITY UNION logo, the first mass movement in the Communist bloc that was not controlled by the government.

LENIN SHIPYARD in Gdansk – the cradle of Soldarity.

✛

Soviet leader. The letter, despite the diplomatic language, was hard in tone. The pope reminded Brezhnev that a state that was signatory to the Final Act of the Conference on Security and Cooperation in Europe could not interfere in the internal affairs of another signatory state. Hence Poland ought to resolve its own problems, the most urgent of which was the moral restructuring of all the social forces in a "spirit of solidarity".

To the leaders at the Kremlin, the letter was a clear challenge, as the pope had undermined the Brezhnev Doctrine, binding in Communist countries, a doctrine of limited sovereignty, which stated that the Soviet Union had the right to intervene militarily in any country where a Communist government was under threat. Moscow thus justified the invasion of Czechoslovakia in 1968. The pope also wrote of solidarity as a moral restructuring force – though with a small *s* – an obvious allusion to the Solidarity union.

The Soviet Union anxiously kept track of the pope's other activities. They were particularly annoyed with papal decisions concerning Catholics in areas of Soviet influence. On March 2, 1979, the pope

STRIKERS' FAMILIES supporting them outside the shipyard railings.

FR. HENRYK JANKOWSKI – later Solidarity chaplain – said Masses for the strikers in the shipyard.

MEMORIAL CROSS in front of the shipyard entrance – in honor of the workers that were murdered in December 1970.

303

JOSYF SLIPYJ,
Ukranian Greek
Catholic cardinal,
spent 18 years in
Soviet forced-labor
camps.

addressed a pastoral letter to the Czechs and Slovenians, wherein he encouraged them to follow the example of their patron, St. John of Nepomuk, who in defending the Faith opposed a tyrant. The Holy Father addressed a similar message to Hungarians a year later.

On March 19, 1979, John Paul II wrote a letter to the Ukrainian Greek Catholic cardinal Josyf Slipyj concerning the millennium celebrations of the baptism of Kievan Rus' in 1988, which was a slap in the face to the Soviets. Firstly, they thought that only they could decide on celebrations that concerned their own history, not a foreigner attempting to break their monopoly as to the interpretation of Russian history. Secondly, the pope saw Kiev and not Moscow as the spiritual center of Rus. The Soviets considered that to be an assertion of Ukraine's superiority over Russia, which could well arouse Ukrainian aspirations for independence and in turn undermine the stability of the Soviet empire. Thirdly, the papal initiative was seen as an attack on their ideological legitimization, since Christianity to them was a superstition, an "opium for the people". In their view, the millennium ought to be an occasion to express sorrow as to the backwardness of ancestors, rather than an occasion for grand celebrations.

On November 13, 1979, there was a meeting of the Secretariat of the Communist Party of the Soviet Union at the Kremlin. Viktor Chebrikov, deputy head of the KGB, presented the document "Resolution to Counteract Vatican Policy Regarding Socialist Countries". He proposed an increase in anti-Vatican propaganda, particularly among Catholics throughout the world in order to bring about divisions amongst them. He also instructed the KGB to perfect its methods in its struggle against the papacy. The action plan presented in the document was approved by, amongst others, Mikhail Suslov (chief ideologue of the Party) Konstantin Chernenko (general secretary of the Communist Party of the Soviet Union), and Mikhail Gorbachev.

Nearly two weeks later, on November 28, 1979, the Turkish terrorist Mehmet Ali Agca, recently escaped from prison, sent a letter to *Milliyet*, a Turkish daily newspaper in Istanbul, wherein he wrote that he intended to kill the pope, saying that was the sole reason he had escaped from prison.

On May 13, 1981, he appeared in St. Peter's Square, and pulled the trigger of his gun.

ABDI IPEKCI MEMORIAL in Istanbul near the place where he was murdered by Oral Celik and Mehmet Ali Agca on February 1, 1979.

KREMLIN, MOSCOW – the headquarters of world Communism, where decisions were made that affected the entire world.

Request Granted

Request Granted

When John Paul II regained consciousness at the Gemelli Clinic he had no doubt that he owed his life to Our Lady. Later, he often said that one hand had held the gun, while another had directed the bullet. He also said that he had known he would not die, as he had felt Our Lady's protective, motherly presence.

JOHN PAUL II during Mass in Managua, 1983. Images of Nicaraguan revolutionaries, Augusto Sandino and Carlos Fonseca, In the background.

GABRIEL TUROWSKI turned John Paul II's attention to the Fatima apparitions in the context of the attempted assassination in May 1981.

On July 17, 1981, Gabriel Turowski turned the pope's attention to the coincidence of dates between the first apparition in Fatima and the assassination attempt in St. Peter's Square. On June 7, while still in the hospital, John Paul II wrote an act of entrustment to Mary, to be read by the bishops that had gathered in the Basilica of Santa Maria Maggiore in Rome on the occasion of two important anniversaries: the sixteen hundredth anniversary of the First Council of Constantinople and the fifteen hundred fiftieth anniversary of the First Council of Ephesus. The latter Council, in 431, saw the Church's first dogma concerning Our Lady – the Mother of God – which inspired John Paul II to write the act of entrustment and consecration of the whole world to the Blessed Virgin, particularly

309

those people and nations that were in most need of it, which was universally seen as an allusion to peoples enslaved by Communism. The pope personally renewed this act on December 8, 1981, in the same basilica.

His personal secretary, Cardinal Dziwisz, recalled that when the pope familiarized himself with the Fatima message, he immediately saw it as being addressed to him personally, and certain issues then became clear to him. On meeting Bishop Hnilica, John Paul II said that after three months in the hospital

AUGUST 5 – the Feast of Our Lady of the Snows – white flower petals shower down from the dome of Basilica Santa Maria Maggiore.

BASILICA Santa Maria Maggiore, Rome, the most important Marian church in the Eternal City.

310

NAAMAN AND ELISHA paintings by ❶ Abraham van Dijck, ❷ Pieter de Grebber.

NAAMAN AND ELISHA

FROM A POLITICAL or societal point of view there is no connection between prayer and the fall of an empire. There is even incredulity among religious people as to why God would demand an act of consecration to the Immaculate Heart of Mary to occasion the fall of Communism. What is the logic behind it?

Let us take a look at this matter from a theological point of view. We can glean a hint from a Bible story in 2 Kings. It speaks of Naaman, a Syrian general who had leprosy. He set off to Samaria to see Elisha, who, according to his servant, could heal people with incurable diseases. But the Israeli prophet did not even bother to welcome Naaman. Rather he instructed that he be told to wash himself in the Jordan seven times in order to be healed. Naaman was outraged at this advice, which he saw as absurd. Why did Elisha not even see him? Why was he to bathe in the Jordan, and not in another river? And why seven times? Angry, he wanted to return home, but his servants persuaded him to listen to the prophet. After all, if he had been told to do something much more difficult, he would

have done it. So why could he not do such a simple thing? The general bathed in the Jordan and was healed.

This story shows that God does not condition His favors on gigantic tasks. Only trust and humility are needed to carry out instructions that at times, from a human point of view, could well seem to be absurd. As St. Paul writes: "God chose what is foolish in the world to shame the wise, God chose what is weak in the world to shame the strong, God chose what is low and despised in the world, even things that are not, to bring to nothing things that are, so that no flesh might boast in the presence of God" (1 Cor 1: 27–29).

he came to understand that he had to respond to the Fatima call, and that in his opinion it was the only way to save the world from wars, catastrophes, and atheism.

John Paul II recalled Fr. Petrus Pavlicek, who visited him on May 7, 1981, six days before the assassination attempt. The Austrian monk did not have to tell the pope that his country had been delivered from Communism thanks to the consecration to Our Lady of Fatima, as the pope knew this perfectly well. The aged Franciscan, so ailing that that he could not fulfill his priestly ministry, offered up his own suffering for the pope.

Meanwhile the world was awaiting Mehmet Ali Agca's trial, which began on July 20, 1981, in the Palace of Justice in Rome. He testified that he worked alone and that he did not intend to kill the pope. He also stated that the Italian court was not

P. PETRUS PAVLICEK OFM.

FR. PETRUS PAVLICEK, an Austrian Franciscan, offered up his suffering before his death for John Paul II.

PALACE OF JUSTICE, Rome, where Mehmet Ali Agca's trial took place.

authorized to examine his case, as he shot the pope on Church property, hence the Vatican ought to hear his case. So he refused to answer any questions.

Two days later, Judge Severino Santapichi announced the verdict – a life sentence. On July 23, at Rebibbia Prison, Agca stated that he would not appeal the sentence. The Italian judiciary, however, had no doubts that Agca had not worked alone but was the last link in an elaborate plot. Hence investigations continued.

Meanwhile the situation in Poland was becoming more and more strained. The government was troubled by the rapid development of Solidarity, the very existence of which was a challenge to Communist rule. The mood was such that the union leaders had to curb anti-Communist inclinations and the independence aspirations of the people, afraid that bold

SOLIDARITY LEAFLET of March 1981, about the beatings of union activists by the police in Bydgoszcz, Poland.

SOVIET ARMED intervention in Afghanistan, 1979.

313

ROMAN FORUM – heart of ancient Rome.

CIA DIRECTOR William Casey personally informed John Paul II of the plans to introduce martial law in Poland.

RYSZARD KUKLINSKI was exposed by Fr. Jausz Bolonek, a Communist agent in the Vatican. Later, Fr. Bolonek became an archbishop and an apostolic nuncio in five countries.

positions and bold talk about freedom could well annoy the authorities and provoke repressions.

The Soviet Union would have readily intervened militarily in Poland, as in Hungary in 1956 and Czechoslovakia in 1968. But as it was engaged in armed conflict in Afghanistan from December 1979, it pressured Gen. Jaruzelski into dealing with the incipient rebellion himself. In 1981 Jaruzelski had total power, being the prime minister, the first secretary of the Polish United Workers' Party, and the minister of defense, hence he was in charge of the government, the Communist Party, and the Polish Army. He prepared to do battle with Solidarity.

Col. Ryszard Kuklinski, who worked for the General Staff of the Polish Armed Forces, learnt of the plans to suppress Solidarity, which he immediately passed on to his American contact, including information about imminent martial law. On hearing about Jaruzelski's intentions, William Casey, director of the CIA, flew to Rome to convey personally the

information to John Paul II, as he had no trust in the telecommunications system.

Unfortunately a Polish priest, recruited in 1971 by the security service as a spy, under the pseudonym "Lamos", took part in the meeting between the pope and Casey as a translator and informed his contact about it. He also provided the Polish government with more than three hundred pages of highly confidential information. When the security service archives in Warsaw were made available after the fall of Communism, it turned out that during the postwar period about one hundred Communist agents had been active in the Vatican.

A secret dispatch from Rome informed Gen. Jaruzelski that there was an American spy at the highest level in the Polish Army, because the top secret plan that Casey revealed to the pope was known by only a few high-ranking officers in Warsaw. Counterintelligence began intensive investigations, with those under suspicion placed under round-the-clock

REAGAN AND WOJTYLA

DURING WORLD WAR II, Hollywood actor Ronald Reagan was engaged in helping displaced persons who had fled from National Socialism or Communism in Europe to the United States. On hearing about the realities of life in areas of Soviet influence, he decided to support nations enslaved by the Soviet Union.

His American political career began on October 27, 1964, with his television speech "Time for Choosing", when he said that Americans could not buy peace and security by coming to an understanding with the Soviet regime, as they would thus contemptibly leave a billion people behind the Iron Curtain at the mercy of Communism. No other American politician spoke so loudly and so clearly against Communism as an enemy of humanity. It was he who first called the Soviet Union the "evil empire".

When he was a candidate for the US presidency, he watched John Paul II's pilgrimage to Poland and was deeply moved by the pope, whose views he shared. In 1981 both of them experienced an assassination attempt, and both forgave their assassins, which brought them closer together. While Reagan was president, the United States and the Holy See established diplomatic relations with each other (1984).

observation. Kuklinski felt that the Poles were closing in on him. He managed to inform the Americans that he could be arrested at any moment, aware that there would be but one punishment: a death sentence.

To this day it has not been revealed how the colonel managed to flee Poland (November 7, 1981). What is known is that a few dozen CIA officers were involved in the operation. On November 11, Kuklinski, his wife, and their two sons ended up safely in the United States.

On December 13, 1981, Gen. Jaruzelski followed through on his plan and imposed martial law in Poland. Solidarity was delegalized and its main leaders (led by Lech Walesa) were interned. Strikes broke out, but they were brutally pacified. Basic civil rights were suspended and a curfew was imposed. At the Wujek coal mine in Katowice the army and the police killed nine recalcitrant miners.

The suppression of Solidarity confirmed the pope in his decision to fulfill the Fatima message. On the first anniversary of the assassination attempt, John Paul II went to Fatima to thank God and Mary for his life being saved. But on May 12, 1983, he found himself in danger once again. When walking

TANKS ON Polish streets during martial law were not a rarity.

ANTI-COMMUNIST LEAFLET from the time of martial law in Poland.

FATIMA ATTACKER

IN 1982, Fr. Juan Krohn was sentenced to six years imprisonment for attempting to kill the pope, but he was released after just three years for good conduct. A Portuguese journalist fell in love with him when visiting him in prison in order to write an article about him. He eventually left the priesthood and married her.

In 1985 they settled in Brussels, where Krohn became a sought-after lawyer, famous for his eccentric behavior in court. In 1986 he was accused of setting fire to the headquarters of the Basque Herri Batasuna Party, which was connected with terrorists, but he was eventually cleared of the allegations.

In 2000, however, he was sentenced to five years imprisonment for attempted murder. When the king of Spain Juan Carlos arrived in Brussels, Krohn broke through a line of bodyguards and ran towards the king and the Belgian royal couple, King Albert II and Queen Paola, waving his hands and shouting that the king of Spain had murdered his own younger brother, Alfonso, in order to become king.

To this day there is no evidence that Krohn participated in a plot on the pope's life. It appears that he acted alone.

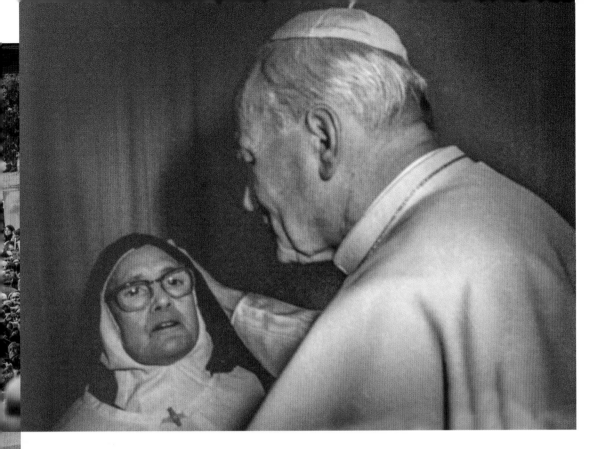

up the steps towards the main altar in the basilica, a priest, shouting, bayonet in hand, threw himself at the pope. A Vatican bodyguard, Camillo Cibin, grabbed the would-be assassin's hand and quickly disarmed him. The pope, slightly hurt, turned around and blessed the attacker with a sign of the cross. The priest shouted: "Down with the pope! I accuse you of destroying the Church!"

The attacker was thirty-two-year-old Fr. Juan Fernandez Krohn, whose life abounded with many strange events. A Belgian lawyer of Spanish descent, he was ordained in the Catholic Church in 1978. Horrified by the crisis in the Church in Western Europe, for which he blamed Vatican II, he became a member of the Society of St. Pius X, which protested against some Vatican II resolutions. But the Lefebvrists dismissed him, as they thought that he was mentally unbalanced. He then became affiliated with ultraradical traditionalists, the Sedevacantists, who claim that the last valid pope was Pius XII and that those since have been anti-popes. In court, Fr. Krohn admitted that he wanted to kill the pope, seeing him as a Soviet spy out to destroy the Church from within.

JOHN PAUL II thanking Our Lady of Fatima for saving him on May 13, 1982 – first anniversary of the assassination attempt.

SR. LUCIA met John Paul II three times: 1982, 1991, and 2000.

319

On the morning of May 13, 1982, John Paul had a twenty-minute meeting with Sr. Lucia, the details of which are unknown. Then the Holy Father celebrated Mass at the basilica in Fatima, attended by over one million people. He also consecrated the world to the Immaculate Heart of Mary, which – as he said – was equivalent to consecrating the world to the Savior's pierced Heart, the source of salvation.

The consecration was not in union with all the bishops throughout the world, however. The Holy Father had intended the full participation of the world's bishops, but his letters to them arrived too late. Hence Sr. Lucia stated that the consecration did not comply with Our Lady's demands.

The evening of the same day, the pope prayed for forty-five minutes before the statue of Our Lady in the Chapel of

Apparitions. As a sign of gratitude for his life being saved, he had the bullet that Agca had fired at him inserted in an aperture, which had been made in Our Lady's crown.

During his visit to Portugal the pope received a statue of Our Lady of Fatima, which he placed on a small table by his bed in the Vatican. He kissed the hands and the feet of the statue every evening and recited the Rosary there before retiring.

PORTUGAL

Fatima

•Lisbon

In January 1983, Judge Ilario Martella, who headed the investigation of the plot to kill John Paul II, maintained that he could identify those behind the attempted assassination and could reconstruct the course of their activities on the basis of Agca's testimonies between December 1981 and January 1983.

At first the assassin's testimonies seemed logical and coherent. While in Tehran, Iran, he claimed, he met Wladimir Kuziczkin, a KGB agent who directed him to Bulgaria. Agca said he then went to Sofia, where he met with Bulgarian secret police who offered him three million West German marks to kill John Paul II. Agca, who had already killed a Turkish journalist, said he willingly accepted the offer. From then on, he said, the Bulgarians oversaw all his actions leading up to May 13, 1981.

GOLD CROWN – Our Lady of Fatima. Made in 1942 from jewelry donated by Portuguese women, it weighs 2.5 pounds and consists of 2,650 precious stones (including 950 diamonds and 313 pearls). In the center an aperture houses one of the bullets fired at the pope by Mehmet Ali Agca.

ANOTHER BULLET from Acga's gun – John Paul II Family Home Museum, Wadowice.

After October 20, 1983, however, Agca's testimony unraveled. On that day two Bulgarians visited him at the Rebibbia Prison. Officially they were judges, but Martella and others believed that they were high-ranking secret police officers. One was Col. Jordan Ormankov, the other, his subordinate, was Stefan Markov Petkov. They claimed the reason for their visit was an inquiry in Sofia concerning Agca, who was alleged to have used a false passport in Bulgaria.

At one point during the interrogation by the Bulgarians, Martella proposed a coffee break. Ormankov went for coffee,

321

STASI SEAL – East German Ministry for State Security.

STASI HEADQUARTERS in East Berlin.

STASI CONFERENCE room.

while Petkov, who was officially the translator, remained alone with Agca for thirty minutes. It is not known what they talked about, but from then on Agca changed his testimony, constantly making up new narratives, full of inaccuracies and fabrications. Finally, he claimed to be the Messiah, hence he was regarded as being out of his mind, his testimonies not credible. The "Bulgarian connection" was never proved in court, and only Agca was sentenced.

Years later, in 2005, the Italian press reported that released East German security service (STASI) documents linked Agca with Bulgarian and East German agents working under orders from the KGB. According to these documents, in 1983 Ormankov met with STASI officers to request a disinformation campaign in the West to cover up the "Bulgarian tracks" in the assassination attempt.

Shortly afterward, numerous conspiracy theories appeared in articles, books, and even films. These blamed the attempted murder of the pope on various individuals and organizations: CIA, NATO, P2 (a Masonic group), Islamic fundamentalists, Turkish right-wing extremists, Lefebvrists, and Italian special services. Later, however, the Berlin office managing the STASI

archives said it had no evidence linking the STASI or the Soviet and Bulgarian secret police to the assassination attempt.

Agca implicated another person during the course of his investigation and trial. On November 25, 1982, the Italian police detained Sergei Antonov, a Balkan Airlines representative in Rome, after Agca accused him of being involved in the plot to kill the pope. Antonov was acquitted in March 1986 after investigators failed to find convincing evidence of his guilt and Agca withdrew his earlier testimony against him.

Although Communist antipathy for the pope could not be proved by Agca's actions, it was demonstrated in another way. In March 1983 John Paul II was directly confronted with Communist hostility when he visited Nicaragua, where after the overthrow of the dictator Anastasio Somoza, the Sandinista National Liberation Front, sponsored by the Soviets, assumed power.

SERGEI ANTONOV, a Rome-based representative for Balkan Airlines, was arrested in November 1982 and charged with participating in the assassination attempt on the pope. His trial lasted from May 1985 to March 1986. He was acquitted because of a lack of evidence.

323

FIDEL CASTRO
– a great hero
to liberation
theologians.

**CELEBRATIONS IN
MANAGUA** – 10th
anniversary of
the Sandinista
revolution.

Catholic priests served in the new government, for example, Fr. Miguel d'Escoto (foreign minister) and Fr. Ernesto Cardenal (minister of culture), one of the most influential advocates of liberation theology. Fr. Cardenal claimed that the Gospel had led him to Marxism and maintained that the common aim of Christianity and Communism was the building of God's kingdom on earth. According to Cardenal, Fidel Castro's regime in Cuba (which ruthlessly persecuted the Church) realized New Testament premises. It was sinful to criticize the Soviet system, he said, and the very thought of the existence of forced-labor camps in the Soviet Union was evidence of an immoral person.

On March 4, 1983, there was a papal Mass in Central Park, Managua. There was no cross on the altar, but enormous images of Marx, Lenin, Augusto Sandino, and other Communist heroes towered above it. The best sectors were occupied by the ruling party activists, who had microphones hidden on them while the organizers secretly controlled an alternative sound system. From the very beginning of the Mass, the pope was drowned out. State leaders, headed by President Daniel Ortega, set the tone, shouting "Power to the people" with party activists joining in. When the pope tried to outshout the Sandinistas during the homily, his microphone was silenced while the concealed alternative system was amplified. Hence the pope could not communicate with the multitude that was far from the altar. Unable to hear the pope, they could but cheer him.

The Nicaraguan government saw the Managuan operation as a propaganda success. But it was mistaken, as the Mass, transmitted live throughout Latin America, provoked public outrage against the Sandinistas' treatment of the pope, which in turn occasioned that the pope was more enthusisatically welcomed than expected in other Latin countries.

Three months later (June 1983), when martial law was in force in Poland, the pope raised his compatriots' spirits, plunged in sorrow and even despair because of the break-up of Solidarity. He called for the defense of human dignity, but without

AGAINST LIBERATION THEOLOGY

IN 1982, JOHN PAUL II requested Cardinal Joseph Ratzinger, prefect of the Congregation for the Doctrine of the Faith, to draw up the Church's stance regarding liberation theology in order to establish whether it was in accord with Catholic teaching; a Holy Office document was announced on the matter on August 6, 1984.

The document, *Instruction on Certain Aspects of the Theology of Liberation*, was a strong criticism of the movement. It warned that one could not reduce Christianity to a political dimension, nor instrumentalize it in the name of social justice. It mentioned that the class struggle was not the main driving force in history, nor could it justify force on the grounds that the aim justifies the means. It stated that it was not possible to build God's kingdom on earth as some Marxist theologians maintained. It declared that unjust political, social, and economic structures were not the sources of evil, but human hearts.

One week after the announcement of the *Instruction*, the Holy See ordered all religious to resign from government positions in Nicaragua. Fr. Miguel d'Escoto and Fr. Ernesto Cardenal, both government ministers, did not comply with the order.

LIBERATION THEOLOGIANS depicted Christ as a socialist.

OSCAR ROMERO, archbishop of San Salvador, murdered in 1980 by a Salvadoran death squad – beatified by Pope Francis.

FR. ERNESTO CARDENAL – minister of culture in Nicaragua's Communist government from 1979 to 1987.

Rome

ITALY

JOHN PAUL II
consecrating the world (including Russia) to the Immaculate Heart of Mary in St. Peter's, Rome, on March 25, 1984.

326

recourse to force, and he spoke about a moral renewal, the power of the spirit, and the building of community. He appealed against being carried away by hate. All in all, the approach was completely different from the one liberation theologians advocated in Nicaragua. He did not advocate the class struggle, but social solidarity, embodied by the Solidarity union.

The pope himself gave an example of forgiving persecutors. On December 27, 1983, he visited Agca in prison. At one point the pope was alone with him; both sat, leaning towards each other, whispering to each other. We still do not know what they talked about.

John Paul II was determined to accomplish the consecration to Our Lady according to her conditions of 1917, which he did on March 25, 1984, the Feast of the Annunciation, in St. Peter's, Rome. Over three months earlier invitations had been sent to all the Catholic bishops throughout the world to participate in the consecration. Some of the hierarchs personally attended the occasion at the Vatican, while the majority united with the pope in their own dioceses. Five patriarchs of the Orthodox Church also joined in the consecration. Thus, the consecration was made in union with bishops throughout the world.

Bishop Pavel Hnilica was one of those who most desired to participate in the consecration. He had discussed it several times with the pope, who informed him that numerous bishops and Catholic theologians were against consecrating Russia to the Immaculate Heart of Mary. On hearing of the pope's intention, he came up with an insane idea. Since the consecration concerned Russia, that it might cease to spread its errors throughout the world, then one should approach the main source of the said errors: Moscow, the Kremlin!

In February 1984, Bishop Hnilica found himself in Calcutta, where he often helped Mother Teresa. He asked the sisters of the Missionaries of Charity to say a novena for the success of his mission. In India he managed to obtain a visa to the Soviet Union.

On March 22, at 4:00 a.m., he landed at Sheremetyevo International Airport in Moscow, accompanied by the Austrian

priest Fr. Leo Maasburg. The bishop was in civilian clothes, and possessed an Italian passport, yet a customs official was unhappy about something. He detained the bishop and phoned somewhere. As it was very early in the morning nobody took his call. Meanwhile, the bishop prayed the Rosary, on beads Mother Teresa had given him. Eventually the official gave up trying to contact someone and allowed the bishop through customs.

There was still the baggage check, however. Fortunately, the customs officer turned out to be a believer, so he did not raise the alarm when he saw a Bible, the bishop's crucifix, and several dozen religious medals. The bishop gave him several mementoes from the Vatican and left the airport without any problems.

When the pope was preparing for the consecration in Rome, Bishop Hnilica and Fr. Leo Maasburg appeared at the Kremlin. They entered the part designated for tourists, where they had

CONSECRATION OF THE WORLD TO THE IMMACULATE HEART MARY

1. "We have recourse to your protection, holy Mother of God".

As we utter the words of this antiphon with which the Church of Christ has prayed for centuries, we find ourselves today before you, Mother, in the Jubilee Year of the Redemption.

We find ourselves united with all the pastors of the Church in a particular bond whereby we constitute a body and a college, just as by Christ's wish the Apostles constituted a body and college with Peter.

In the bond of this union, we utter the words of the present Act, in which we wish to include, once more, the Church's hopes and anxieties for the modern world.

Forty years ago and again ten years later, your servant Pope Pius XII, having before his eyes the painful experiences of the human family, entrusted and consecrated to your Immaculate Heart the whole world, especially the peoples for which by reason of their situation you have particular love and solicitude.

This world of individuals and nations we too have before our eyes today: the world of the second millennium that is drawing to a close, the modern world, our world!

The Church, mindful of the Lord's words: "Go… and make disciples of all nations… and lo, I am with you always, to the close of the age" (Mt 28:19–20), has, at the Second Vatican Council, given fresh life to her awareness of her mission in this world.

And therefore, O Mother of individuals and peoples, you who know all their sufferings and their hopes, you who have a mother's awareness of all the struggles between good and evil, between light and darkness, which afflict the modern world, accept the cry which we, moved by the Holy Spirit, address directly to your Heart. Embrace, with the love of the Mother and Handmaid of the Lord, this human world of ours, which we entrust and consecrate to you, for we are full of concern for the earthly and eternal destiny of individuals and peoples.

In a special way we entrust and consecrate to you those individuals and nations which particularly need to be thus entrusted and consecrated.

"We have recourse to your protection, holy Mother of God": despise not our petitions in our necessities.

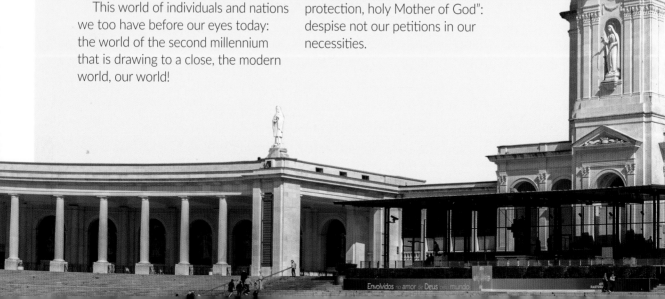

Envolvidos no amor de Deus todo o mundo

2. Behold, as we stand before you, Mother of Christ, before your Immaculate Heart, we desire, together with the whole Church, to unite ourselves with the consecration which, for love of us, your Son made of himself to the Father: "For their sake", he said, "I consecrate myself that they also may be consecrated in the truth" (Jn 17:19). We wish to unite ourselves with our Redeemer in this his consecration for the world and for the human race, which, in his divine Heart, has the power to obtain pardon and to secure reparation.

The power of this consecration lasts for all time and embraces all individuals, peoples and nations. It overcomes every evil that the spirit of darkness is able to awaken, and has in fact awakened in our times, in the heart of man and in his history.

How deeply we feel the need for the consecration of humanity and the world—our modern world—in union with Christ himself! For the redeeming work of Christ must be shared in by the world through the Church.

The present year of the Redemption shows this: the special Jubilee of the whole Church.

Above all creatures, may you be blessed, you, the Handmaid of the Lord, who in the fullest way obeyed the divine call!

Hail to you, who are wholly united to the redeeming consecration of your Son!

Mother of the Church! Enlighten the People of God along the paths of faith, hope and love! Enlighten especially the peoples whose consecration and entrustment by us you are awaiting. Help us to live in the truth of the consecration of Christ for the entire human family of the modern world.

3. In entrusting to you, oh Mother, the world, all individuals and peoples, we also entrust to you this very consecration of the world, placing it in your motherly Heart.

Immaculate Heart! Help us to conquer the menace of evil, which so easily takes root in the hearts of the people of today, and whose

MONUMENT OF JOHN PAUL II – in front of the basilica in Fatima, which he visited during his three pilgrimages to Fatima.

immeasurable effects already weigh down upon our modern world and seem to block the paths towards the future!

From famine and war, deliver us.

From nuclear war, from incalculable self-destruction, from every kind of war, deliver us.

From sins against the life of man from its very beginning, deliver us.

From hatred and from the demeaning of the dignity of the children of God, deliver us.

From every kind of injustice in the life of society, both national and international, deliver us.

From readiness to trample on the commandments of God, deliver us.

From attempts to stifle in human hearts the very truth of God, deliver us.

From the loss of awareness of good and evil, deliver us.

From sins against the Holy Spirit, deliver us, deliver us.

From sins against the Holy Spirit, deliver us, deliver us.

Accept, Oh Mother of Christ, this cry laden with the sufferings of all individual human beings, laden with the sufferings of whole societies.

Help us with the power of the Holy Spirit to conquer all sin: individual sin and the "sin of the world", in all its manifestations.

Let there be revealed, once more, in the history of the world the infinite saving power of the Redemption: the power of merciful Love! May it put a stop to evil! May it transform consciences! May your Immaculate Heart reveal for all the light of Hope![48]

John Paul II
March 25, 1984

to leave their hand luggage. The bishop began a friendly chat with a guard who quickly took a liking to him. Hence the bishop asked him if he could keep some personal things on him. The security guard allowed the bishop to take his baggage inside.

Once inside the Kremlin they made their way to the nearest church, St. Michael the Archangel, which had been turned into a museum. Fr. Maasburg kept watch while the bishop took a copy of *Pravda*, a Communist Party newspaper, out of his bag. Inside the newspaper there was a page from *L'Osservatore Romano* that contained the consecration text. The bishop read the text, strongly accenting the word "Russia", spiritually uniting himself with the Holy Father and all the hierarchs throughout the world.

Then the two "tourists" made their way to the Church of the Dormition (Assumption) of Our Lady, and the consecration of Russia to the Immaculate Heart of Mary was repeated. The bishop then approached the patriarchal throne, laid a Marian medal on it, and prayed that the true patriarch might shortly ascend the throne.

PRAVDA MASTHEAD – Soviet Communist Party official newspaper.

TSAR CANNON, Kremlin, Moscow – never fired.

CHURCH of the Dormition of Our Lady (Assumption), Kremlin – a museum after World War II.

331

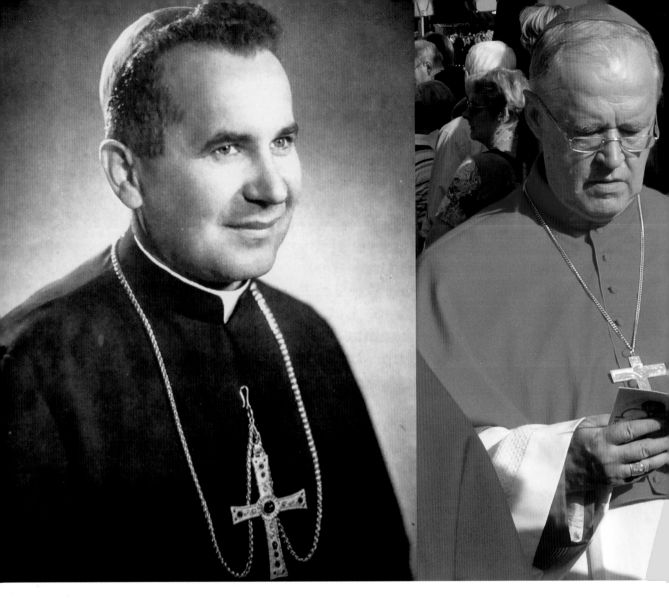

SLOVAKIAN BISHOP
Pavol Hnilica –
organized a daring
visit to the Kremlin in
March 1984.

**GERMAN
CARDINAL**
Paul Josef
Cordes –
John Paul
II's trusted
associate.

As they had not drawn attention to themselves, they decided on a yet more audacious step. The bishop took two aspirin bottles – which contained water and wine – out of his bag as well as a little nylon pouch that contained hosts. He again opened the newspaper, which also contained a Latin Mass form for the Feast of the Assumption. Face hidden behind the pages of the newspaper, from afar he looked as if he were a hardened Communist who could not refrain from reading the Soviet press even in a church. In reality he was saying Mass, virtually at the very center of Communism: the Kremlin.

During the consecration on March 25, 1984, John Paul II did not mention Russia directly but spoke of nations that most

urgently needed to be consecrated to the Immaculate Heart of Mary. Cardinal Paul Josef Cordes recalled that shortly after the consecration the pope confided to him that he considered mentioning Russia but gave up the idea on the counsel of his advisers who persuaded him that the Soviets would have seen it as an ostentatious provocation.

Hence many question the spiritual efficacy of the consecration. Others maintain that it brought graces, not full, but partial graces, as did the consecrations of 1942 and 1952 by Pius XII. Bishop of Leiria Alberto Cosme do Amaral stated that the pope – who became silent for a moment during the consecration – mentioned Russia mentally. Sr. Lucia said at the time that Pope John Paul II would do all that he could. She later said that he had granted Our Lady's request and that his consecrations had been accepted by heaven.[49]

JAN HNILICA – the bishop's brother, and Fr. Jaroslaw Cielecki, who was one of Bishop Hnilica's closest cooperaters from 1998 to 2006 (Grzegorz Gorny in the middle).

333

Fall of the Evil Empire

CHAPTER 13

Fall of the Evil Empire

As late as 1988 the majority of Sovietologists in Western countries did not expect the demise of Communism. They forecast that the Soviet Union would exist for many years to come. Many politicians did not want it to break up as they feared that would mean a terrible war, with a countless number of victims. Yet it was soon to be otherwise.

BERLIN WALL – its demolition symbolized the end of Communism in Europe.

From 1983 to 1984 great tension grew between NATO and the Warsaw Pact. US President Ronald Reagan realized that the policy of detente had not brought the desired results as Communism continued to spread its influence throughout the world. Hence he initiated a new chapter in international policy – the Reagan Doctrine, which helped any nation, government, or movement that fought against Communism. He urged Western governments to impose an embargo on the supply of advanced technologies to Communist countries and came to an understanding with Saudi Arabia to increase petroleum output. He thus reduced its cost, which mainly affected the Soviet Union, whose economy was based on the export of oil.

337

MONUMENT of Communist leader Felix Dzerzhinsky, Warsaw – pulled down in 1989.

But Reagan primarily renewed the arms race. Moreover, he referred to the rhetoric from George Lucas' films, calling the Soviet Union an "evil empire". He initiated the Star Wars program, that is, a defense system capable of destroying ballistic missiles aimed at the United States or its allies, not hiding the fact that his objective was to bring the Soviet Union to its knees.

An intrinsic feature of Communism, evident in all centralized economies, is its inefficiency, which results in the poverty of the majority of its inhabitants and the chronic lack of basic goods. Before World War I, Russia was the granary of Europe, with an enormous surplus of grain, but under Communism it had to import it. In Ethiopia, home of the coffee plant, coffee became scarce under the rule of Mengistu Haile Mariam. The technological gap

SOVIET BALLISTIC missile.

BALLISTIC MISSILE – parade in Red Square, Moscow, displaying the Soviet Union's military power.

NORTH SEA Heroes
Monument –
Severomorsk naval
base.

SOVIET JET – pride
of the USSR Air
Force.

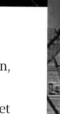

between the West, where there was universal computerization, and the East, where one could but dream of it, increased.

Kremlin leaders were aware that in the long run the Soviet economy would not withstand American competition, particularly the arms race. Some of them concluded that the only way to save the system was to attack the West while they still had a military advantage, both nuclear and conventional.

Marshal Nikolai Ogarkov advocated a preemptive attack by the Warsaw Pact forces on Western Europe. Simultaneously, a Soviet fleet, together with air cover, was to cut off Western Europe from American supplies, while the main burden of the battle for the Atlantic was to rest on the Northern Fleet that was based in Severomorsk. But Moscow could not decide on such a step as there was a dispute between the supporters and the opponents of the attack.

Frequent changes of the Communist Party's general secretary, that is, the actual leader of the government, did not favor the decision-making process. Seventy-five-year-old Leonid Brezhnev

MARSHAL NIKOLAI
Ogarkov, author of
USSR war doctrine.

339

STRING OF DEATHS
Three USSR leaders died within just two-and-a-half years of one another: Leonid Brezhnev, Yuri Andropov, and Konstantin Chernenko.
Their early deaths heralded the decline of the empire.

died on November 10, 1982. His successor was sixty-eight-year-old Yuri Andropov, head of the KGB, responsible for, among other things, putting down the uprising in Hungary in 1956. But after only three months in office he needed dialysis treatment due to kidney failure and died fifteen months later. He was succeeded by seventy-three-year-old Konstantin Chernenko, who was seriously ill and did not have the strength to fulfill adequately the responsibilities of a leader, dying not quite one year after assuming office.

SOLIDARITY MARTYR

THE INCEASING WEAKNESS of the Communist system did not cause a reduction in brutality. From 1981 to 1989 there were over 100 political murders in Poland. The best-known victim of the security service was Fr. Jerzy Popieluszko, who was kidnapped and then murdered in October 1984.

During martial law the churches in Poland were oases of freedom, where, after the break-up of Solidarity, society was spiritually sustained, where the opposition found shelter, and where the repressed and their families were helped. Fr. Popieluszko was one of the priests who was very active, whose motto was, after St. Paul, "Overcome evil with good."

The murder of Fr. Popieluszko – the Solidarity chaplain – was the only political crime in the Polish People's Republic that ended up in court. In 1985 four security service officers were sentenced to imprisonment, though the circumstances surrounding the murder had not been fully explained, as is still the case today. Fr. Popieluszko was beatified on June 6, 2010.

JERZY POPIELUSZKO, Solidarity chaplain – political murder victim.

CROSS near the dam in Poland, where the murderers threw Fr. Popieluszko's body into the Vistula.

FR. POPIELUSZKO'S funeral, Warsaw, 1984 – thousands attended.

President Reagan encouraged an arms race with the Soviet Union because he did not believe that the Soviets would start a war, as a nuclear conflict would have ended in catastrophe for the whole world. His assumption would have been correct had his opponents reasoned rationally. But they were guided by a utopian ideology, which was linked with imperialistic ambitions.

Reagan's assumption was based on information that had been supplied by Col. Kuklinski, thanks to which the Soviet Union's defense system was transparent to the United States. Kuklinski became a Pentagon adviser, having spent many years working for the Warsaw Pact General Staff. Hence he was familiar with the thinking and planning of Russian military strategists, and he was able to predict the moves of the Soviet top brass.

At that time incidents that could well have led to a global war were still on the increase. On September 1, 1983, a Soviet fighter jet shot down a South Korean passenger plane, a Boeing 747, killing all 269 people aboard. The plane was flying from Anchorage,

PASSENGER PLANE
– Korean Air Lines.

KOREAN AIR LINES

HL7456

大韓航空

ARCTIC OCEAN

KAL 007,
246 passenger
23 crew

Ultimate
destination

USSR

Sea of

Sakhalin

CHINA

Sea of Japan

Seoul
SOUTH
KOREA   Tokio

JAPAN

Alaska, to Seoul, South Korea, but in passing over the island of Sakhalin it violated Soviet Union air space.

The shooting down of a passenger plane was of great significance to the balance of power in Europe. Hitherto the Soviet Union had a decided advantage regarding medium-range nuclear missiles, which were aimed at Western European capitals. NATO countries were at a disadvantage as they refused to install missile launchers on their territories. President Reagan's administration sought to establish such installations, but European governments were under the influence of leftists and pacifists. The situation changed when the Boeing was shot down. Great Britain, Germany, Italy, Holland, and Belgium agreed to accept American medium-range cruise missiles in Europe beginning in November 1983. The Soviet Union realized that its military advantage was diminishing, that it was losing its trump cards in the rivalry with the West. Contrary to Reagan's expectations, they thought of attacking as soon as possible.

MAP DEPICTING the Boeing 747 flight from Anchorage, Alaska, to Seoul, South Korea.

SOVIET fighter Su-15.

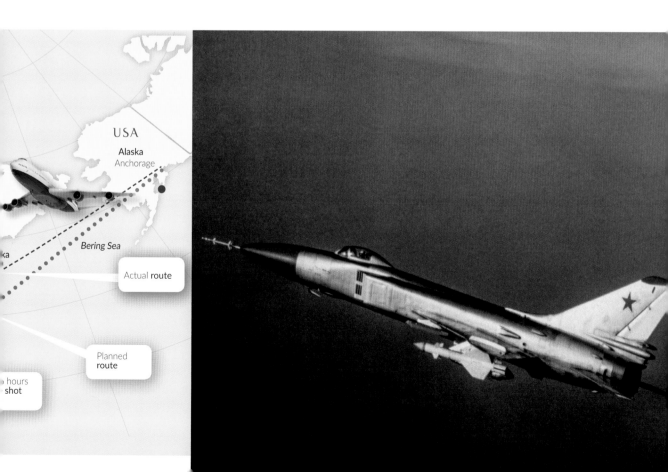

USA
Alaska
Anchorage

Bering Sea

Actual **route**

Planned **route**

hours **shot**

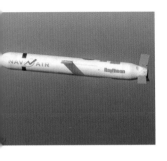

BGM-109 TOMAHAWK
– American cruise
missile.

**PACIFIST
DEMONSTRATIONS**
in Western
countries were
often instigated by
the Soviet special
services.

**CATASTROPHE
IN SEVEROMORSK**
on May 13, 1984,
destroyed the
Russian Northern
Fleet's battle
capacity.

Severomorsk

• Moscow

SOVIET RUSSIA

It was precisely then, when a global nuclear war was imminent, that John Paul II consecrated the whole world to the Immaculate Heart of Mary (Rome, March 25, 1984). Shortly afterwards, there was a series of events that changed the course of history.

May 13, 1984, the first anniversary of the Fatima apparitions, saw the Soviet fleet's greatest postwar catastrophe. It was probably caused by a sailor's cigarette, which caused a major fire at the Severomorsk naval base, and which in turn caused the stockpile of naval missiles to explode. Five hundred eighty of the nine hundred anti-aircraft missiles were destroyed, as well as three hundred twenty of the four hundred surface-to-surface missiles, which could carry atomic warheads. Two to three hundred perished. The Northern Fleet lost its strike capacity in a single day. From then on the Soviet Union was not capable of conducting a war for the control of the Atlantic. Marshal Ogarkov's doctrine was impossible to realize.

Col. Kuklinski gave the final blow to the Soviet expansion plans. The Russian top brass was unaware that he had been revealing the Warsaw Pact's top secrets to the CIA for ten years. At a certain point during negotiations between Moscow and Washington, the Americans revealed files – code-named Albatros, concerning detailed plans of the location of a system of bunkers as a command center for the Soviet Army – that changed the course of the negotiations. It became clear to the Moscow generals that if they attacked NATO countries they would be killed on the very first day.

Years later, Sr. Lucia wrote: "Everyone knows perfectly well that we went through one of the most critical moments in human history, when the great, mutually hostile powers planned a nuclear war that would have destroyed the world, if not the whole world, then the greater part of it. And what would have remained? What chances of survival? And who could have dissuaded those arrogant people, surrounded by their war plans …? Who, if not God?"[50]

In 1985, in a Coimbra convent, Sr. Lucia had another apparition of Our Lady, who told her that the entrustment and consecration carried out by John Paul II saved the world from a nuclear war.

Sr. Lucia disclosed this in a discussion with two cardinals, Antony Padiyara from India and Ricardo Vidal from the Philippines. But she also stated that the danger still existed, as the devil did not sleep but continually attacked people and God.

The Kremlin elite knew that they would not win against the West, with the economy falling apart at the seams and generation changes at the top level. On March 11, 1985, fifty-one-year-old Mikhail Gorbachev became the leader of the Soviet Union. He soon announced his *glasnost* (openness) and *perestroika* (restructuring) policies to reform the system, but it was essentially unreformable.

345

Stanowimy organizację
SOLIDARNOŚĆ WALCZĄCA
Naszą dewizą: „wolni i solidarni".
Wyrośliśmy z powszechnego ruchu
społeczno – wyzwoleńczego,
z NSZZ „Solidarność"/.../. Zmierzar
niepodległej, demokratycznej Polsk
Dążymy do wyswobodzenia narodó
z pęt komunizmu.

SOLIDARNOŚĆ WALCZĄCA

WARSAW UNIVERSITY students' strike. Main Gate covered with banners.

UNDERGROUND LEAFLET – Fighting Solidarity.

Gorbachev attempted to maintain the ruling Communist Party's monopoly, limiting the spheres where freedom of action was allowed. But the nations that were enslaved by Moscow did not want partial freedom; the Poles, Hungarians, Czechs, Slovaks, Romanians, and Bulgarians wanted to make their own decisions. An independence ferment arose among peoples that had been incorporated into the Soviet Union: Ukrainians, Lithuanians, Latvians, Estonians, Georgians, Moldavians, Armenians, Azerbaijanis, and Belarusians. There were also separatist tendencies in Central Asia, while the Russians themselves increasingly demanded that which was inconsistent with Communism – political, economic, and religious freedom.

Gorbachev made a chink in the system, but under social pressure it became a great breach. In an age of satellite television, the

MIKHAIL GORBACHEV – last Soviet Union leader.

POSTAGE STAMP – advocating a *perestroika* (restructuring) of the Soviet system.

SAMIZDAT PLACARD – advocating *glasnost* (openness), that is, transparency in the Soviet system.

government could not maintain an information monopoly, the basis of propaganda. Nor did it have the power to stop the processes – which it instigated – by force. As from 1988 it virtually ceased to attack religion, though in law it was possible to do so. The Ukrainian Greek Catholic Church emerged from the underground, and the authorities slowly began to return seized churches and to allow the building of new ones.

In 1988 the Soviet authorities agreed to the millennium celebrations of the Christianization of Kievan Rus, centered on Moscow,

347

MIRACULOUS CURE OF EMILIA SANTOS

ON MARCH 25, 1987, a 57-year-old woman, Emilia Santos, lay paralysed in bed in one the wards at St. Francis Hospital in Leiria. Only able to move her hands and head, she persistently prayed for a cure at the intercession of the three Fatima visionaries, particularly Jacinta. She suddenly heard a child's voice: "Sit up! Sit up! You can do it!" She felt a tingling in her legs, and then heat spreading throughout her body. At first she thought that she had gone out of her mind. After a while she sat up, which she had not done for almost 40 years. But she still could not feel anything from her waist down.

Almost two years later, on February 20, 1989, the anniversary of Jacinta's death, Emilia Santos said: "If you solicit a cure for me, I shall be the happiest woman in the world." After the prayer, she stood up and walked about without any problem. The hospital staff were shocked, while her doctors saw it as inexplicable from a medical point of view.

The cure was later instrumental in the beatification of the Fatima visionaries.

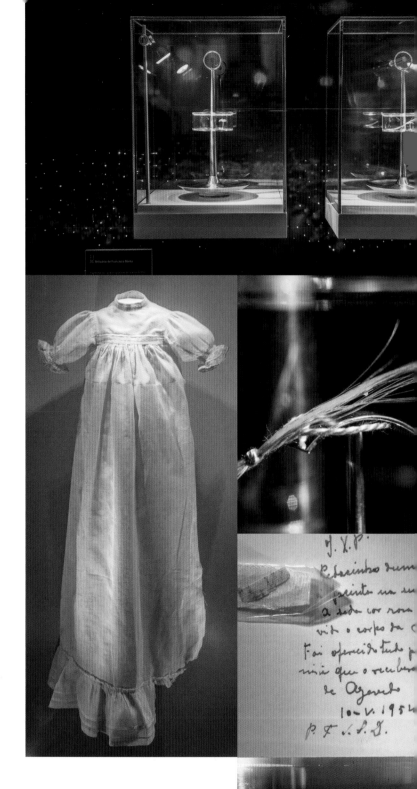

RELICS – Bl. Jacinta and Bl. Francisco – House of Light, Fatima.

Leningrad, and Kiev. From June 5 to 12, the majority of the Orthodox Church patriarchs throughout the world arrived in Russia for the occasion.

John Paul II also celebrated the occasion, first at the Greek Catholic St. Sophia Cathedral in Rome and then at St. Peter's. He then stated that the Church ought to breathe with "two lungs", East and West. He referred to the "Apostles of the Slavs", Saints Cyril and Methodius (whom he made copatrons of Europe in 1985), hence to the times when Christianity was still divided into Latin and Greek parts. The pope made it clearly understood that Orthodox Russians, Belarusians, and Ukrainians, as well as Greek Catholic Ukrainians, were the spiritual heirs of St. Vladimir, who Christianized Kievan Rus.

In the international arena, Moscow agreed to disarm under American conditions dictated by President Reagan. In December 1988, Gorbachev announced a unilateral reduction of conventional arms at the UN General Assembly. American policy

SAINTS CYRIL and Methodius – John Paul II made them patrons of Europe.

THREE POLITICIANS: George Bush, Ronald Reagan, and Mikhail Gorbachev – their meeting in New York in 1988 heralded the end of Communism.

349

ROUND TABLE, Warsaw – the government came to an understanding with some of the opposition.

SOLIDARITY ELECTION placard depicting Gary Cooper.

W SAMO POŁUDNIE 4 CZERWCA 1989

had precipitated such a great economic crisis that there were no resources in the USSR budget for day-to-day needs. Moscow had to seek more credit and in exchange was forced into geopolitical concessions.

The year 1989 went down in history as the Autumn of Nations. Central European Communism was dismantled at a rapid pace. The Round Table talks in Poland saw partially free parliamentary elections on June 4, when the nation decidedly rejected Communism. Tadeusz Mazowiecki's government was of a mixed nature – Solidarity representatives, Communists from the Polish United Workers' Party, and members of other parties.

Events in Hungary proceeded somewhat differently; there the Round Table talks resulted in completely free parliamentary elections. In March 1989, the anti-Communist opposition won the elections, and Jozsef Antall became the prime minister. On

May 2, the new government removed the barbed wire entanglements on the Austrian border, allowing thousands of East Germans to flee to West Germany via Hungary. East Germany quickly began to be depopulated again, so it was decided to open the border between the two German countries. Hence the Berlin Wall was dismantled, together with the Communist system, opening the way to a united Germany.

Those events encouraged other Central European nations. On November 17, 1989, Prague saw the bloodless Velvet Revolution, which brought Vaclav Havel, a well-known playright and anti-Communist dissident, to power; he became president of Czechoslovakia on December 29. Parliamentary elections on June 8, 1990, removed Communists from power for good.

On November 18, 1989, the first Bulgarian anti-government demonstrations broke out in Sofia. After talks, the first democratic elections took place in June 1990, won by the former Communist Party, which had "transformed itself" into a social democratic party and thereby maintained government continuity, though within a different political reality.

REFUGEES FROM the GDR fleeing to the FRG via Hungary and Austria.

PRAGUE INHABITANTS laying flowers on the place where Jan Palach, a student, burnt himself to death (1969) in protest against the invasion of Czechoslovakia.

VACLAV HAVEL, a well-known playwright and anti-Communist dissident, became president of Czechoslovakia.

JOZSEF ANTALL – the first post-World War II non-Communist prime minister of Hungary.

LITHUANIAN commemorative coin minted for the 10th anniversary of the "human chain" protest.

MOSAIC READING: *Stebuklas*, that is, "miracle" – Cathedral Square, Vilnius, where the "Baltic chain" began.

Romania was the last Communist country in Europe to see sudden changes as its leader Nicolae Ceausescu long resisted the fall of Communism. Towards the end of 1989, a revolt broke out, which ended in a coup d'etat. Some of the dictator's coworkers led the protests. Their leader was Ion Iliescu, who founded the National Salvation Front. On December 25, Ceausescu and his wife, Elena, were arrested, and after a two-hour trial they were sentenced to death and shot. Former Communists assumed power; as in Bulgaria, they had transformed their party into Social Democrats.

All the changes in Central Europe would not have been possible without the consent of the Kremlin. Communism, imposed on those countries, could have been maintained only as long as the Soviet Union was in a postion to enforce it. With its loss of power, the fall of Communism was but a question of time.

On December 1, 1989, there was an event that had hitherto been inconceivable – a Vatican meeting between Gorbachev and John Paul II, when Gorbachev, though the leader of world Communism, assumed a profoundly humble attitude. When the pope told Gorbachev that it was necessary to change the laws in the Soviet Union, and guarantee religious freedom, he readily agreed, adding that every citizen ought to have the possibility of

ION ILIESCU, a Communist activist who rebelled against Nicolae Ceausescu, the Communist Party leader.

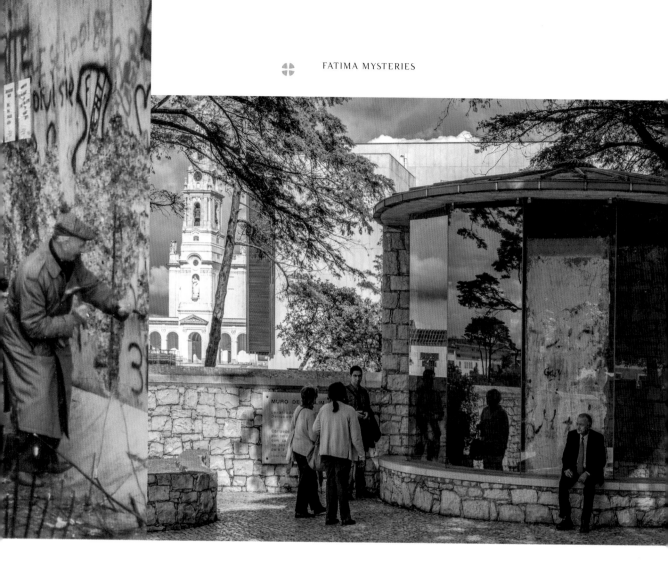

fulfilling his spiritual needs, a view that completely contradicted Leninist ideals.

The changes were not restricted to Eastern Europe, for they also began to affect the Soviet republics. On August 23, 1989, the fiftieth anniversary of the Molotov-Ribbentrop Pact, two million inhabitants from Lithuania, Latvia, and Estonia formed a human chain to protest the Soviet occupation. The Lithuanians on March 11 and the Latvians on May 4 declared independence. Other USSR nations increasingly demanded independence. The empire was falling apart at the seams.

Hence on August 19, 1991, hard-headed Communists at the Kremlin staged a coup d'etat in order to rebuild the former foundations of the Soviet system. It collapsed after three days, with

CITIZENS OF a united Germany breaking up the Berlin Wall.

CONCRETE SLAB from the Berlin Wall in Fatima – a memorial of the victory over Communism at the intercession of Our Lady.

353

YANAJEV'S COUP – Boris Yeltsin and associates on a tank in front of the White House in Moscow.

BORIS YELTSIN – first president of Russia after the collapse of the Soviet Union.

only three fatalities. The president of the Russian Soviet Federative Socialist Republic, Boris Yeltsin, became a symbol of resistance against the putsch.

Members of the World Apostolate of Fatima have noted a curious coincidence of dates: August 19 (start of the putsh) was the anniversary of the fourth Fatima apparition and the commemoration of St. John Eudes (the first propagator of the Immaculate Conception of the Blessed Virgin Mary), while August 22 (collapse of the putsch) was the Feast of the Queenship of Mary. For some, the coincidences were but accidental, to others, a clear sign.

DISSOLUTION of the USSR. The document that ended the Communist empire was signed by three leaders: Boris Yeltsin (Russia), Leonid Kravchuk (Ukraine), and Stanislav Shushkevich (Belarus).

The failure of the putsch made everyone aware that the collapse of Communism was inevitable. Shortly, Estonia, Ukraine, Belarus, Moldavia, Armenia, Georgia, Azerbaijan, Kazakhstan, Kyrgyzstan, Tajikistan, Uzbekistan, and Turkmenistan proclaimed their independence. The fall of the empire was sealed on December 8, 1991, the Feast of the Immaculate Conception, when the leaders of Russia, Ukraine, and Belarus, that is, Boris Yeltsin, Leonid Kravchuk, and Stanislav Shushkevich, respectively, met in the Bialowieza Forest and decided to dissolve the Soviet Union.

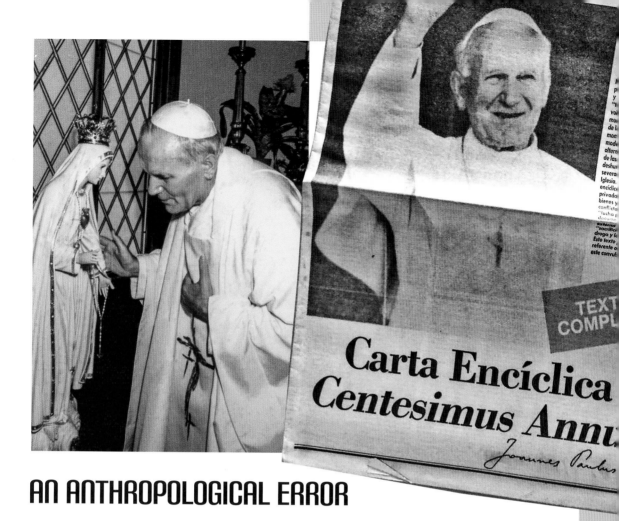

AN ANTHROPOLOGICAL ERROR

ON MAY 1, 1991, John Paul II announced the encyclical *Centessimus annus*, wherein he gave some thought to, amongst other things, the causes of the fall of Communism. He stated that a basic anthropological error lies at the heart of it, that is, a false conception of human nature and society, which gives rise to erroneous solutions in the political and economic spheres, and deforms law and morality. But, according to the pope, atheism is the root of evil, the prime source of a false ideology.

A little later, May 12–13, the pope visited Fatima for the second time and renewed the consecration of the whole human race to Our Lady. Though the Soviet Union had collapsed, the pope was aware that the spirit of Communism was still alive. In his homily, he warned that Marxism could shortly be replaced by a new version of atheism. On the one hand, it would advocate freedom, on the other, strive to destroy the very roots of human and Christian morality.

The pope continued that theme during his first general audience on returning to Rome. He then said that the same errors, of which Mary had warned in Fatima, were being spread throughout the world in the 20th century and were still a danger, as they were turning people away from the Creator, cutting Him off from humanity, and building a godless society, even one that was anti-God.

JOHN PAUL II and a statue of Our Lady of Fatima.

PAPAL ENCYCLICAL *Centesimus annus* (1991) summed up, among other things, the phenomenon of Communism in the context of its demise.

Third Secret

SR. LUCIA WITH JOHN PAUL II in Fatima, 2000 – beatification of Jacinta and Francisco Marto.

PORTUGAL

Fatima

Lisbon

CHAPTER 14

Third Secret

The Soviet Union disintegrated, and the Communist system in many countries was done away with. Yet many wondered whether the Church would finally reveal the third Fatima secret.

HOLY SEE SPOKESMAN Joaquin Navarro-Valls accompanied John Paul II to Fatima on two occasions.

In 1991, when John Paul II was in Fatima for the second time, he made a vigil at Our Lady's shrine (May 12). He said, among other things: "Today, with this multitude of brothers, I came to your throne acclaiming: Hail, Holy Mother! Hail, safe Hope that never disappoints! Totus Tuus, O Mother! Thank you, Heavenly Shepherdess, for having guided with maternal affection the people to freedom!... Fatima, in its message and its blessing, is conversion to God. Here you feel and witness the redemption of man, through the intercession of and with the help of her who with her virginal foot crushes the head of the ancient serpent."[51]

Joaquin Navarro-Valls, John Paul II's press liaison, participated in the pilgrimage. He recalled that two things made a particular impression on him. The first was the Holy Father's silent prayer in the Chapel of Apparitions, where he was alone, alone with Our Lady, though crowds were all around. The second was the meeting with Sr. Lucia, who conversed with the pope for ten minutes. Navarro-Valls recalled photographs of Sr. Lucia, serious and attentive in virtually all of them. But then – a permanently cheerful smile.

OFFICIAL LOGO of the World Apostolate of Fatima – a rosary and two doves, a scapular and an inscription: One World Praying (*Orbis Unus Orans*).

In those days the members of the Blue Army were also cheerful. After the fall of Soviet Communism, the Blue Army became the World Apostolate of Fatima, with a membership of ten million, an apostolate that has no equal in spreading the Fatima message throughout the world.

In 1993 John Paul II paid his first visit to the former Soviet Union. He visited Lithuania, Latvia, and Estonia, where he said that he saw the finger of God in the fall of Communism.

A year later, the Italian writer Vittorio Messori had a series of interviews with John Paul II. He wanted to know, among other things, why the pope had frequently used the words "miracle" and "mystery", in the context of the collapse of Soviet Communism. The pope, though not directly asked about it, referred to the three Fatima visionaries in his reply, that they could not have known of Russia and its conversion, as they had no knowledge of history and geography. Yet that which they spoke of came about. The pope connected his fate with the Fatima message, recalling the attempt on his life in Rome, adding that those events were perhaps needed in order that we could understand the actions of God in history.

JOHN PAUL II – Gate of Dawn, Vilnius, pilgrimage to Lithuania in 1993.

SR. LUCIA'S LAST YEARS

SR. LUCIA LIVED in the Carmelite convent in Coimbra from 1948 to 2000. She left the Carmel but four times for meetings with Paul VI and John Paul II in Fatima. The passing years did not reduce her activities. She participated in the convent housework, made devotional items – which were sold – and also replied to every letter that she received, of which there were thousands from all over the world. Despite her advanced age she learned to use a computer.

At the same time she led an extraordinarily deep spiritual life, which included consecutive Marian apparitions. Her nurse disclosed that Sr. Lucia wrote down all her experiences and reflections, which, however, have not been published.

SR. LUCIA: praying before a statue of Our Lady of Fatima; corresponding with people throughout the world; reading a letter from John Paul II on her deathbed.

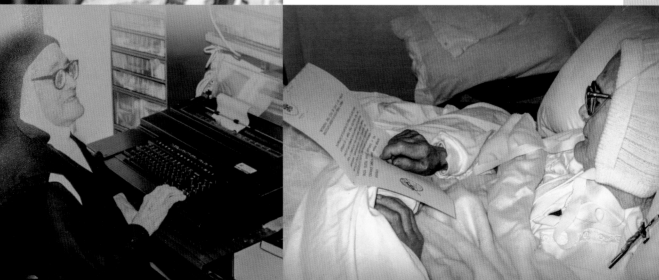

OBNINSK in Kaluga Oblast – was the strangest place that the pilgrim statue of Our Lady visited. During Communist times it was a closed city to which unregistered people had no access. There was a large armed forces research center and the world's first nuclear power plant. When the USSR collapsed, part of the officers' club was turned into an Orthodox church.

John Paul II saw a combination of factors, natural and supernatural, as the cause of Communism's collapse. He was of the opinion that it fell because of its own errors and abuses. Further on in the interview, he emphasized that that did not automatically indicate a bright future, as the phenomenon of Communisn could not be reduced to "Russia's errors".

"The fall of Communism opens before us a *retrospective panorama of modern civilization's typical way of thinking and acting,* especially in Europe, where Communism originated. Modern civilization, despite undisputed successes in many fields, has also made many mistakes and given rise to many abuses with regard to man, exploiting him in various ways. It is a civilization that constantly equips itself with power structures and structures of oppression, both political and cultural (especially through the media), in order to impose similar mistakes and abuses on all humanity. How else can we explain the increasing gap between the rich North and the ever poorer South? Who is responsible for this? Man is responsible – man, ideologies, and philosophical systems. I would say that *responsibility lies with the struggle against God, the systematic elimination of all that is Christian.* This struggle has to a large degree dominated thought and life in the West for three centuries. *Marxist collectivism is nothing more than a "cheap version" of this plan.* Today a similar plan is revealing itself in all its danger and, at the same time, in all its faultiness."[52]

Hence John Paul II had not succumbed to the euphoria at the fall of Soviet Communism. He did not, like other thinkers, announce "the end of history", but rather foresaw new dangers arising from the same old root. In the interview with Messori, the pope grieved over the fact that he had even been rejected in his own homeland. When he visited an enslaved Poland in 1979, 1983, and 1987, he was enthusiastically greeted, and even the Communist media refrained from criticizing him in any way. But when he returned to a free Poland in 1991, ordinary people were indeed as enthusiastic and spontaneous as before, but some of the elite responded otherwise. That was evident in many press articles, wherein the pope was criticized for not understanding either the contemporary world or his own country.

He said of this reception: "When, during my last visit to Poland, I chose the Decalogue and the commandment of love as a theme for the homilies, all the Polish followers of the 'enlightened agenda' were upset. For such people, the Pope becomes *persona non grata* when he tries to convince the world of human sin."[53]

After the demise of Communism the pope's homeland saw a struggle between two visions of social order, visions based on different anthropological foundations. In 1993 Poland was the first democracy to move from pro-abortion law towards the protection of the unborn. What is more, most people were in favor of it

In December 1996 a statue of Our Lady of Fatima left Portugal to circulate around the former Soviet Union until July 1997. It was welcomed enthusiastically, carried in procession in numerous Russian cities, from Kalingrad on the Baltic to Perm near the Ural Mountains. It found its way to places where Communism had left its bloody mark: the forced-labor camps where millions of

PROVISIONAL PLYWOOD iconostasis in the officers' club in Obninsk, where an Orthodox parish was established. People there received the statue of Our Lady with deep emotion.

OUR LADY of Fatima – Red Square, Moscow, December, 1996.

EUROPE

Moscow

Perm

ASIA

USSR

innocent people were deprived of their freedom and even their lives; Katyn, where Polish prisoners of war were murdered; Yekaterinburg, where the tsar and his family were executed; and major World War II battlefields. Here and there the arrival of the statue was announced in advance with the agreement of the local authorities, but at times there were unexpected changes in the plans.

Janusz Rosikon, a photographer, recalled one such occasion: "We left Perm for one of those strange, closed Soviet towns, built for the researchers and workers of a nearby secret atomic research center. We travelled in an old car, the statue, wrapped up in a blanket, lay in the trunk. The police detained us at a tollbooth. Fortunately I had a large red identity card in Cyrillic: *Internacjonalnyj Zurnalist* [International Journalist]. It was invalid, but it had a lightning effect – we were allowed into the town without being checked. There were no churches, of course, in that strange place. When a political

STATUE of Our Lady of Fatima was looked after in Russia by a Polish priest – he accompanied Our Lady on trains and planes.

RUSSIAN ORTHODOX monk and Argentinian Catholic priest during a Marian procession in Perm.

'thaw' came, the inhabitants appropriated half of the officers' club and, using plywood boards and printed pictures, they 'built' a little church. We were greeted in it by three Orthodox priests, who raised the statue on a plinth. People came up to it and reverently touched Our Lady's feet, and then prayers were said."[54]

The statue was joyously welcomed by Catholics and Orthodox alike, transported mainly by rail all over Russia, hidden in a double bass case. At one airport, the priests were detained by the security guards who checked passenger baggage with an X-ray machine. They were convinced that they had a child's remains in the case.

The statue's arrival in Moscow occasioned a particularly memorable state of affairs. The authorities had not agreed to any public event that involved the statue, but the local Franciscans recalled what St. Maximilian Kolbe had once said, that is, that a statue of Our Lady

would one day stand in Red Square. Hence Janusz Rosikon attempted to persuade the monks to take the statue to the former center of the Soviet Empire, to Red Square. The monks hesitated, afraid of being arrested. Eventually, Fr. Grzegorz Cioroch, the prior, prevailed. Hence they set off for Red Square.

After furtively taking photos of themselves with the statue, they returned to their car. But Janusz Rosikon had misgivings. He persuaded the Franciscans to return and to stand the statue ostentatiously in the middle of Red Square. On doing so, people distanced themselves from it, as they still dreaded being associated with religion, even though it was then six years after the fall of Communism. Janusz Rosikon arranged a photo session, and not one policeman interfered. Later, the photos circulated throughout the world – Our Lady of Fatima at the foot of the Kremlin wall, hailing her victory over Communism.

John Paul II visited Poland in 1997. On June 7 – the first Saturday of the month, the liturgical memorial of the Immaculate Heart of Mary – he consecrated the Church of Our Lady of Fatima in Zakopane. He then emphasized that the church was a votive offering for his life being saved on May 13, 1981: "At that time I experienced mortal danger and suffering, but also the great mercy of God. By the intercession of Our Lady of Fatima my life was given back to me."[55] The pope wiped tears from his cheeks during his homily.

In subsequent years John Paul II repeatedly returned to the subject of Fatima. In October 1997 – the eightieth anniversary of the Miracle of the Sun – the pope sent a letter to the bishop of Leiria Serafin de Souza Ferreira e Silva, in which he wrote: "On the threshold of the third millennium, as we observe the signs of the times in this twentieth century, Fatima is certainly one of the greatest, among other reasons because its message announces many of the later events and conditions them on the response to its appeals: signs such as the two world wars, but also great gatherings of nations and peoples marked by dialogue and peace; the oppression and turmoil suffered by various nations and peoples, but also the voice and the opportunities given to peoples and individuals who in the meantime have emerged on the international scene; the crises, desertions and many sufferings of the Church's members, but also a renewed

RUSSIAN Orthodox and Catholic procession in Perm.

PERM railway station – the statue being prepared to continue the journey.

367

FLAG OF EUROPE
– designed by Arsene Heitz, a Frenchman, who was inspired by St. John's Apocalypse, which depicts a woman with a crown of twelve stars around her head.

and intense feeling of solidarity and mutual dependence in Christ's Mystical Body, which is being strengthened in all the baptized, in accordance with their vocation and mission; the separation from and abandonment of God by individuals and societies, but also the in-breaking of the Spirit of Truth in hearts and communities to the point of sacrifice and martyrdom to save 'God's image and likeness in man' (cf. Gn 1:27), to save man from himself."[56]

In the same letter, the pope notes that Fatima threw light on the events of the twentieth century, where a theme from the history of salvation is repeated: "It is not the first time that, feeling rejected and despised by man but respecting his freedom, God allows man to feel distant from him, with the consequent obscuring of life which causes darkness to fall on history, but afterwards provides a refuge. This already happened on Calvary, when God Incarnate was crucified and died at the hands of men. And what did Christ do? After invoking the mercy of heaven with the words: 'Father, forgive them, for they know not what they do' (Lk 23:34), he entrusted humanity to Mary, his Mother: 'Woman, behold, your son'" (Jn 19:26).[57]

TWOFOLD COMING OF OUR LADY

LOUIS-MARIE GRIGNION DE MONTFORT,
a French religious who lived at the turn of the 17th century, wrote that the first coming of Christ was preceded by Mary, who gave birth to Him. She herself stayed in her Son's shadow throughout her life. Even the Evangelists did not write much about her. She gave birth to Jesus in poverty and isolation. Such was the case with the first appearance of God incarnate on earth; Christ lived and ministered in meekness and humbleness of heart.

Christ's second coming will be in glory, in all His divine majesty. That too will be preceded by Mary, according to de Montfort. Just as He will come in His power and might, not as a small baby, but as King of the universe – so she too will appear earlier in royal splendor.

That which de Montfort predicted began to be fulfilled from the 19th century on, when a whole series of Marian apparitions occurred for the first time in history (for example, the Rue du Bac (Paris), La Salette, and Lourdes apparitions), mainly centered on the propagation of a profounder knowledge of the Blessed Virgin's attributes. As de Montfort wrote, Jesus desired that His Mother might thus be more deeply loved. Such is the nature of the Fatima apparitions.

FRANCISCAN SAINT Louis-Marie Grignion de Montfort.

WEEPING MADONNA – La Salette, France.

CANDLE PROCESSION – Lourdes, France.

CARDINAL SECRETARY of State Tarcisio Bertone met Sr. Lucia to discuss the third Fatima secret.

The same theme – the culminating point of which is Golgotha – links the beginning and the end of our history. It had already been foretold in the Book of Genesis when, after the fall of Adam and Eve, a prophecy appeared about a Woman whose seed shall crush Satan's head. It is also repeated in the Apocalypse, with the appearance of a Woman clothed with the sun, a crown of twelve stars around her head.

In May 1999, John Haffert, the founder of the Blue Army, met Sr. Lucia in Coimbra. She was joyful throughout the meeting, he recalled, in contrast with his first meeting with her in 1974, when she did not smile for three hours, while anxiously speaking of what needed to be done to avoid war. Haffert said later that her behaviour in 1999 was to him a clear sign that the greatest danger, of which the Fatima message spoke, had passed.

On the occasion of the Great Jubilee in 2000, John Paul II made a decision that had been awaited for several decades throughout the world. On April 27, Cardinal Tarsicio Bertone arrived at the Carmel in Coimbra to confirm the authenticity of a text that was shortly to be made public. He had a long conversation with Sr. Lucia, which he later related to Cardinal Joseph Ratzinger.

On May 13, 2000, John Paul II led the beatification Mass of Francisco and Jacinta Marto in Fatima. During his homily the pope particularly thanked Jacinta for having prayed for popes, including him.

The Vatican Secretary of State Cardinal Angelo Sodano was present at the beatification Mass, where he announced that the third Fatima secret would shortly be revealed. In the meantime, he elucidated its meaning, saying that the secret concerned the war waged against Christianity by atheistic systems, the immense suffering endured by the faithful, and a pope killed along with the martyrs.

During his stay in Fatima the pope again met Sr. Lucia at the basilica in a small room that directly adjoined the tombs of Francisco and Jacinta Marto. Joaquín Navarro-Valls, who was at the meeting, recalled that both spoke little, as if they knew everything about each other; there was nothing of curiosity or inquisitiveness in their discussion. Navarro-Valls had the impression that he was a witness to the dialogue of two saints, who were evidently in the presence of God on a daily basis, which not only transformed them inwardly but was also reflected in their faces.

On June 26, 2000, the prefect of the Congregation for the Doctrine of the Faith Joseph Ratzinger called a Vatican press conference.

PORTUGAL

Fatima ✠

Lisbon

STATUE of Our Lady towering over the faithful – Fatima, October 13, 1995.

JOHN PAUL II praying before Our Lady during his visit to Fatima in 2000.

371

✠

In the presence of a large number of journalists he read the text of the third Fatima secret, revealed to Lucia dos Santos on July 13, 1917, at the Cova da Iria, which was written down on January 3, 1944, in Tui. The text reads:

"After the two parts which I have already explained, at the left of Our Lady and a little above, we saw an Angel with a flaming sword in his left hand; flashing, it gave out flames that looked as though they would set the world on fire; but they died out in contact with the splendour that Our Lady radiated towards him from her right hand: pointing to the earth with his right hand, the Angel cried out in a loud voice: 'Penance, Penance, Penance!' And we saw in an immense light that is God: 'something similar to how people appear in a mirror when they pass in front of it' a Bishop dressed in White 'we had the impression that it was the Holy Father'. Other Bishops, Priests, men and women Religious going up a steep mountain, at the top of

which there was a big Cross of rough-hewn trunks as of a cork-tree with the bark; before reaching there the Holy Father passed through a big city half in ruins and half trembling with halting step, afflicted with pain and sorrow, he prayed for the souls of the corpses he met on his way; having reached the top of the mountain, on his knees at the foot of the big Cross he was killed by a group of soldiers who fired bullets and arrows at him, and in the same way there died one after another the other Bishops, Priests, men and women Religious, and various lay people of different ranks and positions. Beneath the two arms of the Cross there were two Angels each with a crystal aspersorium in his hand, in which they gathered up the blood of the Martyrs and with it sprinkled the souls that were making their way to God."[57]

THREE FATIMA apparitions – *O secreto de Fatima*, painted by Cristina Rubalcava in 2003.

Cardinal Ratzinger provided the secret of Fatima text with a theological commentary, which he emphasizes is but an "attempt". According to him, the word "penance" is the key to understanding the third secret. He refers to his meeting with Sr. Lucia, who told him that the purpose of all the apparitions was to help people grow in faith, hope, and charity. In that context, a call to penance was a call to conversion.

Cardinal Ratzinger analyzes the images that appeared in the vision. On the one hand, an angel with a flaming sword represents the threat of judgment that looms over the world, while on the other,

J.M.J.

A terceira parte do segredo revelado a 13 de Julho de 1917 na Cova de Iria – Fátima.

Escrevo em acto de obediência a vós Deus meu, que mo mandais por meio de sua Exª. Revª. o Senhor Bispo de Leiria e da Vossa e minha Santíssima Mãe.

Depois das duas partes que já expus, vimos ao lado esquerdo de Nossa Senhora um pouco mais alto um Anjo com uma espada de fôgo na mão esquerda; ao cintilar, despedia chamas que parecia iam incendiar o mundo; mas apagavam-se com o contacto do brilho que da mão direita expedia Nossa Senhora ao seu encontro: o Anjo apontando com a mão direita para a terra, com voz forte disse: Penitência, Penitência, Penitência! E vimos n'uma luz imensa que é Deus: "algo semelhante a como se vêem as pessoas n'um espelho quando lhe passam por diante" um Bispo vestido de Branco "tivemos o pressentimento de que era o santo Padre". Vários outros Bispos, sacerdotes, religiosos e religiosas subir uma escarpada Montanha, no cimo da qual estava uma grande cruz de troncos toscos como se fôra de sobreiro com a casca; o Santo Padre, antes de chegar aí, atravessou uma grande cidade meia em ruínas e meio trémulo com andar vacilante, acabrunhado de dôr e pena, ia orando pelas almas dos cadáveres que encontrava pelo caminho; … aos pés da … lhe disparavam … e … morrendo … Bispos sace… religiosas e … res, cavalhe… dames e po… ços da cruz cada um … de cristal … nhavam o san… êle regavam … navam de …

ORIGINAL TEXT
– Sr. Lucia on the three Fatima secrets. Written in 1944 and revealed in 2000.

the splendor of the Mother of God, summoning all to penance in order to be saved. According to the cardinal it signifies that the future was not a foregone conclusion, as it could be shaped by man, who is free to choose. Thus an apparition is not a fatalistic vision of the inevitable, but indicates an alternative path that leads to that which is good. Hence we have a call to mobilize our strengths, to transform ourselves, to be converted.

The cardinal also analyzes the images of a steep mountain, a great city, and a cross. The first two images symbolize the arena of human history. The hill signifies life as an arduous ascent to the summit, while the city signifies community and coexistance. The fact that it is in ruins reminds one that man has the ability not only to create but also to destroy. The cross is a symbol of salvation, the ultimate goal and guide of mankind.

The next element of the vision is a procession of the clergy ascending the steep mountain with difficulty amid ruined buildings and dead bodies. It ends with a massacre of Christians. The cardinal writes that this Via Crucis is the Church's journey through the history of the twentieth century, a century of martyrs, a century of suffering and persecution of Christians, of numerous armed conflicts, of two world wars. In this context Cardinal Ratzinger refers to Sr. Lucia's letter to John Paul II on May 12, 1982: "The third part of the secret refers to Our Lady's words: 'If not [Russia] will spread her errors throughout the world, causing wars and persecutions of the Church. The good will be martyred; the Holy Father will have much to suffer; various nations will be annihilated.'"[58]

The cardinal notes that an anguished Holy Father had a special role in the vision, as he sees all the popes of the twentieth century in this figure, from Pius X to John Paul II, whose ministry was marked by suffering. Karol Wojtyla has a unique place among them, as the fact that he survived an assassination attempt thanks to Providence is, according to Joseph Ratzinger, the best proof that the future has not been determined once and for all, that an immutable destiny does not exist. It shows that faith and prayer are powerful forces that can shape history, that "prayer is more powerful than bullets and faith more powerful than armies."[59]

POPE BENEDICT XVI – main interpreter of the third Fatima secret.

375

STATUE of Our
Lady of Fatima

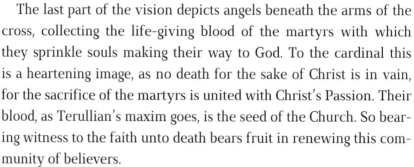

The last part of the vision depicts angels beneath the arms of the cross, collecting the life-giving blood of the martyrs with which they sprinkle souls making their way to God. To the cardinal this is a heartening image, as no death for the sake of Christ is in vain, for the sacrifice of the martyrs is united with Christ's Passion. Their blood, as Terullian's maxim goes, is the seed of the Church. So bearing witness to the faith unto death bears fruit in renewing this community of believers.

Cardinal Ratzinger notes that the contents of this secret would no doubt be a disappointment for those who expected some sort of apocalyptic vision. The purpose of revelations, however, is not to satisfy our curiosity, but to help us to attain salvation. The cardinal also says that the individual events described in the vision belong to the past.

The last theme of the commentary concerns the Immaculate Heart of Mary, a theme that links the beginning and the end of Cardinal Ratzinger's commentary. He explains: "In biblical language, the 'heart' indicates the centre of human life, the point where reason, will, temperament and sensitivity converge, where the person finds

NIGHT PRAYER vigils in Fatima attract several thousand people.

his unity and his interior orientation. According to Matthew 5:8, the 'immaculate heart' is a heart which, with God's grace, has come to perfect interior unity and therefore 'sees God'. To be 'devoted' to the Immaculate Heart of Mary means therefore to embrace this attitude of heart, which makes the *fiat*—'your will be done'—the defining centre of one's whole life…. But from whom might we better learn in every age than from the Mother of the Lord?"[60]

Cardinal Ratzinger also referred to an expression in the secret – "my Immaculate Heart will triumph." "What does this mean? The Heart open to God, purified by contemplation of God, is stronger than guns and weapons of every kind. The *fiat* of Mary, the word of her heart, has changed the history of the world, because it brought the Saviour into the world—because, thanks to her *Yes*, God could become man in our world and remains so for all time. The Evil One has power in this world, as we see and experience continually; he has power because our freedom continually lets itself be led away from God. But since God himself took a human heart and has thus steered

377

« Je suis l'Immaculée Conception. »

THE DOGMA OF THE IMMACULATE CONCEPTION

ALTHOUGH the Immaculate Conception of the Blessed Virgin Mary had been believed by Christians from the very beginning, it became a Catholic Church dogma as late as December 8, 1854 (Pius IX – *Ineffabilis Deus*). The dogma states that Our Lady was preserved from original sin by virtue of a singular grace of God and the future merits of Jesus as the Savior of mankind.

THE GOSPEL refers to Mary as "full of grace". The Church Fathers described her as pure, innocent, without stain. The Immaculate Conception was universally acknowledged in the Orthodox Church, hence there was no need of a dogma. In the Greek Catholic Church, a feast in honor of the Immaculate was established in the eighth century.

IT WAS otherwise in the Latin Church, where there was no lack of opponents of this truth (for example, St. Thomas Aquinas and St. Bonaventure). The final theological justification of the dogma was worked out by St. Duns Scotus. But as criticism of it continued in the West, Pius IX decided to announce the dogma, which was confirmed by the apparitions in Lourdes in 1858, when Our Lady said to Bernadette Soubirous: "I am the Immaculate Conception."

IMMACULATE CONCEPTION – Rubens, Prado Museum, Madrid.

ST. BERNADETTE SOUBIROUS reported what Mary had told her: "I am the Immaculate Conception."

GREAT DEVOTEES of Mary: Bl. Duns Scotus ❶, and St. Stanislaw Papczynski. ❷

human freedom towards what is good, the freedom to choose evil no longer has the last word. From that time forth, the word that prevails is this: 'In the world you will have tribulation, but take heart; I have overcome the world' (Jn 16:33). The message of Fatima invites us to trust in this promise."[61] Both the text of the third Fatima secret and the theological commentary on it encounter much criticism in some circles. Among the critics we find, for example, Antonio Socci, Solideo Paolini, and Fr. Paul Kramer. Even Vittorio Messori wrote in the *Corriere della Sera* newspaper that we were a long way from a complete solution to this problem.

What doubts do such critics raise? How do the Church hierarchs respond? There are several main charges. The most outrageous claim is that the Vatican has not revealed the whole text, that there is a fourth Fatima secret (in other words, the third secret has been only partly revealed). Cardinal Tarsicio Bertone strongly denied that, as Sr. Lucia – with whom he spoke in April 2000 – confirmed that the text that was revealed two months later was authentic. Pope John XXIII's former personal secretary, Cardinal Loris Capovilla, who

SHRINE RECTOR
Fr. Carlos Manuel Pedrosa Cabecinhas is certain that the Fatima message is relevant today.

379

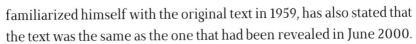
familiarized himself with the original text in 1959, has also stated that the text was the same as the one that had been revealed in June 2000.

Another criticism concerns Cardinal Ratzinger's interpretation. In the secret there is mention of a pope who was killed by bullets and arrows, whereas John Paul II was but wounded. Moreover, Cardinal Ratzinger sees the assassination attempt on the pope as the culmination of the martyrdom of Christians in the twentieth century, whereas in the secret the murder of a pope is but the beginning of the slaughter of bishops, priests, monks, nuns, and lay believers.

Sr. Lucia made it clear that she but described the vision, while she left the interpretation completely to the Church. Cardinal Tarcisio Bertone, who showed her Cardinal Ratzinger's commentary, said that she saw it as a correct interpretation. Cardinal Ratzinger maintains that the visions cannot be treated like photographs or films, because the images are often unclear. He also notes that a supernatural impulse is filtered by one's perceptual powers, conditioned by circumstances, personality, temperament, imagination, manner of expression, and the like. John Paul II identifies himself with the figure of the killed pope for – as he himself said on May 13, 1994 – he was dying, on the threshold of death.

PILGRM IN
Fatima with a statue of Our Lady in his rucksack.

As Wincenty Laszewski, a Polish Mariologist, noted: "Anyone who is familiar with the Fatima documents is aware of two things. First, that all the warnings and promises are conditional, as God made them dependent on people's cooperation. Hence the third part of the secret of July 1917 was not fulfilled. That is why the bishop in white was stopped on the verge of death, why World War II broke out, and why Communism spread its errors for many years. Such is human dignity! Man is God's partner, coresponsible for the world's history."[62]

We can find similar themes in the Old Testament. On the one hand, we have the story of Sodom and Gomorrah, whose inhabitants did not convert despite many warnings and so suffered the penalty sent from heaven. On the other hand, the inhabitants of Nineveh behaved totally otherwise. They listened to Jonah the prophet , converted, and so avoided being destroyed.

MARY AND POLITICAL CORRECTNESS

OUR LADY OF FATIMA most certainly did not adhere to the principles of political correctness.

Firstly, the advocates of political correctness maintain that the Church should not meddle in politics, whereas Mary spoke of, among other things, the political situation, of the necessity of Catholics to be involved in politics.

Secondly, Our Lady condemned "Russia's errors", leaving no doubts that she had Communism in mind, while political and academic leaders still embrace leftist ideology.

Thirdly, she indicated that the devotion to her Immaculate Heart, which no doubt hinders ecumenical dialogue, was the only way out of humanity's crisis, not social or political programs or charity initiatives.

Fourthly, at a time when priests and catechists strive to tell children as little as possible about hell and sin in order to spare them unnecessary anxiety and emotional trauma, Mary showed the young visionaries a terrifying scene of the infernal abyss and the agony of the damned, an approach that would occasion the loss of parental rights in many countries.

AMERICAN YOUTH demonstrate in the defense of life.

UNBORN MEMORIAL – Ste. Genevieve, Missouri.

VISION OF HELL – Hans Memling's *The Last Judgment*.

NUNO PRAZERES, director of the World Apostolate of Fatima.

There are other doubts as to the Vatican interpretation. Many claim that Our Lady's promises have not been fulfilled because John Paul II's consecration of 1984 was not fully in accord with her instructions, as the pope did not mention Russia by name. Hence, according to them, the graces granted were but partial ones. Communism fell, but has Russia been converted? Religious freedom does indeed exist there, but practical atheism prevails – in Moscow only 4 percent of the faithful attend church at Easter, the most important feast day in Christianity. The authoritarian government, the pillar of which is the former KGB elite, does not shrink from political assassinations and even genocide, as evidenced by the war in Chechnya.

Furthermore, Russia's errors are still being spread throughout the world. Cultural Marxism did not disappear with the Soviet Union. It is not merely a subject for academic considerations, as it is systematically becoming an element in education programs, the media, and the legal system. The sexual revolution too is enjoying great success in more and more countries, and the legalization of abortion continues to extend to more regions throughout the world. (Paradoxically, abortion is banned in Islamic countries, though the Decalogue is not part of the Koran, while it is permitted in countries based on Christian culture.) The family is the object of merciless attacks, its form and essence ceaselessly undermined. It was no accident that in her letter to Fr. Carlo Caffarra (the then president of the Pontifical John Paul II Institute for Studies on Marriage and Family) Sr. Lucia wrote – mindful of the fact that she had a vision of the Holy Family during the October apparition in 1917 – that the future of the Church and the world would be determined in marriages and families.

However, one should bear in mind that it is not possible to eliminate quickly the destructive effects of a system that had wrecked people's lives for three or four generations. One can compare it to a confession; in one moment one's sins could be taken away, but

FR. LUCIANO GUERRA, the former long-standing rector of the Shrine of Our Lady of Fatima, thinks that Fatima has not as yet had its last word, and that the future will see Fatima connected with many momentous events.

FR LUCIANO GUERRA with Grzegorz Gorny and Samuel Pereira.

383

✠

their effects could well hang to the end of one's life. It is not possible to erase quickly the signs of a system that had left its destructive mark on social life for seventy years.

Sr. Lucia responded to such criticisms as follows: "After all that there are still those who are still blind, who do not see, or do not want to see, who say: 'There are wars apart from this one, whereas Our Lady promised peace.' Yes, Our Lady promised peace, but this concerned the war that the Communists had unleashed throughout the world, not civil wars, which we have always had, and will have until God deigns to transform the world.… But that day has yet to come, but it will, when it pleases God, in accord with His plans of great mercy.… And peace will reign for a time. The promise regarding peace refers to the wars waged throughout the world by Communists, it is with regard to those wars that Our Lady, Her Immaculate Heart, will be victorious."[63]

The conclusive argument as to the effectiveness of the consecration of Russia should be Lucia's own words in her *Message from Fatima*: "The consecration was carried out publicly by John Paul II in Rome, on March 25, 1984, before the image of Our Lady that is

venerated in the Chapel of Apparitions in Fatima, which the Holy Father – after writing to all the bishops to unite with him in the consecration – ordered to be brought to Rome in order to underline the fact that the consecration fulfilled the requests that Our Lady made in Fatima."[64]

Further on in her text, Sr. Lucia wrote that when John Paul II was carrying out the consecration the world was on the verge of a nuclear war. In that context, Sr. Lucia posed a question: "And who would have been able to dissuade those arrogant people, intent on war, dissuade them from their revolutionary designs, their atheistic ideologies that propagate enslavement and their dominion over people, and see themselves as masters of the whole world? Who would have been able to change that into something completely different? Who would have complied to a request for a meeting, in order to embrace in a gesture of peace?" And she answers: "One could say more. God saw to it that one of the main Communist leaders decided to go to Rome to meet the Holy Father, who perhaps would have, irrespective of that, consecrated Russia to the Immaculate Heart of Mary, as she requested in Fatima – a leader who saw the Holy Father

385

as the highest representative of God on earth, that is, Jesus Christ, the Founder of the one true Church."[65]

Fr. Krzysztof Czapla, director of the Fatima Secretariat in Poland, pointed out that Sr. Lucia underlined the intention of consecrating Russia as well as the collegial aspect of the consecration, and not the literal presence of the name of the country in the consecration. After all, she questioned the effectiveness of Pius XII's consecration in 1942, not because of the omission of the name of Russia, but the lack of communion with the bishops throughout the world.

A certain, significant fact frequently escapes many critics of Cardinal Ratzinger's interpretation. It is true that not all Our Lady's promises have been fufilled, but they were dependent on two conditions: the consecration of Russia to the Immaculate Heart of Mary and Communions of reparation on First Saturdays. Catholics throughout the world usually concentrate on the first point, on the pope's actions. But they forget about the second point, that is, the devotion of the Five First Saturdays. Our Lady's requests are addressed to the Holy Father and the people of God, that is, the Church. Can we in all certainty say that the second condition has been adequately fulfilled? Taking into account the creeping secularization of Europe and America, and what that entails – less and less people who pray – one would expect that the devotion is practised less and less. Fr. Krzysztof Czapla also points out that the basic aspect of the Five First Saturdays very often escapes the faithful and even priests, that is, the necessity of making reparations to Mary for the affronts to her Immaculate Heart. So the Fatima message continues to be a challenge.

It is worth remembering the significant discussion of October 11, 1993, when Sr. Lucia told Cardinal Ricardo Vidal that Fatima was a "Divine Week", and added: "Fatima is still in its Third Day. We are now in the post consecration period. The First Day was the apparition period. The Second was the post apparition, pre-consecration period. The Fatima Week has not yet ended…. The Fatima Week has just begun. How can one expect it to be over immediately? … I may not get to see the whole Week."[66] According to John Haffert, the next Fatima day will come when the appropriate number of people throughout the world respond to Our Lady's call and

PORTUGUESE PERIODICAL dedicated to Fatima.

practice Communions of reparation for sins against the Immaculate Heart of Mary.

Critics of the Vatican interpretation also cite Sr. Lucia statements, wherein she was to have spoken of yet other future events. But much of this is not firsthand information, and has not been authorized by her. Moreover, it is necessary to keep in mind that Sr. Lucia was a mystic who had had many apparitions, the contents of which – the majority – are as yet unknown. Angela Pereira da Silva, vice postulator for Sr. Lucia's beatification process, once said that Sr. Lucia left thousands of pages of spiritual notes that have never been published. Fr. Luciano Guerra, rector of the Shrine of Our Lady of Fatima, believes that her writings will soon become part of the canon of Christian mystical literature alongside the works of, for example, St. John of the Cross and St. Teresa of Avila. Manuscripts of her work of 1955, written on the instructions of the superior general of the Carmelite Order, the future Cardinal Anastasia Ballestrero, are to be found in the Vatican archives. They might well contain information that could disperse some of the doubts concerning Fatima. But there is no doubt that we shall never know of some of the details, as Sr. Lucia admitted that she wanted to remain silent about certain reminiscences and secrets forever.

ANA REIS of the World Apostolate of Fatima comes from the Marto family.

VICE POSTULATOR of Sr. Lucia's beatification process: Sr. Angela Pereira da Silva.

The most frequently omitted element of the third Fatima secret is that which is its very essence, that is, the angel's exclamation: "Penance! Penance! Penance!" It was no accident that it was repeated three times. It was a very dramatic call to conversion, to an acknowledgement of one's sins, a call for remorse and reparation. We must keep in mind that it is easier point out the negligence of popes than it is to decide to change one's life and faithfully follow the path pointed out by Christ.

Let us leave the Fatima secret controversey and return to the events themselves. Several months after the disclosure of the secret, about 1,400 hierarchs gathered in Rome, including 76 cardinals, to participate in the consecration of the Church and the world to Our Lady for the new millenium; it was the largest gathering of Catholic hierarchs since Vatican II. No pope had hitherto summoned so many bishops to solemnly implore Our Lady to intercede with her Son. At times, signs mean more than words – everything took place before the statue of

PILGRIMS MAKING their way, on their knees, to the Chapel of Apparitions at the Cova da Iria.

ABOUT 300,000 PEOPLE gather at the Fatima basilica during an evening Rosary (May 12, 2017).

Our Lady of Fatima, which was brought from Portugal for the occasion. John Paul II's statements also stuck in one's mind, requesting Mary's aid because – as he said – mankind has found itself, more so than at any other time in history, at the crossroads.

According to Fr. Luciano Guerra – the rector of the Fatima shrine – Fatima has not as yet had its last word. He is convinced that, as in the past, when many momentous events were connected with the apparitions, something important will occur in the future.

In 2001 the Vatican Congregation for Divine Worship and the Discipline of the Sacraments issued *The Directory on Popular Piety and the Liturgy,* wherein the Five First Saturdays devotion was officially permitted for the first time, not by local bishops, as hitherto, but by the Holy See.

Near the end of her life, Sr. Lucia received permission from her superiors to write down her reflections, which are usually replies to questions in letters from all over the world. Thus arose her book *The Message of Fatima: How I See the Message from the Perspective of Time and Events.* It was not finished, but it contains many valuable reflections.

PEOPLE ARRIVE in Fatima with various requests. Some, for example, pray for their children to be cured, others, to give thanks for their healing.

PILGRIMS from Mexico – Fatima.

389

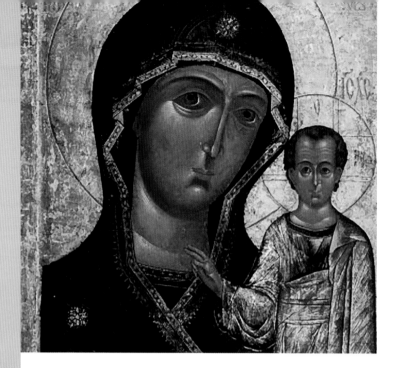

OUR LADY OF KAZAN ICON

IN 2004, ON THE INSTRUCTIONS OF JOHN PAUL II, Cardinal Walter Kasper arrived in Russia bearing a gift from the pope: an icon of Our Lady of Kazan, one of the most precious sacral works of the Russian Orthodox Church. The icon survived a great fire in Kazan in 1579. It ended up in Moscow in 1612, when Polish soldiers who had been stationed there for two years were forced to leave the Russian capital. In 1633, the icon was housed in the Cathedral of Our Lady of Kazan in Moscow. In 1721 Tsar Peter the Great had it moved to St. Petersburg the newly built capital of the empire. In 1811, the Cathedral of Our Lady of Kazan, then the largest church in the country, was built, and housed the icon, which was stolen in 1904.

It was found after World War II, when John Haffert, the founder of the Blue Army, bought it on the black market. He intended to return it to its rightful owners, but not while Communists ruled in Russia. Hence he built a special chapel for the icon in Fatima and later presented it to John Paul II, who in turn gave it to the Russian Orthodox Church two years before his death.

MASS IN FATIMA on October 13, 2014 – 70,000 with umbrellas and paper lanterns despite the constant heavy rain.

As to the question of why, according to the Fatima apparitions, World War II was to be a "much worse war" than World War I, Sr. Lucia replied: "Because it will be an atheistic war, against the Faith, against God, against the people of God, the aim of which will be to uproot Judaism, whence came Jesus Christ, Our Lady, as well as the Apostles, who passed on the Word of God, the gift of knowledge, hope and mercy."[67]

Asked if God wanted the war so as to punish the world, she wrote: "It does not mean that God wanted a war, as He is Lord of peace, goodness and love: 'Love one another as I have loved you.' That is the Lord's law, His first and last commandment. Yet He allows wars, just as He allows sin, on account of the gift of freedom that He endowed us with, so that we might serve Him, be obedient to Him, and love Him freely. If we use this gift to wrong people, then we are responsible before God, before our consciences, before humanity, which suffers the consequences of our errors."[68]

At the beginning of 2005, Sr. Lucia, almost ninety-eight, fell ill. On November 10, she received a letter from John Pau II, wherein he expressed his solidarity with her in her illness. She

THE LARGEST LENIN monument in Kiev was pulled down on December 8, 2013, the Feast of the Immaculate Conception. There followed the "Leninfall", which saw 374 monuments of Lenin pulled down throughout Ukraine.

died three days later. Her last words were: "For the Holy Father!... Our Lady, Our Lady, Holy Angels, Heart of Jesus, Heart of Jesus! We are going, we are going ... to heaven ... with Our Lord ... Our Lady ... and the little shepherds."[69] In an official communique, Sr. Lucia's reference to the Holy Father was removed, as the pope was still alive, though his condition was worsening. He died on April 2, 2005, the first Saturday of the month. After his death, Sr. Lucia's reference to him was written in again.

On April 19, 2005, Cardinal Joseph Ratzinger became pope and took the name Benedict XVI. In May 2010 he visited Fatima. During the flight to Portugal the Holy See's press secretary Fr. Federico Lombardi asked the pope whether the suffering of the popes in the Fatima apparitions could also be connected with the suffering of the Church on account of the sins concerning child sex abuse.

Benedict XVI replied: "Apart from the great vision of the Pope's suffering, which we can primarily ascribe to Pope John Paul II, [the apparitions] indicate events of the future of the Church, which develop and are revealed little by little.... Thus it is the sufferings of the Church that are being announced. As for the novelties we can discover in this message today, we may see that attacks against the Pope and the Church do not only come from outside; rather, the sufferings of the Church come from inside the Church, from the sin that exists in the Church. This was always common knowledge, but today we see it in truly terrifying form: the greatest persecution of the Church does not come from external enemies, but is born of sin within the Church."[70]

During his homily of May 13, 2010, Benedict XVI said: "We would be mistaken to think that Fatima's prophetic mission is complete.... May the seven years which separate us from the centenary of the apparitions hasten the fulfilment of the

OCTOBER 13, 2013, Pope Francis entrusted the world to Our Lady of Fatima on the Marian Day of the Year of Faith: "Let us respond to the gift as did St. John the Apostle, who took Mary 'into his home', that is, by renewing our personal consecration."

prophecy of the triumph of the Immaculate Heart of Mary, to the glory of the Most Holy Trinity."[71]

He then explained what he meant by it: Sin, on the one hand, exists and activates a cycle of death and terror, but on the other hand, God ceaselessly seeks the just in order to save the city. So it was with Fatima, where three little shepherds offered to bear all sorts of suffering to convert and save sinners. This is still relevant, and addressed to each one of us.

Pope Francis, on the occasion of the Year of Faith Marian Day, had the statue of Our Lady of Fatima brought to Rome. On October 13, 2013, he consecrated the whole world to her. He then said:

"Blessed Virgin Mary of Fatima, with renewed gratitude for your motherly presence we join in the voice of all generations that call you blessed. We celebrate in you the great works of God, who never tires of lowering himself in mercy over humanity, afflicted by evil and wounded by sin, to heal and to save it."[72]

THE WAY OF PENANCE in Fatima is about 1,300 feet long. Pilgrims traverse the square in front of the basilica on their knees to the Chapel of the Apparitions, some in supplication, others in thanksgiving.

LUCAS' MIRACULOUS CURE

MARCH 3, 2013. Juranda, a town in Brazil. Two children, sister and brother, Lucas and Eduarda, were playing together in their grandfather's house. At a certain moment the five-year-old boy fell, head first, out of a window onto concrete from a height of over 20 feet.

The boy, in a coma, was taken to a hospital in Campo Mourão. Doctors described his condition as critical. They stated that he had little chance of survival and that even if he did survive, he would be severely brain damaged. At best he would be mentally handicapped for the rest of his life.

The boy's parents, Joao Batista and Lucila Yurie, were aware that only a miracle could save their child. The father, from the outset, prayed mentally to Our Lady of Fatima as well as to Francisco and Jacinta Marto for their intercession. He rang the Carmel in Campo Mourão with a request for prayers. But at that time there was a silent hour, and the nun who took the call did not pass on the devastated father's request to her community. On hearing of Lucas' condition, she was

PRESS CONFERENCE with Sr. Angela de Fatima Coelho da Rocha Pereira da Silva, the canonization postulator, and Lucas' parents.

LUCAS' PARENTS: Joao Batista and Lucila Yurie.

convinced that the boy would soon be dead, so she resolved to pray for his family.

Over the followig days the boy's condition worsened, but he did not die. On March 7 the parents rang the Carmel once more with a request for prayers. This time a sister passed on their request to the rest of the nuns, who gathered before the relics of Bl. Francisco and Bl. Jacinta Marto, beseeching their intercession for the cure of Lucas.

On March 9 the boy suddenly stirred and began to speak normally. Two days later he left the intensive care ward, and on March 15 he left the hospital unaided. His cure was sudden and complete, and his accident had not left any negative effects. Lucas was completely fit, physically and mentally.

A team of doctors, including nonbelievers, acknowledged that the case could not be explained from a scientific point of view. The inexplicable cure of the five-year-old Brazilian boy was deemed to be a miracle by the Holy See. The cure opened the way for the canonization of Francisco and Jacinta Marto.

NINE-YEAR-OLD LUCAS in Pope Francis' arms.

A MULTITUDE OF BELIEVERS from throughout the world attended the canonization Mass for Francisco and Jacinta Marto.

OUR LADY OF FATIMA
procession after
the canonization
Mass (May13,
2017).

**CANONIZATION
PORTRAITS OF
JACINTA AND
FRANCISCO MARTO**
on the basilica
in Fatima
by the Portuguese
artist Silvia
Patricio. The little
shepherds are
depicted against
a dark background,
signifying their
gloomy times.
The saints are
holding rosaries
and lanterns;
Jacinta's lantern
depicts the moon,
a symbol of
Our Lady,
while Francisco's
depicts the sun,
a symbol of the
Lord Jesus.

May 2017 saw the hundredth anniversary of the Fatima revelations. Pope Francis led the centenary celebrations in Fatima, Portugal. On May 12 he led the Rosary in which over three hundred thousand participated. Immediately afterwards, Cardinal Piero Parolin, the Holy See's secretary of state, celebrated Mass. During his homily he stressed that the Fatima revelations conveyed a message of hope, as they proclaimed the triumph of the Immaculate Heart of Mary and foretold the victory of Divine Mercy over the powers of evil. The world's fate, particularly the destinies of individual nations, communities, and persons, was however dependent on the extent to which people would be prepared to cooperate with God. Hence Our Lady of Fatima calls all to participate in the spiritual battle over the future of mankind, primarily through persistent prayers, particulary by reciting the Rosary daily. Though one does not often see the results of this devotion immediately, it is never, as Cardinal Parolin said, useless: "Sooner or later it will yield its fruit. Prayer is capital that is in God's hands, which will bear fruit at the appropriate time, according to His designs, which are very different from ours." The hierarch is certain that seemingly useless or ineffective means, such as conversion, penance, and entrusting oneself to God do indeed "have the power to change the world and prevent evil". Francisco and Jacinta Marto are examples of the power of holiness realized in this life.

The next day, May 13, over one million gathered in Fatima to witness the canonization of the little visionaries. The two Portugeese shepherds are the youngest belivers in the Church's history to be raised to the

altars. There have been cases of younger children being beatified or canonized, but they were always little martyrs who had suffered death at times of persecution together with other followers of Jesus. But in this case an eleven-year-old boy and a ten-year-old girl who did not perish for the faith were canonized. The Church presents them as models to imitate, examples of Christian maturity. Eighteen theologians, in their testimony for the Congregation for the Causes of Saints, wrote that the children practiced the three theological virtues and the four cardinal virtues to a high degree.

These two children fully understood, experienced, and realized the Fatima message in their lives. Sr. Lucia wrote that Francisco solely thought about comforting Jesus and Our Lady, who seemed to be sad because of people's sins, while Jacinta was intent on but one matter: the conversion of sinners and saving them from hell. They each focused on a different aspect of the message: he on one's duties to God, and she, to one's neighbor. One, however, cannot exist without the other. Love is that which links them, while it is expressed through prayer and sacrifice.

The hundredth anniversary of the Fatima revelations has aroused interest throughout the world. Hundreds and even thousands of press articles, internet materials, and radio and TV programs have appeared. But has not that which is most essential often escaped people in the media hullabaloo: the apocalyptic battle for the world's soul, the warning against eternal damnation, the call to atonement and conversion, as well as the proclamation of the ultimate victory of the Immaculate Heart of Mary?

POPE FRANCIS in his popemobile amongst believers at the 100th anniversary of the apparitions. He is the fourth pope to visit Fatima, after Paul VI, John Paul II, and Benedict XVI.

ACKNOWLEDGMENTS

The authors and editors wish to thank the following institutions for their help in the realization of this book:

House of Light, Fatima
John Paul II Family Home Museum, Wadowice
Shrine of Our Lady of Fatima, Zakopane
Shrine of Our Lady of Fatima, Fatima
John Paul II Shrine, Krakow
Association of Marian Helpers
World Apostolate of Fatima
Work of Jesus the High Priest (Opus J.S.S.)
National Library, Warsaw

The authors and editors wish to thank the following people for their help in the realization of this book:

Fr. Grzegorz Bartosik, OFMConv, Fr. Pawel
Cebula, OFMConv, Fr. Jaroslaw Cielecki,
Fr. Krzysztof Czapla, SAC, Fr. Zbigniew
Derylo, OFMConv, Fr. Luciano Guerra,
Fr. Kazimierz Kurek, SDB, Fr. Pavol Benedikt
Liptak Fr. Carlos Lumbreras, Fr. Benno Mikocki,
OFM, Fr. Marian Mucha, SAC, Fr. Carlos Manuel
Pedrosa Cabesinhas, Fr. Jacek Pietruszka, Fr. Jan
Rokosz, MIC, Fr. Pawel Stepkowski, OSPPE,
Fr. Roman Tkacz, SAC, Fr. Ryszard Wrobel,
OFMConv, Sr. Maria da Conceicao Ferreira Pinto,
s. Angela de Fatima Coelho da Rocha Pereira da
Silva, Sr. Sofia Guedes, Sr. Adelio Oliveira da Silva,
Sr. Maria Dolores Pedrosa, Marek Adamski,
Elzbieta and Stanislaw Bialaszek, Jaime Vilalta
Berbel, Krzysztof Dzielinski, Stanislaw Grygiel,
Jan Hnilica, Barbara and Jaroslaw Klaput,
Marcin Kolpanowicz, Janusz Kotański, Wincenty
Laszewski, Tomasz Makowski, Maria da Luz Moreis,
Fernando Pequin, Samuel Rodrigo Pereira, Nuno
Prazeres, Ana Reis, Leopoldina Reis Simoes,
Wlodzimierz Redzioch, Catia Sofia Filipe da Silva,
Deolinda Silva, Hanna Suchocka, Gabriel Turowski,
Joanna Valinho, Joaquin Navarro-Vals, Slawomir
Wawer, L'ubomir Welnitz, Krystyna Zelenka

NOTES

1. Mary Lucia of the Immaculate Heart, *Fatima in Lucia's Own Words: Sister Lucia's Memoirs*, ed. Louis Kondor, trans. Dominican Nuns of Perpetual Rosary (Fatima: Postulation Centre, 1976), p. 62. **2.** Ibid., p. 162. **3.** Ibid. **4.** Ibid., p. 163. **5.** Ibid. **6.** Ibid., p. 165. **7.** Ibid., pp. 165–66. **8.** Ibid., p. 166. **9.** Ibid. **10.** Ibid. **11.** Ibid. **12.** Ibid., p. 168. **13.** Ibid., p. 169. **14.** Ibid. **15.** English translation of the *Catechism of the Catholic Church*, 2nd ed. (Vatican City: Libreria Editrice Vaticana; Washington, D.C.: United States Catholic Conference, 2000), no. 67. **16.** Lucia, *Fatima*, p. 171. **17.** Ibid., p. 172. **18.** Ibid. **19.** Almeida Garrett's full account may be found in Antonio Maria Martins, *Novos documentos de Fatima* (Sao Paulo: Edicoes Loyola, 1984). This translated excerpt is from "The Miracle of the Sun: An Eyewitness Account by Dr. Jose Maria de Almeida Garret", Fatima Network, www.fatima.org/essentials/facts/miracle.asp. **20.** Quoted in *100th Anniversary of Fatima*, https://www.ewtn.com/fatima/sixth-apparition-of-our-lady.asp. **21.** Lucia, *Fatima*, p. 172. **22.** Ibid., p. 147. **23.** Ibid., p. 113. **24.** Grzegorz Gorny, Janusz Rosikon, *300 lat wytrwalosci. Warszawska Pielgrzymka Piesza 1711–2011* (Izabelin, Poland: Rosikon Press, 2011), pp. 167–168. **25.** Lucia, *Fatima*, p. 191. **26.** Ibid. **27.** Ibid., p. 169. **28.** Ibid., pp. 198–99. **29.** Ibid., p. 199. **30.** Mary Lucia of the Immaculate Heart, *Lucia Speaks: Memoirs and Letters of Sister Lucia* (Washington, N.J.: AMI Press, 1976), p. 238, quoted in Guido Del Rose, *Fatima: The Five Sins against the Immaculate Heart of Mary*, http://www.catholicapologetics.info/catholicteaching/privaterevelation/fatima.htm. **31.** Lucia, *Fatima*, p. 199. **32.** Faustina Kowalska, *Diary: Divine Mercy in My Soul* (Stockbridge, Mass.: Marian Press, 2012), p. 322, 818. **33.** Pius XI, *Divini Redemptoris*, 22, https://w2.vatican.va/content/pius-xi/en/encyclicals/documents/hf_p-xi_enc_19370319_divini-redemptoris.html. **34.** Robert J. Fox and Antonio Maria Martins, SJ, *The Intimate Life of Sister Lucia* (Hanceville, Ala.: Fatima Family Apostolate, 2001), p. 256, quoted in Andrew Apostoli, CFR, *Fatima for Today: The Urgent Marian Message of Hope* (San Francisco: Ignatius Press, 2010), p. 158. **35.** Robert J. Fox and Antonio Maria Martins, SJ, *Documents on Fatima and the Memoirs of Sister Lucia* (Alexandria, SD: Fatima Family Apostolate, 1992), p. 329. **36.** Lucia, *Fatima*, p. 169. **37.** Cf. Pope Pius XII, *Preghiera per la Consacrazione della Chiesa e del Genere Umano al Cuore Immacolato di Maria* (radio message), October 31, 1942, http://w2.vatican.va/content/pius-xii/it/speeches/1942/documents/hf_p-xii_spe_19421031_immacolata.html. **38.** Cf. Petrus Vigorita, "Deceetum", *Acta Apostolicae Sedi: Commentarium Officiale*, 41, 2, 16:334 (Vatican City: Libreria Editrice Vaticana, 1949), http://www.vatican.va/archive/aas/documents/AAS-41-1949-ocr.pdf. **39.** Cf. Stefan Kardynal Wyszynski, *Wszystko postawilem na Maryje* (Paris: Editions du Dialogue; Warsaw: Soli Deo, 1998), p. 23. **40.** Cf. Sebastiao Martins dos Reis, *O Milagre do sol e segredo de Fatima* (Porto, Portugal: Edicoes Salesianas, 1966), pp. 127–28. **41.** "*Neues Europa* (1963)", Published Testimony series, Fatima Network, http://www.fatima.org/thirdsecret/neueseuropa.asp. **42.** Cf. Wincenty Laszewski, *Ukryta tajemnica Fatimy. Nowy lepszy swiat* (Radom, Poland: Polwen, 2013), p. 43. **43.** Cf. Jan Hnilica and Frantisek Vnuk, *Pavol Hnilica. Biskup umlcanej Cirkvi*, vol. 2 (Trnava, Slovakia: Dobra Kniha, 1996), pp. 189–90. **44.** Cf. *La Documentation Catholique* 19, no. 3 (1967): 542. **45.** Cf. Fr. Ksawery Wilczynski, "Niebiansko-rzymski I europejski rodowod – kontekst NMP Krolowej Polski", Forumdlazycia Tradycji Katolickiej, https://forumdlazycia.wordpress.com/2015/08/17/niebiansko-rzymski-i-europejski-rodowod-kontekst-nmp-krolowej-polski-ks-ksawery-wilczynski/. **46.** Pope Paul VI, Declaration on Religious Freedom (*Dignitatis Humanae*), no. 1, http://www.vatican.va/archive/hist_councils/ii_vatican_council/documents/vat-ii_decl_19651207_dignitatis-humanae_en.html. **47.** Cf. *Uchwala Programowa I Krajowego Zjazdu Delegatow Niezaleznego Zwiazku Zawodowego "Solidarnosc"* (Program Resolution of the First National Convention of Solidarity), Gdansk, Poland, September 1981. **48.** Pope St. John Paul II, "Consecration of all Individuals and Peoples of the World to the Immaculate Heart of Mary", March 25, 1984, http://www.ewtn.com/library/papaldoc/consecra.htm#JP2c. **49.** Tarcisio Bertone, *The Last Secret of Fatima* (New York: Doubleday, 2008), p. 56, quoted in Andrew Apostoli, *Fatima for Today* (San Francisco: Ignatius Press, 2010), p. 198. **50.** Cf. Maria Lucia of Jesus and the Immaculate Heart, *The Message of Fatima: How I See the Message from the Perspective of Times and Events* (Fatima: Secretariado dos Pastorinhos, 2006), p. 55. **51.** Cf. John Paul II, Address at Shrine of Our Lady of Fatima, May 12, 1991, http://w2.vatican.va/content/john-paul-ii/pt/speeches/1991/may/documents/hf_jp-ii_spe_19910512_veglia-fatima.html. **52.** John Paul II, *Crossing the Threshold of Hope* (New York: Alfred A. Knopf, 1994), p. 71, http://www.excerptsofinri.com/printable/crossing_the_threshold_ofhope-popejpii.pdf. **53.** Ibid., p. 34. **54.** Wlodzimierz Redzioch, Janusz Rosikon, "Matka Boza Fatimska byla juz w Moskwie", *Niedziela* 43 (2003). **55.** John Paul II, Homily, June 7, 1997, http://w2.vatican.va/content/john-paul-ii/en/homilies/1997/documents/hf_jp-ii_hom_19970607_fatima.html. **56.** Pope John Paul II, Letter to Serafin de Souza Ferreira e Silva, Bishop of Leiria, https://w2.vatican.va/content/john-paul-ii/en/speeches/1997/october/documents/hf_jp-ii_spe_19971001_fatima.html. **57.** Lucia, "Third Part of the Secret" quoted in Congregation for the Doctrine of the Faith, *The Message of Fatima*, http://www.vatican.va/roman_curia/congregations/cfaith/documents/rc_con_cfaith_doc_20000626_message-fatima_en.html. **58.** Joseph Ratzinger, Congregation for the Doctrine of the Faith, "Theological Commentary", *The Message of Fatima*, http://www.vatican.va/roman_curia/congregations/cfaith/documents/rc_con_cfaith_doc_20000626_message-fatima_en.html. **59.** Ibid. **60.** Ibid. **61.** Ibid. **62.** Cf. Wincenty Laszewski, *7 dni Fatimy* (Gora Kalwaria, Poland: Maryjna Oficyna Fons Omnis, 2007). **63.** Cf. Lucia, *The Message of Fatima*, pp. 56–57. **64.** Cf. Ibid., pp. 54–55. **65.** Cf. Ibid., pp. 55–56. **66.** John Haffert, "Sister Lucia and Third Day of the Week of Fatima", Mother of All Peoples, http://www.motherofallpeoples.com/2005/06/sister-lucia-and-the-third-dayof-the-week-of-fatima/. **67.** Cf. Lucia, *The Message of Fatima*, p. 53. **68.** Cf. Ibid. **69.** Richard Salbato, *Lucy's Last Words*, http://www.unitypublishing.com/Newsletter/Lucia'sLastWords.htm. **70.** Vatican Information Service, "Pope Replies to Questions from Journalists", May 12, 2010, http://www.bishopaccountability.org/news2010/05_06/2010_05_12_VaticanInformation_PopeReplies.htm. **71.** Benedict XVI, Homily, May 13, 2010, http://w2.vatican.va/content/benedict-xvi/en/homilies/2010/documents/hf_ben-xvi_hom_20100513_fatima.html. **72.** Francis I, Homily, October 13, 2013, http://w2.vatican.va/content/francesco/en/homilies/2013/documents/papa-francesco_20131013_omelia-giornatamariana.html

BIBLIOGRAPHY

ALLEGRI, Renzo, Roberto Allegri. *Reportage da Fatima. La Storia e i prodigi nel racconto del nipote di suor Lucia*. Milan. Italy: Ancora, 2000.

AMORTH, Gabriele. *Dietro un sorris. Alexandrina Maria da Costa*, Turin, Italy: Editrice Elledici, 2006.

APOSTOLI, Andrew, CFR. *Fatima for Today: The Urgent Marian Message of Hope*. San Francisco: Ignatius Press, 2010.

BAUER, Josef. *Geeintes Gebet wirkt Wunder. P. Petrus Pavlicek – Leben und Werk*. Vienna: RSK, 2007.

BERTONE, Tarcisio, Giuseppe De Carli. *L'Ultima veggente di Fatima*. Milan, Italy: RSC Libri, 2007.

CZAPLA, Krzysztof, SAC. *Fatima. Wielka obietnica*. Zakopane-Zabki, Poland: Sekretariat Fatimski Apostolicum, 2013.

DE FIORES, Stefano. *Il segreto di Fatima*, Alba, Italy: Edizioni San Paolo, 2008.

DOS REIS, Sebastiao Martins. *O Milagre do sol e o segredo de Fatima*. Porto, Portugal: Edicoes Salesianas, 1966.

DROZD, Jan, SDS. *Oredzie Niepokalanej. Historia objawien fatimskich*. Krakow, Poland: Salwator, 2005.

FOSTER, Claude R. *Mary's Knight: The Mission and Martyrdom of Saint Maximilian Maria Kolbe*. Libertyville, Ill.: Marytown Press, 2002.

GÓRNY, Grzegorz, Janusz Rosikoń. *300 lat wytrwalosci. Warszawska Pielgrzymka Piesza 1711–2011*. Izabelin, Poland: Rosikon Press, 2011.

HAFFERT, John M. *God's Final Effort*. Asbury, NJ: The 101 Foundation, 1999.

HELLER, Michal, Aleksander Niekricz. *Utopia u wladzy*. Translated by A. Mietkowski. London: Polonia, 1985.

HNILICA, Jan, Frantisek Vnuk. *Pavol Hnilica. Biskup umlcanej Cirkvi*. Vol. 1–2. Trnava, Slovakia: Dobra Kniha, 1996.

John Paul II, Vittorio Messori. *Crossing the Threshold of Hope*. Polish Edition. Lublin, Poland: Redakcja Wydawnictw KUL, 1994.

John Paul II. *Jesus Christ, Yesterday, Today and Forever: Addresses from the Holy Father's Apostolic Pilgrimages to Poland in 1997*. Polish Edition. Zabki, Poland: Apostolicum, 1997.

KOWALSKA, Faustina. *Diary: Divine Mercy in My Soul*. Marian Press, Stockbridge, Mass.: Marian Press, 2007.

LASZEWSKI, Wincenty. *7 dni Fatimy*. Gora Kalwaria, Poland: Marian Publishing Fons Omnis, 2007.

_____. *Fatima. Objawienia 1915–1929. Dokumenty i komentarze*. Warsaw, Poland: Fronda, 2016.

_____. *Ukryta tajemnica Fatimy. Nowy lepszy swiat*. Radom, Poland: Polwen, 2013.

_____. *X Krucjata*. Szczecinek, Poland: Fundacaja Nasza Przyszlosc, 2011.

MARTINS, Antonio Maria. *Documents on Fatima and the Pope and the Memoirs of Sister Lucia*. Alexandria, South Dakota: Fatima Family Apostolate, 1992.

_____. *Fatima: Way of Peace*. Devon, England: Augustine Publishing Company, 1980.

Mary Lucia of the Immaculate Heart. *Fatima in Lucia's Own Words: Sister Lucia's Memoirs*. Edited by Louis Kondor. Translated by Dominican Nuns of Perpetual Rosary. Fatima: Postulation Centre, 1976.

NAVARRO-VALLS, Joaquin. *A Passo D'uomo*. Milan, Italy: Mondadori, 2009.

GRAJEWSKI, Andrzej, Michal Skwara. *Agca nie byl sam. Wokol udzialu komunistycznych sluzb specjalnych w zamachu na Jana Pawla II*. Katowice, Poland: Gosc Niedzielny, 2015.

SICCARDI, Cristina. *Fatima e la Passione della Chiesa*. Milan, Italy: Sugarco Edizioni, 2012.

SOCCI, Antonio. *Il Quatro Segreto di Fatima*. Milan, Italy: RSC Libri, 2008.

STANZIONE, Marcello. *I Pastorelli e gli Angeli di Fatima*. Tavagnacco, Italy: Edizioni Segno, 2010.

TINDAL-ROBERTSON, Timothy. *Fatima. Russia and Pope John Paul II*. Still River, Mass.: Raventage Press, 1992.

TUROWSKI, Gabriel. *Zamach, czyli jak zlo w dobro sie obrocilo*. Krakow, Poland: Bialy Kruk, 2010.

WEIGEL, George. *Witness to Hope: The Biography of Pope John Paul II*. Italian Edition. Milan, Italy: Mondadori, 1999

WYSZYNSKI, Stefan. *Wszystko postawilem na Maryje*. Warsaw, Poland: Soli Deo, 1998.

_____. *Zapiski wiezienne*. Warsaw, Poland: Soli Deo, 2001.

Polish edition *Tajemnice Fatimy*
Published 2016 by Rosikon Press, Warsaw, Poland

© **Grzegorz Górny** text
© **Janusz Rosikoń** photographs

Graphic design, maps, and illustrations **Maciej Marchewicz**

Collaboration **Jan Kasprzycki-Rosikoń**

English translation **Stan Kacsprzak**

Scripture citations are from the *Second Catholic Edition of the Revised Standard Version of the Bible*
© 1965, 1966, and 2006 by the Division of Christian Education of the National Council of the Churches
of Christ in the United States of America. All rights reserved.

Archive photographs: Secretariado dos Pastorinhos.
Photographs: Archive – Prof. Gabriel Turowski: 26, 35, 309; ©Fotolia.com: 7 – ©James Thew. 9, 159 –
©petejau. 9, 127, 194-195 – ©Anton Balazh. 36, 53 – ©Joao Freitas. 55 – ©StockPhotoArt, ©Traumbild,
©Artur Bogacki, ©Distraction Arts. 62 – ©LiliGraphic. 208-209 – ©Noel Moor. 280 – ©portokalis. 342 –
©fotogenix. 343 – ©chagpg; Polish Press Agency: 6, 13, 15-16, 18-19, 31; Archive – RSK (Rosary Crusade for
World Peace), Vienna: 217, 246, 247, 249-251; John Paul II Family Home Museum, Wadowice: 21-23, 25, 28;
Archive – Conventual Franciscans, Niepokalanów: 113, 180-182; POLARIS / EAST NEWS: 308; Archive –
Famiglia di Maria in Rome: 32, 223, 225, 226, 270, 332; Wikipedia: 8-11, 28, 30, 36-43, 46, 50, 51, 53, 54, 56-59,
64, 65, 87, 102, 109, 110, 116, 126, 128-157, 162, 163, 165-169, 183-185, 186, 188, 189, 192, 193, 194, 196-199, 201,
202, 205, 209, 213, 215-222, 227, 230-235, 240-243, 256-259, 262-264, 266-269, 271-273, 276-278, 280-282,
284, 287, 288, 290, 291, 294-296, 299, 302-306, 311, 312, 313, 315-317, 322, 324, 325, 327, 332, 334, 336, 338-347,
349, 351, 352, 354, 369, 370, 375, 378, 381, 392, 393; Grzegorz Galazka: 395

© 2017 by Ignatius Press, San Francisco and Rosikon Press, Warsaw

All rights reserved. No part of this publication may be reproduced or transmitted, in any form or by any
means, electronic, mechanical, photographic or otherwise, without the prior permission of the publishers.

ISBN 978-1-62164-163-6

Library of Congress Control Number 2016952278